SLAVERY, FREEDOM & CULTURE

SLAVERY, FREEDOM & CULTURE

among

EARLY
AMERICAN
WORKERS

GRAHAM RUSSELL HODGES

M.E. Sharpe
Armonk, New York
London, England

Library of Congress Cataloging-in-Publication Data

Hodges, Graham Russell, 1946–
Slavery, freedom, and culture among early American workers / Graham Russell Hodges.
p. cm.
Includes bibliographical references and index.
ISBN 0–7656–0112–5 (alk. paper). — ISBN 0–7656–0113–3 (pbk. : alk. paper)
1. Afro-Americans—New York (State)—New York Region—History—18th century.
2. Afro-Americans—New York (State)—New York Region—History—19th century.
3. Afro-Americans—New York (State)—New York Region—Social conditions.
4. Slavery—New York (State)—New York Region—History—18th century.
5. Slavery—New York (State)—New York Region—History—19th century.
6. Working class—New York (State)—New York Region—History.
7. Labor—New York (State)—New York Region—History.
8. New York Region—History—1775–1865. I. Title.
F128.9.N3H64   1998
974′.00496073—dc21   97–47642
CIP
Printed in the United States of America

The paper used in this publication meets the minimum requirements of
American National Standard for Information Sciences—
Permanence of Paper for Printed Library Materials,
ANSI Z 39.48-1984.

EB (c)   10   9   8   7   6   5   4   3   2   1
EB (p)   10   9   8   7   6   5   4   3   2   1

Table of Contents

Acknowledgments

A number of the essays in this book have previously appeared else-where and are reprinted by permission. Several were book chapters. "The Freemanship in New York City: 1648–1800," originally appeared in *Authority and Resistance in Early New York,* Conrad E. Wright and William Pencak, eds. (New York: New-York Historical Society, 1988); "Black Revolt in New York and the Neutral Zone, 1775–1783" was originally printed in *New York in the Age of the Constitution,* William Pencak and Paul A. Gilje, eds. (Cranbury, NJ: Fairleigh Dickinson University Press, 1992); " 'Desirable Companions and Lovers': African Americans and Irish in New York's Sixth Ward," came out in the collection *The New York Irish,* Ronald Bayor and Timothy Meagher, eds. (Baltimore: Johns Hopkins University Press, 1995). Chapter 3 on slavery and freedom in Bergen County is a greatly revised version of a pamphlet written for the Bergen County Historical Society (River Edge, NJ, 1989). Other essays appeared in a number of journals. "In Retrospect: Richard B. Morris and *Government and Labor in Early America,* (1946)" (vol. 25, no. 2 [June 1997]: 360–368); "Violence and Religion in the Black American Revolution," (vol. 20, no. 2 [June 1992]: 157–163); and "Gabriel's Republican Rebellion," (vol. 22 [1994]: 428–432) all appeared in *Reviews in American History.* "Reconstructing Black Women's History in the Caribbean," was published first in the *Journal of American Ethnic History.* (vol. 12, no. 1 [November 1992]: 101–107). "The Decline and Fall of Artisan Republicanism in Antebellum New York City: Views from the Street and Workshop" (vol. 18, no. 2) pp. 211–221, copyright © 1992 by Sage Publications; "Flaneurs, Prostitutes, and Historians: Sexual Commerce and Representation in the Nineteenth-Century Metropolis"(vol. 23, no. 4) pp. 488–497, copyright © 1997 by Sage Publications: both appeared in the *Journal of Urban History* and are reprinted by permission of Sage Publications.

Over the years many people have assisted me with helpful and sharp criticism of this work. They include Paul A. Gilje, Ronald Bayor, William Pencak, Sylvia Frey, Douglas Egerton, Howard Rock, and Margaret Washington. At Colgate, research for the essays in this book was made possible by grants from the Faculty Research Council. Colgate students who assisted in the research for this volume include Paul Townend and JoEllen Kelleher. Alan Brown was enormously helpful with formatting tables. Trudy King was patient and cheerful as she typed endless drafts. At M.E. Sharpe, Peter Coveney and Eileen Maass were excellent editors who knew how to prod dilatory authors in a firm but friendly fashion. My wife, Margaret Washington, and my parents, Graham and Elsie Hodges, helped in immeasurable ways.

Introduction

The essays in this book range widely in focus and over time. Beginning with a study of the significance of the freemanship in the earliest years of colonial New York City and ending with a discussion of interracial marriages in antebellum New York City's Sixth Ward, they touch upon labor, African-American, women's, and urban historiographies. They reflect my own interests and comment upon others' excellent scholarship, which I have been fortunate to review at length. Given the scope of these essays, it is difficult to generalize about their meaning, but I hope the reader will find them original and provocative. Individually and collectively, the chapters make some new comments in each of the subfields of early American history mentioned above. Chapter 1 surveys the intersection of government and labor among the cartmen, a key semiskilled occupation granted responsibility to carry the city's goods and necessities—a right given only to holders of the freemanship in early New York. This grant conferred citizenship on the burly carters and gave them privileges their economic status and education would not have otherwise warranted. As the freemanship was not available to free or enslaved African Americans, David Roediger has accurately described it as an early example of the "wages of whiteness," by which Caucasian Americans created privileges open only to those of their color and so sustained differences based upon race when class status was not dissimilar. In the article, the freemanship's enfranchising powers made the carters and other holders of it equal in political clout to their economic and social betters. In so doing, it made ordinary laborers political operatives and opened the doors to political patronage. Perhaps uniquely to New York City, although it also existed in Albany and Philadelphia, the freemanship helped to create a path toward universal white male suffrage in the early nineteenth century.[1]

Many of my original insights into the importance of the freemanship and the history of the cartmen are owed to Richard B. Morris's seminal work, *Government and Labor in Early America*. Chapter 2 is an appreciation I wrote on the fiftieth anniversary of the publication of Morris's epic. In the essay I emphasize the significance, realized and potential, of Government and Labor to students of labor and racial history. One of the most salient aspects of Morris's huge achievement is what did not get into the final draft. Among the tables and prose cut to curb production costs was material on concerted actions by white and black laborers. As the debates over directions in early black and labor history heat up, the next few essays should offer some insights and raise more questions.

Chapter 3 is about slavery and freedom for the beleaguered African Americans of Bergen County, New Jersey, just across the Hudson from New York City. Related in many ways to my recent book on blacks in Monmouth County, this two-century survey of black life in Bergen poses a counterfactual query: whether American slavery in the North would have survived if the Society of Friends had not existed? Quakers and other liberals on the race question did not have any say in Dutch-dominated Bergen County, where intransigent masters defied abolition insofar as they could stretch the laws. In response, blacks left the county or, if they stayed, turned inward to a vernacular revival of Africanity.[2]

The early history of blacks in America, I contend, turns on the American Revolution. The next three chapters (Chapters 4, 5, and 6) deal with the abilities of blacks to turn the American Revolution into a triangular struggle between Patriots, the British, and themselves. The first essay is on Sylvia Frey's magnificent account of black freedom struggles in the revolutionary southern colonies. The second is my own reconstruction of how defiant African Americans teamed up with white Loyalists in and around revolutionary New York City. From the ashes of the British defeat, blacks in New York and in the South learned military lessons and deeply imbibed republican ideology. That republicanism emerged again in Gabriel's Rebellion, so well rebuilt by Douglas Egerton. Chapter 6 includes my thinking on Egerton's valuable definitive book on Gabriel.

Three of the final four chapters (Chapters 7, 8, and 9) have to do with gender and sexuality in the port cities of the Atlantic. Chapter 7 discusses three significant approaches to black women's history in the

Caribbean and suggests ways North American scholars might employ those lessons. Chapter 8 discusses three major works on the difficult subjects of prostitution and women's roles and representations in nineteenth-century New York and London. Interspersed with these studies is an essay on recent work on artisan republicanism in New York City. Chapter 10, the last chapter in the book, is my own essay on the social politics of interracial marriage in the tumultuous Sixth Ward of antebellum New York City.

SLAVERY, FREEDOM
& CULTURE

1

Legal Bonds of Attachment

The Freemanship Law of
New York City, 1648–1801

In 1844 Philip Hone, while rummaging through some old papers, came across the certificate for the freedom of the city awarded to his grandfather eight years before.[1] Hone mused about the fleeting powers of the freemanship, which by this time had become an honorarium bestowed upon visiting presidents, kings, generals, and commodores. Today we recognize the right of the freeman only through the custom of awarding the "key to the city" to former hostages, rock stars, and astronauts. Yet for the early citizens of New York, the freemanship held special meaning. It served as a contractual bond with the local government. Obtaining the freedom of the city was an exercise in the responsibilities and privileges of a citizen of New York. When the applicant presented his credentials, paid the required fees, and took an oath of loyalty, he received a grant of special powers, which recognized his right to work within the city, a privilege restricted to fellow freemen, and allowed him to vote in local elections regardless of the extent of his freehold.[2]

The rights and duties of the freemanship—monopolistic control of labor, suffrage, and public service—were diffused throughout New York society and formed the basis for an ideological relationship between the classes. In a city considered "too great a mixture of nations," the freemanship united everyone who was blessed with citizenship. Even citizens by freehold had to take further steps to obtain the freemanship right and become vested with its powers. In New York City, the freemanship made occupation, as well as ethnicity and wealth, a basis for self-identification.

Recent students of New York history have neglected this important civic tradition for too long. The prevailing view, first enunciated by Beverly MacAnear, holds that the freemanship, as a relic of English law, passed rapidly into disuse in the colonies. Such historians as MacAnear, Gary B. Nash, Hendrik Hartog, and Jacob Price cite scarcity of labor, ease of mobility, and the constant attraction of the frontier as reasons for the obsolescence of the freemanship by the 1750s. By that time, they argue, only suffrage rights attracted citizens and then only in times of political crisis.[3]

This essays seeks to restore the central importance of freemanship for understanding the corporate values and ideology of New York's early citizenry. Not only did the freemanship remain a live issue during the colonial period, it continued to have fundamental importance as a social and political adhesive well after the Revolution. Freemanship declined in the 1790s only because the ruling Federalists, imposing their political will, chose to deny it to such occupational groups as cartmen, tavern keepers, porters, and grocers. The loss of freemanship contracted the laboring man's political rights and threatened his occupational security. As the nineteenth century opened, the freemanship remained a focal grievance of laborers who sought to have it reinstated to protect their monopolistic position in a rapidly changing economy.

Although this study will survey more than one hundred trades represented on the freemanship rolls, it will emphasize the experience of the cartmen. The cartmen were among the most numerous and essential of all occupations in New York City. They numbered more than one thousand by 1800; without them the city's commerce would have ceased. Carters worked regularly for the city government. They hauled sand and building supplies for municipal construction, and when necessary they "carted" criminals such as Angel Hendricksen, a child murderer, through the streets. While one carter drove her past jeering crowds of citizens, others hauled the lumber for a gallows. As Mrs. Hendricksen suffered her last worldly agonies, the carters and other workers gathered by her feet to drink the "wine and brandies" served by local government in partial payment for their labors. Cartmen were invaluable as carriers of household necessities including wood, hay, and groceries. In times of crisis such as plagues and fires, New Yorkers anxiously sought cartmen to move their belongings. A carter, as Isaac Lyon, the cartmen-historian, pointed out that a carter, "had to know all things about the city, its houses, streets and churches, or be set down as a know-nothing." He had to be, according to Lyon, a "combination of encyclopedia and intelligence-office."[4]

James Kent, author of the first great study of the civic charter, discussed the importance and feudal origins of freemanship in 1836. It was "introduced as an invaluable barrier against the insecurity and oppression of the feudal system. . . . Corporate cities offering the freedom to feudal serfs became refuges to the oppressed." Kent noted that New York City's earliest charters provided for the freemanship and that "there was something sacred and dear attached to the very mention of its chartered rights and privileges."[5]

New York lawmakers took much of their legislation intact from London precedent. In New York as in London, one obtained the freemanship either by birth in the city, apprenticeship, or direct grant from the mayor or an alderman. The "Dun and Scot" provision of the freemanship, which required local residency, enabled citizens in New York and London to protect their occupations against "outsiders." In New York, outsiders included farmers, transients, slaves, and free blacks, all of whom were excluded from the privileges of citizenship.[6]

A second English ideal, that of "corporate government," greatly affected the New York experience. Independent English municipalities emerged between the thirteenth and fifteenth centuries. Mayors and aldermen, who were usually merchants, passed many laws to promote commerce. City officials used the freemanship to create a viable work force guaranteed exclusive privileges. Each freeman was part of the corporate body; inclusion made laborers and artisans roughly equal to wealthier merchants, at least for the purpose of citizenship. Each freeman held an equal vote and similar right to work in the city. The freemanship became a "bond of attachment," or mutual dependency, uniting laborers and the municipal corporate body. Each freeman had an obligation to the whole and shared in the benefits of mutual efforts.[7]

When the English captured New Amsterdam in 1664, they found that the burgher right that the Dutch had enacted bore close resemblance to their own customs. Reinforcing earlier city laws designed to keep out peddlers and sailors desiring to work in New Amsterdam, the Dutch burgher right rewarded local inhabitants who had served against the English and Indians with exclusive control over their occupations. The burgher right, in effect, created the privileges and responsibilities of citizenship.[8]

Between 1657 and 1661 more than 260 men, most of them carpenters, cordwainers, and tailors, claimed their burgher right at town meetings. The Dutch also granted the burgher right and guild status to coopers, cartmen, porters, and even to more humble occupations, including chimney sweeps and drummers. Only the blacks of the city were excluded. These patterns of protection and exclusivity continued into the English era.[9] After the English takeover, the new oath of allegiance recognized the burgher rights of the Dutch, and 135 Dutch and English laborers took the new freeman's oath.[10]

The mayoralty of William Merrett from 1695 to 1698 saw the greatest number of new freemen since the initiation of the burgher right forty years before: 365 New Yorkers, representing twenty-eight trades ranging from merchants and gentlemen at the apex of society down to cartmen, blacksmiths, and laborers at the bottom, applied for and received the freemanship. Carpenters and cordwainers were the largest groups, reflecting the predominance of small-scale crafts in the city. Large numbers of workers, however, also came from the mercantile sector. Coopers, blockmakers, sailmasters, and mariners formed increasing percentages of the freemanship rolls.[11]

Ease of admission produced a steady increase in the number of freemen over the next forty years. Between 1695 and 1735 more than seventeen hundred New Yorkers became freemen.[12] Slaves and free blacks continued to be restricted from all but the most menial trades, but white applicants easily obtained work. Although some immigrants acquired the freemanship, the great majority were local residents. Despite its need for laborers, early eighteenth-century New York City became so notorious for restrictive work laws that few immigrants or indentured servants considered settling there.

The range of occupations represented on the freemanship rolls at this time reflected the power of the corporate ideal of government. Tradesmen of all types sought protection from competition. The service-sector retailers, building tradesmen, transportation, and assorted other workers provided the largest number of freemen, 70 percent of the total. Within the service sector many workers who faced little competition, including booksellers, organists, chocolatiers, dancing masters, printers, and razor-grinders, became freemen. It is hard to believe that New York's economy could support more than seventeen goldsmiths and sixteen silversmiths. More common trades included cartmen, bricklayers, surgeons, carpenters, and tavern keepers. Some trades seem to have been entirely composed of freemen. At the top of society, sixty-two "gentlemen" became freemen.

For members of licensed occupations, including cartmen, bakers, butchers, tavern keepers, bellmen, and porters, the freemanship also meant initial entrance into the patronage rolls of the city government. Dutiful service by a freeman was usually rewarded by a sinecure. Examples include forty cartmen, among them Jacob Bennett, Abraham Blanck, Isaac DeLa Montagne, Peter DeLa Montagne, Rynier Knox, William Milliner, Joseph Paulding, and John Ten Broek, elected to city positions such as constable, assessor, and collector. Samuel Benson obtained an appointment as surveyor of highways, Caspar Burger became a corn measurer, and Dirck Cooke attained the posts of bellman, deputy commissioner of markets, and collector. Such posts provided them additional income.[13]

In times of economic reversal, the city government gave preference to local freemen. During the depressed years of the 1730s complaints to the Common Council about the decay of trade and the inability to find work spurred city officials to increase the fees for the freemanship to £3 for merchants and 20S. for craftsmen. At the same time, the Common Council gave preference to native-born applicants. Freemen born in the city outnumbered immigrants by a ratio of more than three to one.[14]

The construction of the city streets, wharves, and piers was also reserved for freemen. Work on city projects increased during periods of economic distress. Cartmen, carpenters, and bricklayers, for example, all full subscribed to the freemanship, benefited from public works expenditures.[15]

Political considerations contributed to the powers of freemanship. In the 1730s, acrimony often raged in the assembly, where factions fought over the policies of Governor William Cosby, but at the municipal level, stability reigned. Mayors often served for five or even ten years. The length of the typical alderman's term increased dramatically. Lower city offices were characterized by nepotism, long terms of service, and sinecures.

During the middle of the eighteenth century, some trades found their "ancient freedoms" under attack. In 1747, for example, the carpenters and bricklayers were aggrieved by the illegal incursions of "inhabitants of neighboring provinces and more especially of the Jerseys," who "pay no taxes" yet entered the city with "their nails and tools to sell

their labor at 20 to 30 pounds less per year than the agreed upon rates."
The carpenters and bricklayers petitioned the governor as freemen
seeking relief and protection from encroachers. The governor passed
the complaint back to the Common Council, which noted that it was
signed by "many persons obscure to us" and that freemen were already
protected by local law. Despite this defeat, the carpenters and bricklayers vigilantly, if informally, excluded outsiders. The petition
demonstrates the power of the freemanship, the expectation of protection, and the custom of fixed rates. It was signed by more than one
hundred carpenters, bricklayers, and other freemen, including future
revolutionary Alexander MacDougall.[16]

The cartmen, however, feared little from outsiders. Although several
signed the petition in support of carpenters, their occupation remained
well protected by the local government. Prospective cartmen received
very few new freemanships between 1720 and 1750, as the trade
fought successfully to keep its numbers down. Many new freemen
were the sons of cartmen. Families including the Bantas, Ackermans,
Montanjes, and Bogarts contributed second-and third-generation cartmen, as fathers passed their rights to their sons. With such stability, the
political strength of the trade grew even more potent. By 1752 it was
so notorious that William Livingston criticized the Common Council
in the *Independent Reflector* as men "who stand in more Awe of A
band of Carmen than of an Armed Host; because that proceeds not so
much from natural Timidity, as a more political one."[17]

Some of this awe may have come from the growing interdepend-
ence between the mayor and cartmen. The Montgomerie Charter of
1731 gave the mayor the exclusive right to license cartmen and tavern
keepers, and the fees he collected from them constituted his salary. The
practice of multiple officeholding provided the mayor, who was appointed by the governor and not beholden to the Common Council,
with rich patronage opportunities.[18]

Mayor John Cruger, Jr., who entered office at the outset of the
Seven Years' War, used these opportunities to great advantage. Cruger served during a war that gave enormous impetus to the city's
economy and brought it previously unknown levels of prosperity. As
the British army's demand for goods and services soared, local wages
reached unheard-of rates. When New York became the principal supply depot for British troops, tavern keepers and grocers prospered
from the rain of shillings coming from visiting soldiers. Shipbuilding

became a major New York industry. Moreover, the city had to supply few troops in comparison with beleaguered Boston, and taxes remained relatively low.[19]

As the economy expanded, so did the demand for cartmen. Previously, the trade had averaged between twenty and thirty members. In the first few years of Cruger's term, more than two hundred men received cartmen's licenses and the freemanship.[20] This dramatic increase made carting one of the largest occupations in the city, surpassed only by the hundreds of mariners. Not only did Cruger take over licensing, he also reserved for himself the granting of freemanships to carters. The Common Council did not record many of these freemen, yet they voted in local elections and for the assembly.

In 1761 Cruger ran for the colonial assembly. The first assembly election in some time and the first since the recent death of the powerful politician James De Lancey, Sr., the contest promised to be interesting. At the time, Cruger was not only mayor but also a leading merchant and the head of the British commissariat in New York, a position that allowed him to hire numerous local tradesmen. Just before the election, he hired fifty carters to haul munitions to the embattled British for at Albany, for which he paid them the equivalent of at least one month's wages in town.[21]

The carters, beholden to Cruger in several ways, lined up to vote for him en masse. More than fifty of the seventy-four cartmen voting cast their ballots for Cruger, providing about 5 percent of his total and a healthy margin over the losing candidates, Philip Livingston and Lawrence Lispenard.[22]

Although the number of cartmen rose from about 40 or 50 to 386 between 1754 and 1763, other groups continued to be strongly invested in the freemanship. Many artisans became freemen in one occupation and then moved into others without reapplication. Some used it as a hedge against the failure of their original businesses. A number of cordwainers, bakers, blacksmiths, and carpenters, for example, acquired cartmen's licenses after becoming freemen. Carting became a refuge for distressed freemen. Cruger granted more than nine hundred freemanships in his nine-year tenure as mayor. Among them were seventy-nine cordwainers, thirty tailors, twenty-six coopers, thirty-four bakers, twenty-five blacksmiths, and fifty-five carpenters. Twenty-eight merchants undertook the right. Although these numbers indicate that not all tradesmen became freemen, their representation was still strong.[23]

During Cruger's last years as mayor, long-standing animosities toward English rule intensified and were manifested in the Stamp Act riots, hatred between the English soldiers and local tradesmen, and the growing political involvement of all classes. Political participation became wider and more intense. As a means for laboring men to gain the franchise, the freemanship took on added significance. On October 1, as agitation against the Stamp Act grew stronger, 164 New Yorkers became freemen, joined by 143 others in that month alone, in time for the next elections three months away.[24]

The freemen came out in large numbers for the two elections in 1768. They outnumbered the freeholders by more than 400 and produced 1,411 votes. The cartmen were particularly active. Ninety-four cast ballots in 1768. James De Lancey's successful party took advantage of his leading role in the Stamp Act riots and identified his unpopular opponent, lawyer John Morin Scott, with British tyranny.

At the dawn of the revolutionary era, New York was still wedded to a corporate social order. From top to bottom, white laborers possessing the freemanship held monopolistic job security, political opportunities, patronage, and full rights of citizens. Free blacks excluded from licensed occupations remained near the bottom of society, above only those slaves employed as house servants. Farmers, transients, and recent immigrants viewed New York as a hard place to find work. The city's Dutch were restricted from several occupations in which Anglo-American laborers received priority, and local residents received preference over outsiders.

In the years between 1770 and 1776, the city divided first between popular and conservative Whigs and then between patriots and loyalists. Of all the northern ports, New York remained the most tied to the British economy and society. As the most conservative city, it fell far behind Philadelphia and Boston in its reaction to British oppression. Although New Yorkers were deeply angered by the presence of English troops and their propensity to undercut the wages of local tradesmen, the city's loyalties remained uncertain as late as 1775.[25]

As the events of the revolutionary years rapidly unfolded, New Yorkers faced wrenching choices about their allegiances. Many freemen joined the patriot armies and served under such local heroes as Marinus Willett and Alexander MacDougall. Some, no doubt encumbered by poverty, expressed no preference. At least one hundred cartmen stayed in the city to make fat profits serving as wagoners for the

British.[26] The British recognized the rights of the freemanship as much as possible. The English commanders in chief even awarded new rights to the freemen during the war. The military commander and the Chamber of Commerce shared regulation of local commerce by negotiating market rates with committees representing various trades, particularly the cartmen.[27]

While the British occupied New York, patriot leaders met in exile in Fishkill to plot the state's future. The delegates to the state constitutional conventions designed new governing bodies and laws more liberal than the colonial charters with their restrictive freehold requirements. One provision, however, was conservative. In vain, James Duane and other New York City delegates tried to abolish franchise privileges for freemen of Albany and New York. Although their argument does not survive, the events of the 1760s and the tradesmen's loyal support of James De Lancey's faction, consisting largely of men who turned Tory in the 1770s, clearly affected Duane's proposal.[28]

The Revolution caused many changes in American life, but historians have considered none as far-reaching as the transition from a communal, corporate society to a world of self-interest. First merchants and lawyers, then middling tradesmen, and finally artisans adopted new ideas about the merits of the free market. Most scholars argue that by the close of the revolutionary war the American people were as devoted to self-interest as they were to the egalitarian goals of liberty and political equality. As a result, medieval concepts of bonded labor gradually became obsolete. Indentured servitude, apprenticeship, and slavery all lost their legitimacy in the northern states. So, too, the freemanship was discarded.[29] Yet not all groups within society developed at the same rate. The abandonment of medieval labor relations and movement toward a capitalist ethos by many citizens of New York does not imply that others more humble desired the same. Nor would society have let them.[30]

After Evacuation Day, November 25, 1783, the entering patriots fond the city in complete disarray. Seven years of war had left barricaded streets, crumbling wharves, fire-gutted housing, and ubiquitous filth.[31] At the first meeting of the temporary council ruling the city, the first issue raised was the regulation of cartmen, who, it was claimed, were abusing Tories and patriots alike by rate-gouging, refusing to provide service, and outright theft. Regulation of trade had broken down completely under the British in the later stages of the war, and economic anarchy existed. While the council was drawing up regulations and fixed rates for the cartmen consistent with prewar law, it also had to consider a petition from various tavern keepers, grocers, and other mechanics of the city to restrict the licensing of those trades to freemen and patriots. Many market and labor laws passed in the city by a popular Whig council immediately after the evaluation by the British duplicated earlier colonial monopolistic regulations.[32]

James Duane, who had sought to have the freemanship stripped of its political powers, became the first postwar mayor. Duane decided to start fresh with the carters. He announced that all cartmen who wished to be licensed by the city and made freemen should register at his office at once. Within a few months, 325 veterans, old-time residents, impoverished tradesmen, sons of former New Yorkers, and even a few Tories who had friends among the patriots appeared at the Common Council to take the freeman's oath. The only difference from the prewar oath was the insertion of United States government for King George III. Other trades apparently did not need to register for the freemanship, but city law required all potential cartmen to do so. By mid-1784, 385 cartmen had become freemen, bound to the city by an oath of allegiance. Other cartmen frequently endorsed their petitions for licenses, which often cited service in the American army and loyalty to the new government. The government was thus able to create stability out of chaos and to extract loyalty from a most difficult trade.[33]

The reestablishment of the freemanship for the cartmen brought them great political and economic benefits. As city employees they were expected to vote according to Duane's instructions, but they still held the potential for massive political clout. Carters who held the freemanship excluded everyone else from working the streets. Their close ties to the city government assured them jobs and patronage. As in the prewar era, carters with the freemanship moved easily into sinecures such as inspectorships and the watch. Duane, moreover, appointed cartmen such as Alexander Lamb street commissioners and put them in charge of other carters doing road repairs.[34]

By 1787 Duane ceased offering the freemanship to cartmen. Perhaps he wished to limit its numbers, or perhaps he simply imposed his original wishes dating back to the state constitutional convention of 1777. Between 1785 and 1788, however, he did grant the right to about 150 tradesmen from fifty-three other occupations. As in the colonial era, freemanship rolls revealed the economic breadth of society.

After the adoption of the new federal constitution and the ascendance of the Federalist party, Duane had designs on higher office. But George Washington rejected his attempt to become a New York senator and instead appointed the mayor a supreme court justice for the middle states. His successor as mayor was the longtime city recorder, Richard Varick, who assumed office in August 1790 and remained until 1801, the longest tenure of any New York City mayor before Fiorello La Guardia.[35]

Although the Federalist party won sweeping victories in the elections of 1788 and 1789 and clearly held the loyalty of the mechanics and cartmen of the city, its grip on power was insecure. Mechanics and cartmen alike demanded greater representation in office; they had begun to seek places on the assembly ticket as early as 1785. As one newspaper declared, "The pedantic lawyer, the wealthy merchant and the lordly landlord have their needs attended to, but the mechanics and cartmen do not."[36] The *New York Packet* that same year nominated a number of mechanics and cartmen for the assembly. Interestingly, none of the supposed cartmen on that ticket was a freeman. The ties between the Federalists and cartmen blessed with the freemanship were beginning to distress those carters without them.

To the Federalists, talk of mechanics and cartmen in the assembly was heresy. The party insisted on loyalty. Richard Varick, a loyal party man, set out to do his best. The most vulnerable voters were the various licensed workers. Varick informed incumbent cartmen that disloyalty to the Federalists would result in termination of their licenses. Because the city charter gave him that power, and the mayor was appointed by the Council of Appointment and not elected by voters, the license holders had little recourse.[37]

As the economy grew, Varick appointed three hundred new cartmen by 1792 to answer the needs of city merchants and the burgeoning populace. He refused, however, to grant them the freemanship, thereby effectively disfranchising every cartman without a £40 freehold, which few had. As Varick denied them the vote and drove rebellious older cartmen from the ranks, the trade itself became politically threatened. Even worse, loss of the freemanship made the trade more vulnerable to becoming swamped by unlicensed drivers and outsiders. In this political and economic context, a major labor dispute broke out in 1791.[38] The previous winter had been very hard on New Yorkers, and the city's poor detested Varick. Sometime over the summer of 1791 he gathered together the entire force of six hundred cartmen and informed them that anyone who did not vote for the Federalist ticket in the fall election could expect to have his license revoked.[39]

The elections themselves were not especially important. The Anti-Federalists were in retreat and as yet did not have an effective strategy for attracting urban voters. The previous year, however, the Livingston family, one of the most powerful forces in state and city politics, had broken with the Federalists. One of the urban members of the family, William S. Livingston, decided to gain political capital by condemning the Federalists' blatant manipulation of the cartmen.[40]

Using the pseudonym "Lucious," Livingston blasted Varick in the newspapers for wielding the "iron rod of power . . . in dreadful suspense over the head . . . of cartmen, butchers, tavern-keepers and all who work . . . under the sanction of a license." He reminded the carters and others that they were "freemen and should not have their rights retrenched in any way." The following day, "Cato" supported Livingston by assuring the freemen that "the chief magistrate was within the reach of the laws and could be impeached if guilty."[41] This warning set off a furor. For the next decade the cartmen attempted repeatedly to have Varick impeached as mayor.

The denial of freemanship, the legal bond of attachment in New York City for over a century, had now become a major political controversy. The insurgent Republicans, allied with the Livingstons, took the side of the cartmen. The Federalists in turn revealed their policy over the next decade. Instituting what the Republicans called a "Reign of Terror," the majority party in the city attempted to impose political loyalty on municipal workers by using their licenses as a club. Without the protection of the freemanship, the cartmen and other licensed trades worked at the mercy of the mayor.

Despite its official deterioration, the freemanship continued to have great political and economic importance. It remained dear to the cartmen because it was a means of achieving political equality. It also represented occupational monopoly, which the carters desperately needed to maintain their prosperity in the face of the city's erupting population.

In the spring elections of 1792, William S. Livingston revived his support for the goals of the cartmen. Addressing his demands directly to the Society of Cartmen, newly organized in March 1792 to further their interests, Livingston argued that the mayor should be elected, not appointed, to make him more responsive to the needs of "freemen." Calling Varick a tyrant, he charged that the mayor was abusing the rights of citizens. No one should deny the freemanship to anyone who had served an apprenticeship, who had fought against "foreign powers," who had resided continually in the city except for wartime service, and who filled the "most respectable and industrious of offices." Nor should freemen be denied the right to pass their status on to their heirs.[42] Each of these charges spoke to the cartmen's difficulties. As long-term, loyal citizens, they expected their rights and privileges to be protected. As a reward for his sponsorship, eligible cartmen gave Livingston an overwhelming majority of their votes for the assembly, probably providing his margin of victory. Other cartmen, disfranchised, appeared at political rallies and loudly proclaimed their anger at Varick's actions.

To be sure, not all cartmen turned against the Federalists. In the next few years Varick maintained the loyalty of the ninety or so cartmen who held the freemanship even though he lost the favor of the others. The prominent cartman Alexander Lamb, for example, remained loyal. A lifelong resident of the city, he was the son of Alexander Lamb, Sr., for many years the doorkeeper of the colonial-era Common Council. Alexander Lamb, Jr., showed leadership qualities in his service of the patriot army by his ability to find hay and firewood for the beleaguered New York State militia. After his return to New York City in 1783, Lamb gained the freemanship and began supervising teams of cartmen employed by Mayor Duane. At the same time he organized petition drives that successfully limited the numbers of cartmen, legalized the use of iron rims for cartwheels, and increased the maximum fees allowed for cartage. In 1787 Duane made Lamb the first foreman of the first "class" of cartmen. Duane also appointed Lamb head of the watch, a lucrative post paying more than a dollar a night. A year later, Varick made Lamb the captain of a new militia troop, and in 1793, Lamb became superintendent of street cleaning for the sixth ward, giving him large patronage powers.[43] Lamb's career illustrates the immense value political loyalty and the freemanship could hold for a few select cartmen.

As close as Varick and Lamb may have been, the Federalists had not fully realized the value of the latter's popularity. In April 1795, when the Republicans met with the Society of Cartmen to seek support for their ticket, they readily agreed to the cartmen's demand that Lamb replace Benjamin Blagge, a longtime but aged friend of the trade, as the sixth ward's candidate for the assembly. In the election that followed, Lamb's candidacy caused a furor. A letter supposedly written by the Federalists, but no doubt forged by the Republicans, asked merchants to unite to defeat Lamb, for "would it not be a reflection on all of us, if a cartman and his associates were in the assembly."[44]

Lamb swept to a huge victory, outpolling all other candidates except Jotham Post, a butcher. His rise to the assembly did not pollute that august body, however. Lamb actually supported many Federalist measures while in office. Indeed, Republican newspapers accused Lamb of intimidating even neutral cartmen who did not actively support the opposition. The following year Lamb was reelected, this time as a Federalist. His career as a party functionary ensured his loyalty to those who gave him power—power that came from his freemanship.[45]

By the mid-1790s, the increasing number of cartmen without the freemanship produced a split within the trade. By 1795 there were more than one thousand cartmen, but a steadily declining number held the freemanship. Those who had it fared well; those without it felt no loyalty to the city government.

Events in 1797 revealed the government's weakening hold over the cartmen. For the previous two years the cartmen had kept up their attacks on Varick, joining in the furor over the Jay Treaty and in protests over his granting permission to the captain of the *Thetis,* a British naval vessel, to take prisoners from the city jail for his crew. By late 1797 Varick and most of the cartmen were enemies.[46] That November, after the Republicans racked up gains in the local elections and nearly secured Varick's recall, he revoked all the cartmen's licenses. Varick's action had an economic basis. The city's population accused the cartmen of rate-gouging, of refusing service to the poor, of reckless driving, and of insulting behavior. Varick announced his decision to terminate their licenses by public notice in newspapers and in broadsides.[47]

In 1799 Varick finally began to recognize his mistakes. Although he did not reinstitute the freemanship or allow the cartmen the franchise, he wrote many elements of freemanship into new city laws governing the cartmen. After 1799, cartmen had to reside in the city, be citizens, and own at least one cart and horse "free and clear of all debts." Long-term residents and veterans received preference. Many of these regulations simply recognized established fact, but the codes retained the substance if not the form of freemanship.[48]

Varick's reforms were not enough, however. By 1801, the cartmen's changed loyalties helped give the Republicans their first real municipal majority. One of their first acts was to rid the city of Varick. Edward Livingston, who had received popular support from the cartmen in the 1790s, became mayor. Republican newspapers commemorated Varick's departure by a full-scale review of his depredations. He had been, charged the *Argus,* worse than "yellow fever itself."[49]

With the Republicans in power, the cartmen called in their political debts. Shortly after Livingston's ascension, the Society of Cartmen circulated a petition, signed by several hundred members, calling for reinstatement of the freemanship and for the status of freemanship as a part of the licensing process. Livingston offered his support and expressed his "willingness to cooperate in a measure which might tend to the welfare and happiness of his fellow citizens." The Committee of Cartmen then gained the support of aldermen Joshua Barker and Mangle Minthorne; approval of only two more aldermen was then needed. At this point the plan floundered. Jotham Post refused to sign the measure, arguing that if the petitioners were made "free," three thousand others would have equal claim. When asked if it was not their right to become freemen, Post responded that "undoubtedly it was . . . but that so it would be attended with consequences very dangerous if so large a body were made free." The cartmen then countered with a compromise by which only they would become freemen; did not Post "suppose that they would elect a proper character to the council?" Post agreed, but argued that the cartmen might well "choose a man not possessed of a freehold . . . who might do damage to those who had." At this point the petition died.[50]

As this incident makes clear, the freemanship was by no means a dead article, even as late as 1801. Although they initially petitioned for all citizens, the cartmen were willing to restrict the privilege to themselves. Rather than listen deferentially to office-holders, they formed a committee to negotiate the return of the freemanship.

The goals of this petition were finally achieved in 1804, when instead of reinstating the freemanship, the Republicans reformed election qualifications in general. Because most city laborers qualified to vote under the new rules, the political potency of the freemanship diminished. With the freemanship incorporated into the city's licensing procedures, few bothered to go before the Common Council to take the formal oath.[51]

Yet the spirit of the freemanship lived on in the monopolistic ideology of local workers. Protected by city law from becoming casual laborers, cartmen, tavern keepers, grocers, and butchers controlled entrance to their trades and kept their numbers down. They maintained favorable relations with the Common Council. Shifting their loyalty in response to political patronage, licensed occupations became "powerful groups of voters." The cartmen, in particular, made use of their intimate bond with city government. In 1816 the Society of Cartmen secured an increase in maximum fees, removed old charges for inspection, and nominated a superintendent of carts to govern them. They began to use their license fees to subsidize their own benevolent fund.[52] A few years later, the passage of city laws reestablishing long-term residence and citizenship requirements for licensure resolved a threat to the carters' monopoly by Irish interlopers. The city again gave preference to sons of cartmen, to veterans, and to those nominated by the trade. The Irish had to be satisfied with "dirt carters" licenses, which allowed them to pick up the garbage and little else.[53]

City workers also continued to prohibit local blacks from many occupations. Except for notable victories in gaining control of chimney sweeping and hackney-coach driving, free blacks in early nineteenth-century New York seldom cracked the racial barriers that city workers set up. As a result, blacks frequently moved into entrepreneurial callings such as catering or challenged the monopolies of grocers and tavern keepers. They were unable, however, to mount a substantial threat to the cartmen. This occupation, deeply imbued with the spirit of freemanship, remained racially exclusive until the 1850s. As late as the early twentieth century, few blacks were able to break into transportation occupations in New York's streets.[54]

The freemanship remained strong among the postrevolutionary generation. New York's workers not only embraced the egalitarian reforms of the age, they also looked to the past for inspiration. Workmen expected full citizenship, protection of their trade, favorable relations with government, and patronage. The freemanship remained the "bond of attachment" between government and labor in New York until the early nineteenth century.

2

In Retrospect

Richard B. Morris and Government and Labor in Early America *(1946)*

On December 20, 1944, Dorothy M. Swart of Columbia University Press informed Richard B. Morris, then Associate Professor of History at the City College of New York, that he needed to cut approximately 40 percent of his original 1,000–page manuscript of *Government and Labor in Early America* or face a subvention fee of $250. Accordingly, Morris cut over four hundred pages, including nearly all tables and a hefty chunk of a chapter on concerted actions by laborers. A few months later, Morris anxiously wrote to Charles G. Proffitt, his editor at Columbia University Press, urging him to publish the book quickly. With the end of World War II in sight, Morris explained, his book has a "great many implications [about] the current problem of wartime controls on wages and prices." Morris worried that the end of the war and the gradual relaxation of such controls would make publication of the book less timely. As months wore on, Morris continued to urge rapid release of his book, only to learn from Proffitt that its appearance was delayed by wartime paper shortages. Both editorial decisions would affect the long-term responses to the book.[1]

Publication finally occurred in 1946 and the book received highly favorable notices from commercial and academic reviews. Typical of these was Joseph Rosenfarb's appraisal that *Government and Labor* would become the "point of departure" for any study of colonial labor and legal history.[2] The book collected additional appreciation over the next few decades. In 1952, it received some votes for "Preferred Books in American History, 1936–1950," in a survey conducted by the *Mis-*

sissippi Valley Historical Review. As Morris rose to prominence in the historical profession, the book was reissued in several editions. *Government and Labor* is now out of print, but it continues to inspire scholars. This essay surveys the significance of the book in the half-century since its first publication, discusses how scholars have accepted or rejected Morris's conclusions, and suggests how Morris's findings might serve as markers for newer studies.[3]

Principally, Morris hoped that the book would convince legal scholars to employ social interpretations of court records. Prodded by negative criticism of the sweeping nature of his previous work, *Studies in the History of American Law* in 1929, Morris gathered voluminous amounts of evidence from court records in all thirteen original colonies to support his contentions. As in his earlier work, Morris tried to pry colonial legal historiography away from dismissive attitudes of Roscoe Pound and push it toward a social understanding of the effect of law. In the estimation of Stephen Botein, legal historians' appreciation of Morris's achievements had to wait until the 1980s. Today, legal scholars such as Christopher Tomlins, Robert J. Steinfeld, and Karen Orren owe much to Morris for their social interpretations of labor law governing master/servant relations, rules of conspiracy, and the power of the remnants of feudalism in America.[4]

Government and Labor's greatest influence has been on social historians. This was not clear for many years. Although duly noted, Morris's book languished as a "neglected classic" until it was rediscovered by the "new" social historians of the 1960s and 1970s. As Gary B. Nash points out, the book introduced scholars to the use of court records to rescue from oblivion the roles of ordinary Americans in the construction of a new society. Morris was also active in this revival. In the preface to a 1981 edition of *Government and Labor,* Morris suggested several ways his book had influenced contemporary scholarship. He claimed that its broadly brushed concerns about economic and social mobility inspired works by James Henretta, Charles G. Grant, James Lemon, Allan Kulikoff, and Nash. Similarly, he contended that the works of Jesse Lemisch and Marcus Rediker on sailors were indebted to *Government and Labor.* Laying claim to the ancestry of a major historiographic debate, he argued (1981 edition, pp. ix-xii) that evidence he unearthed of labor grievances against employers in colonial cities, undergirded studies on "crowd" or "mob" actions by town artisans and mechanics spurring revolutionary unrest, namely studies by Pauline Maier, Dirk Hoerder, Alfred F. Young, Eric and Philip Foner, Charles Olton, and, later, Paul Gilje and Sean Wilentz.[5]

Morris's organizational method in *Government and Labor* was thematic. He introduced the book with a lengthy essay on the varying efforts of mercantilism on colonial labor. Mercantilism, Morris contended, was a mixture of the vestiges of feudalism and the seedbeds of merchant capitalism. Morris maintained that feudal law was most apparent in the revival of the Tudor Industrial code in early America; early Americans, he asserted, sustained a social consensus that supported compulsory labor. Hence, colonial Americans punished idleness harshly, built workhouses, and impressed servants for public work projects. On the other side of this ideology were provisions for poor relief, restraints on dismissal, wage fixing, a presumption of higher wages for skilled workers in America, and a lack of class antagonism in the young colonies.

Morris organized the main body of the text into two sections. The first part, "Free Labor," includes chapters on wage regulation in the colonial era and during the American Revolution, concerted action among workers, terms and conditions of employment, maritime labor relations, and labor and the armed services. The second half offers a taxonomy of "Bound Labor," a definition within which Morris included redemptioners, convicts, debt servants, apprentices, and child laborers. In a key decision, Morris consciously avoided, except in a very few instances, discussion of the status of enslaved Africans, contending that others had studied this subject adequately. Referring readers to his previous work, Morris added little new evidence in *Government and Labor* on female laborers in colonial America.

The book's first chapter, which focuses on wage regulation in the colonial era, has found few adherents. Despite the massive evidence Morris produced for *Government and Labor* and augmented with a number of powerful essays in the next decade, the triumph of Louis Hartz's formulation of liberal capitalism made Morris's achievement *sui generis*. Scholars have accepted Hartz's edict that, from the earliest years of settlement, virtually every American colonist "had the mentality of an independent entrepreneur."[6] Hartz's contention that colonial economic regulation was short-lived and ineffectual remains large accepted today. For example, Daniel Vickers's much praised labor history of Essex County, Massachusetts, directly refutes Morris on wage regulation. Courts in Massachusetts, Vickers points out, rarely imposed wage restraints. The lack of regulation was important in the decline of a "moral economy" in the political economy of the countryside and the nurturing of capitalist practices among rural Americans.

The situation was different in colonial cities. Although Vickers has acknowledged that wage regulation in cities may have been more pronounced, few other historians have built upon Morris's conclusive evidence, which showed how local governments constructed sturdy codes regulating production, performance, and sale of essential goods and services including baking, meat cutting, carting, portering, alcohol sales, and grocers. It is unfortunate, as well, that so little attention has been given to these trades. Their close interaction with government, whose massive intervention into their work lives sustained economic stability for generations, resembles the moral economic qualities found among similar English semi-skilled workers. Moral economic behavior depended on stable prices, and colonial cities, as Morris showed, kept wages and prices down for generations.[7]

Nor did these legal traditions decline by the era of the American Revolution. In the next chapter, which was influenced by his observations on the political economy of World War II, Morris continued his analysis of wage restraints into the revolutionary conflict. Confirming the fears Morris conveyed by letter to Charles G. Proffitt, his arguments have failed to convince other historians, who, influenced by the post-World War II boom economy, regard the American Revolution as the staging ground for the transition into capitalism. In contrast, Morris pointed out the lack of clear consensus about the direction the postrevolutionary economy would take and tried to show that a class interpretation of the Revolution had much validity, although he contended that theories of sharp social dichotomies were oversimplified. Despite the wisdom of his argument, Hartz's model of the transition to capitalism remains surprisingly strong, even among labor historians. By relying on Hartz, labor historians ignore the ample evidence Morris uncovered of price codes and work regulation legislated during the Revolution. One cogent reason for this is the identification of labor history with the subsequent history of industrial laborers, whose presence in America did not become prominent until after the American Revolution. Colonial artisans, as Morris disclosed, were more willing to accept government regulation of their business affairs.[8]

In the book's third chapter, which focuses on concerted action by colonial workers, Morris demonstrated the political effects of government regulation. Even after the manuscript cuts required by his editors, this chapter, at seventy pages, is the longest in the book. Morris divided the chapter into six sections, which encompass discussions of the legal traditions of common law and collective action, combinations to maintain craft monopolies, concerted action by workers in licensed trades, concerted actions by bound servants, exclusive behavior by white workmen against black artisans, political actions by working-class groups in the Revolutionary period, and concerted actions by journeymen for labor ends. Each of these parts bears examination.

Morris's evidence of concerted actions by bound workers has been especially influential. Here he focused primarily on two moments of time in late-seventeenth-century Virginia: the York insurrections of 1661 and the famous Bacon's Rebellion fifteen years later. In each case, Morris carefully discussed the grievances and angry actions of frustrated servants and highlighted their roles in the rebellion of 1676. His evidence and analysis anticipate the structure of Edmund Morgan's persuasive reasoning in *American Slavery/American Freedom.*[9] The high impact of working-class behavior was evident later in this chapter in a section on the political activities of working-class groups in the Revolutionary period. Here Morris's quick study of the activities of mariners and mobs in the Stamp Act Riots of the 1760s directly foreshadows works by social historians mentioned by Morris in the preface of the 1981 edition.

Colonial labor historians have paid less heed to some of Morris's other insights in this chapter. For example, after noting that colonial legislators, influenced by the Tudor Statute of Artificers, attempted to stamp out combinations by skilled craftsmen as seditious, Morris divulged how skilled craftsmen used combinations to maintain exclusive control over their skills. Although he concluded that combinations generally declined in importance by the Revolution and never took root in southern colonies, Morris uncovered substantial evidence of collusion by carpenters and weavers in northern cities over a century apart. Considered apart, these incidents perhaps do not amount to much. Taken as a whole, they suggest a pervasive mentality among skilled workers to control their destinies through monopoly decades before the union movement of the 1830s.

Monopoly was also the aim of semi-skilled urban laborers. Such licensed workers as cartmen, butchers, porters, bakers, and even doctors and lawyers used municipal regulations to limit access to their trades. These trades are badly understudied. There is one book on New York City cartmen (mine) and a chapter in another book on the city's bakers. However, such significant occupations of tavern keepers, bakers, butchers, porters, and liverymen have been completely ignored. This is unfortunate because their ties with municipal government made them highly politicized. Butchers, for example, a trade which resisted industrialization until after the Civil War, were commonly numbered among officeholders in eastern cities. The marriage of government and licensed workers also moved west in the nineteenth century. As Richard Wade has shown, newer cities on the frontier used the same municipal regulations far into the nineteenth century.[10]

The protective behavior of the licensed trades was especially aimed at black Americans. Supported by restrictive municipal legislation, these occupations, as Morris exposed, excluded free and enslaved blacks from work opportunities up and down the Atlantic Coast from the early seventeenth century until after the American Revolution. As David Roediger has shown, such prohibitions helped shape an ideology of racial superiority among white laborers, which he has named the "wages of whiteness." Accurate as that may be, far less understood is the political interaction between workers and local government that legitimized these convictions.[11] Blacks also used the government to protect their economic interests. For example, almost nothing is known about how urban black laborers gained government permission to take over the trades of porters and liverymen after the Revolution.

Historians have given much greater attention to Morris's third chapter, which focused on maritime labor relations. In his dissertation and in several major articles, Jesse Lemisch has charted the political significance of mariners in the mob actions in the decade before the American Revolution, fleshing out Morris's insights on concerted actions by workers during the Revolution. Marcus Rediker's book on Anglo-American seamen and pirates is even more directly indebted to Morris. Rediker borrowed Morris's survey of mercantilism to construct his discussion of the world of mariner's work. Rediker also showed the influence of Morris in his discussion of mariners' work methods, wages, concerted actions by sailors, and captain/mariner relations. Rediker's chapters on seamen's language and the spirit of resistance are outgrowths of Morris's fusion of the work experience and culture. While mariners have received ample attention, still needed, however, are works that advance Morris's insights into the special relationship of soldiers and government.[12]

Next, Morris looked closely at the legal status and experiences of indentured servants. His efforts set the terms of scholarship for decades. Together with Abbott Smith, whose monograph appeared in 1947, Morris, as Richard Dunn says, established the "numerous friction points between colonial laborers and their employers." Sharon Salinger's concise study of indentured servants has shown how indentured labor transformed from a paternalist to a semicapitalist system. Bernard Bailyn's portrait of prerevolutionary servants in New York underscores the significance of bonded labor late in the colonial period. The sole general study, David Galenson's econometric analysis, follows Morris's leads by demonstrating that the typical indentured servants were young, lonely males. Roger Ekirch has found similar traits among transported felons in the eighteenth century.[13]

There are still overlooked leads in *Government and Labor* about the significance of indentured servant resistance just before the Revolution. In several tables that survived his editor's cuts, Morris showed rising numbers of advertisements for fugitive indentured servants in newspapers from New York, New Jersey, Pennsylvania, and Virginia, incidents which became a small flood just before the war. Combined with surging increased in numbers of self-emancipated enslaved blacks, Morris's data suggests sweeping restiveness among bonded laborers in the tumultuous years before 1775. In Morris's unpublished papers, there are tantalizing hints of the development of this tide of runaways. For example, excised tables covering fugitive bondspeople in New York, Connecticut, New Jersey, Pennsylvania, Maryland, and Delaware between 1745 and 1765 showed how average annual instances of flight jumped from around fifteen a year to over forty by the time of the Stamp Act Riots, indicating a general restlessness by bondspeople of both races. How different would be understanding of prerevolutionary crowd activity if white and black laborers were considered together, rather than separately?[14]

Gauging the importance of these roaming servants requires erasing conceptual boundaries between the lives of white and black laborers. By his own admission, Morris provided little coverage of enslaved blacks or Native Americans. At one time he considered a massive study of early American slavery, but abandoned it. Although enslaved and free African Americans crop up occasionally in *Government and Labor,* they are otherwise invisible, and odd omission considering that slavery required government support as much as did indentured servitude. By dropping blacks from his portrait of colonial labor, Morris helped sustain a curious division that exists today between early American labor historiography and the study of slavery. Before *Government and Labor,* historians regularly considered the status of various bond-speople on a spectrum of possibilities. For example, Samuel B. McKee wrote chapters on free, apprentice, indentured, and enslaved labor in his still-useful study of colonial labor in New York. In 1955, in one of the last studies in this mode, Lawrence William Towner categorized indentured and enslaved blacks together as "lower servants."[15]

In a final chapter, Morris completed his massive study with a chapter on persistent problems of labor relations in the light of early American experience. In this evocative chapter, he outlined the lineage of labor law from the colonial era to the close of World War II, noting, for example, the use of regulated wages during wartime. He observed the curious vestiges of the master's quasi-proprietary rights over the services of his servant, powers which shackled baseball players before the reserve clause was dropped in 1974. Recently, a key sticking point in the labor dispute in baseball was the desire of team owners to regulate player salaries. In all professional sports, a league draft assigns entering players to a team for years, somewhat akin to sales of indentured servants on the docks of Chesapeake towns. Morris also observed the continued prevalence of licensed trades in modern America, a practice which still, for example, regulates the economies and work attitudes of taxi-drivers in major cities.

Morris ended his book without a summary. This bothered early critics. In 1947, Elizabeth Donnan lamented that Morris did not attempt anywhere in the book to make conclusions about the meaning of his huge endeavor: "Perhaps he believes that this cannot be done, and he better than anyone else should know what questions his material will answer."[16] The book's openended quality has allowed historians to mine particular aspects of it that interested them. While there has been no whole-hearted embrace of the book's general thesis, still, the impact of *Government and Labor* on the history of colonial labor is large. Manifested in the studies mentioned above, Morris's book has guided significant works on the economic and political behavior of indentured servants, mariners, and skilled craftsmen. What is less understood are the meaning and force of their relations with local and imperial government. One avenue for advancing comprehension of those ties is by greater study of the urban, licensed trades, whose

political associations with government lasted through the colonial period almost until the Civil War. The connections between occupations
and government supported, on the one hand, a moral economy that
held down prices for essential goods, but on the other hand, excluded
African Americans from key jobs for generations. Shut out of entry-
level work, blacks rebelled in a host of ways. They often did so in
concert with poor whites. The connections between the rebellious actions of white and black laborers, some of which were lost in the
editorial cuts mandated by Morris's publisher, should be reaffirmed.
Only by following the paths Morris blazed in *Government and Labor*
can historians recouple the divergent narratives of early American
black and white workers.

3

Slavery and Freedom Without Compensation

African Americans in Bergen County, New Jersey, 1660–1860

During the first two months of 1806, eight massive petitions containing over a thousand signatures were presented to the newly seated New Jersey State Legislature. The petitions, endorsed by a large percentage of the Dutch, Huguenot, and Anglo-American farmers in Bergen County, beseeched the lawmakers to consider the "dangerous consequences" that stemmed from the 1804 Gradual Emancipation Act. The petitioners claimed that as citizens they were entitled to the "services for life" of "Sable Sons of Africa," and of "their offspring, and more," according to the laws of the nation. Moreover masters had especially earned these rights because they "protect, Cloathe, and Support the parents" long after the end of their useful work lives. It was easy, claimed the petitioners, for other citizens who did not own any slaves to "cry out freedom away with slavery," with no concern for the consequences of their actions and with no compensation to the masters and no support for the former slaves. Already, complained the signers, the evils of the act "Strikes Consternation and gives the alarm," an apparent reference to indigent freedmen roaming the county. Without support, newborns and the elderly would become "Chargeable upon the townships." Far better, concluded the citizens, to appeal the Gradual Emancipation Act and return all blacks into servitude.[1]

The torturous close to slavery had begun on July 4, 1804, with passage of the Gradual Emancipation Act. In this law, New Jersey, the last of the northern states to abolish slavery, adopted a plan that awarded freedom to all blacks born after July 4, 1804, and that required females to labor for their masters until the age of twenty-one and males until the age of twenty-five. In a thinly veiled bribe to win support for the Gradual Emancipation Act, its proponents included a compensation package that permitted masters to free newborn slaves, abandon them, and then agree with the state to maintain them for a cash fee. Although the state repealed this clause as soon as its enormous costs became apparent, it was obligated to pay for those infants already freed under the act's provisions. By 1808, such compensation accounted for 40 percent of the state's annual budget; Bergen County alone received over $7,000, the majority of the state's expenditures on compensation. The law left much of the apparatus of servitude intact. All enslaved blacks born before July 4, 1804, remained slaves for life. Masters could buy, sell, trade, and bequeath slaves for life or in the time remaining. As a sign of their determination to maintain control over enslaved Africans, New Jersey masters continued, well into the 1850s, to advertise rewards for the return of fugitives with time left on their indentures.[2]

The petitions failed to convince New Jersey's lawmakers to repeal the Gradual Emancipation Act of 1804. They did, perhaps, curtail any additional liberality. Unlike neighboring New York, which ended slavery completely in 1827, New Jersey retained the vestiges of servitude into the Civil War era. The state rejected the Emancipation Proclamation and the Thirteenth, Fourteenth, and Fifteenth Amendments; it ended slavery only by federal order in 1870. Delaware was the sole state north of the Mason-Dixon Line that resisted emancipation more stubbornly than New Jersey.[3]

Unceasing opposition to abolition made Bergen County, where Dutch and Huguenot farmers were the overwhelming majority, easily the most recalcitrant county in New Jersey and, arguably, in the North. In Bergen's society, revolutionary idealism, urban cosmopolitanism, and Quaker benevolence mattered little. Members of its tiny free black community struggled to survive, unlike their culturally rich cousins across the river in New York City, or even their rural counterparts in Monmouth County. My fascination with Bergen is, in part, a response to haunting questions put to me by John Murrin many years ago: What would have been the fate of slavery in the North if the Quakers had not existed? What if their hectoring pricks of the consciences of the leaders of the young republic had remained silent? Would northern slavery have simply moved westward from the Mid-Atlantic into the Old Northwest and beyond? Complete answers to these counterfactual questions are beyond the scope of this chapter, but the history of Bergen County offers allows us to consider what an American future in which virtually none of the white citizenry opposed slavery or favored black freedoms would have been like. Concomitant with that discussion is an ancillary question: How would the emerging African-American communities have fared in a thoroughly hostile environment? In part I have answered that question in my book on Monmouth, but even there, Quakers aided the heroic struggles of the black community to secure freedom, land ownership, and religious independence. In Bergen, free blacks lacked any support at all.

As has been my method in other studies, I trace the intertwined history of blacks and whites in Bergen County from the original seventeenth-century settlements through the era of English colonial rule, the upheavals of the American Revolution, the establishment of the new revolutionary government, gradual emancipation, and the fate of African Americans in Bergen in the antebellum era. In this essay, I argue that while economic forces ensured the vitality of enslavement in Bergen, just as strong were cultural traditions that made small-scale slavery seem so critical to maintenance of local lifestyles. In response, despite a harsh rule of slavery espoused by the county's masters, African Americans in Bergen County never really accepted their lot and responded violently. This was true in the colonial era, during the American Revolution, and afterward. Strikingly, in a black culture geographically close to, but distant in opportunity from, the birth of African-American culture across the river in New York City in the 1830s, blacks in Bergen mounted a vernacular African revival. This revival was but one of a number of spontaneous responses Bergen's African Americans mounted to the harsh enslavement they faced. Servitude began with the earliest European settlements.

Economic and Ideological Origins of Slavery in Bergen County

Bergen County, located in the northeast corner of New Jersey, is one of its oldest European settlements in the Mid-Atlantic. In 1630, the Dutch West India Company, in a desperate attempt to attract investors to its struggling colony of New Netherland, awarded a patroonship to Michael Pauw across the North (Hudson) River at Pavonia (present-day Jersey City). In this location a few Dutch settlers and about thirty African slaves eked out a precarious existence until the farms were wiped out in the Indian wars in 1643. Learning from this devastating defeat, which drove the Dutch settlement back across the Hudson, incoming Governor Pieter Stuyvesant permitted subsequent home-steads only after farmers cleared land titles with the Lenni Lenape Indians. By 1660 there were about 200 people living in protected towns loosely called Bergen. Following Stuyvesant's specifications, settlers constructed each town as a square, 800 feet on each side, intersected by two main streets with another circumscribing its pali-saded border. Beyond the palisades were "outside" gardens to support small vegetable and livestock farms. Purchasers were required to oc-cupy their farms within six weeks and to have at least one family member capable of bearing arms. Significantly, at this point any Afri-cans, free or enslaved, lived with the Dutch inside the confines of the palisades. The social impact of this architecture was to consolidate social bonds between them.[4]

There were a few free Africans among the first nonindigenous settlers of Bergen. Three of the original shareholders in Tappan in Bergen County were John De Vries, Sr., his son John De Vries, Jr., and Nicholas Manu-els, free black farmers who were descendants of the first free black fami-lies of Manhattan. Frans Van Salee, the son of the famous Antony "The Turk" Van Salee and son-in-law of John De Vries, Sr., also moved to Tappan. These free black families stayed in Bergen for at least two gener-ations. In 1707, Abram Van Salee married Helena De Vries, daughter of John De Vries, Jr., in the Tappan Dutch Reformed Church. Samuel Fran-cisco and the sons of Solomon Pietersen, one of the most prosperous free blacks in Manhattan in the 1680s, moved to the western portion of Bergen County.[5] Youngham Antonious Roberts, a freeborn black, purchased 200 acres of land in the 1670s and became one of the first residents of Hack-ensack, New Jersey. Later, distressed at poor relations with Dutch farm-ers, he moved into the Mattawan Mountains. Another free black, Jochem Antony, was a member of the Bergen Dutch Reformed Church in 1679. The Van Donks (Doncks), a free black family, established a farm near Saddle River during this period.[6]

The presence of free black families notwithstanding, Bergen County, like the rest of the New Netherlands, was inexorably moving

toward a slave society. Governor Pieter Stuyvesant was able to improve the marketability of the lonely North American outpost by the
1650s. Once a backwater of Dutch imperial expansion, New Netherland had become attractive to young families from Holland and from
such neighboring countries as Sweden, Germany, Belgium, and England. To solve the colony's longstanding need for labor, Stuyvesant
summoned Dutch slave traders to import their human cargoes directly
from the West Coast of Africa to New Amsterdam, whence the governor intended to supply local farmers and English colonies north and
south of the port. Licensed merchants and privateers brought several
large shipments of enslaved Africans to New Amsterdam in the 1650s
and the early 1660s. Local artisans, merchants, and frontier farmers
eagerly bought the bondspeople, spreading the popularity of the slave
system throughout Dutch colonial society.[7]

Two distinct patterns of life in the county ensured the long-term viabil-
ity of slavery. The first was the general size of its farms. Hedged in by
Stuyvesant's original orders and, later, by small allotments from the English, the average farm size was significantly smaller in Bergen County
than in English counties. Bergen did have a promising agricultural future.
Its lands were good for grass, wheat, or any grain. Local farmers raised
milk cattle, oxen, sheep, and hogs, to be marketed locally or across the
Hudson River in the city. This rural economy required immense amounts
of manual labor, which, it appeared, due to social conditions of the time,
could only be performed by the farmer aided by some form of bonded
worker. Unlike their Calvinist counterparts in New England, the Dutch in
Bergen county could not look to family labor. With lower birth rates and
the tiny farms, Dutch farmers could neither depend upon sons as laborers
nor afford to enlarge their holdings. Nor could they, as did New England-
ers, hold onto sons and daughters through inheritance. With little land to
be partitioned, each succeeding Dutch generation was forced to move
westward to newer settlements in Somerset and Morris counties. These
departures for the frontier made the remaining Dutch farmers even more
reliant on slave labor.[8]

This fundamental difficulty continued into the era of English governance. After the English conquest of New Netherland in 1664, Governor Richard Nicolls, representing the new owner, the Duke of York,
reconfirmed the property claims of Dutch farmers in Bergen but also
limited later grants to fewer than 100 acres each. This pattern continued in the late seventeenth century, as Dutch farmers filtered into the

county from New York. The allotments given them by the English
government were paltry compared to the average grants of 400 acres
per farm in English-dominated Monmouth and Middlesex counties.[9]

Appearing in the first years after the English takeover was a second
major influence on the future slave society of Bergen. The Duke of
York granted huge plantations of over 15,000 acres to Barbadian immigrants with royal connections. To New Barbadoes Neck in Bergen
County came kinsmen William Sandford and Nathaniel Kingsland
(represented by Isaac Kingsland); nearby was John Berry. These
wealthy settlers, along with Lewis Morris in Monmouth County to the
south, brought dozens of slaves with them from Barbados. Berry had
thirty-two slaves; Thomas Noell, another Barbadian immigrant,
brought fifteen. These men, the current and future leaders of the colony, ensured that the congealing system of slavery would go unchal-
lenged and eventually would be legislated into a code. Their use of
slaves, augmented by the establishment of Arent Schuyler's large farm
and copper mine in Bergen, both based on slave labor, increased the
pressure on Dutch farmers to purchase and use bondspeople. These
men, together with other arrivals from Barbados, all brought along
slaves, cultivated their holdings, and sold bits of land to slave-holding
Dutch farmers.[10]

These factors influencing the development of slavery are very much
in line with causes found in other Atlantic colonies. Allowing for local
variation, the choices made by Bergen's elite and commonplace residents seem related to the compact between rich and poor in 1670s
Virginia. To ensure social stability there, white farmers of all ranks
would gain easy access to land and slaves; an economic caste system
based upon skin color allowed for the "freedom" of white settlers. New
Jersey did not take an official census until 1726, but the best estimates
are that there were about 350 people living in Bergen by 1685. The
black population is even harder to guess, but the presence of the free
black families and the arrivals of enslaved Africans with their Barbadian masters in the previous ten years suggest a population of over
fifty souls.

Enslaved blacks worked primarily on farms, though some served as
servants on gentlemen's plantations while others labored in the mines.
Work practices on the frontier allowed for moments of costly freedom.
One court case shows how Bergen County magistrates increasingly
regarded blacks as slaves. A Bergen County Court of Sessions held on

September 15, 1680, learned that "negroes were sent to care for the hoggs," but as they could not return conveniently until morning, they cared for the hogs in a woods belonging to Colonel John Lawrence. Because the hogs did great damage to Colonel Lawrence's property, the Negroes were sentenced to be "whipt, 20 lashes apiece, and their masters admonished to be aware of their whereabouts."[11]

Slave owners in Bergen County needed a core rationale beyond economics, however important that may have been. They found it in their deeply entrenched Reformed Calvinism, which shaped the personality and society of rural Bergen. As settlement stretched farther into the wilderness, frontier families depended more and more heavily upon the Reformed Church of Bergen for community, and were willing to travel hours in a wagon, or to walk miles, to attend weekly church services. Reformed churches founded at Bergen (1664), Hackensack (1686), and Tappan (1694) were the spiritual cores of county lives. In addition, Huguenot and Lutheran settlers, lacking a sufficient population to build a church, worshipped at Reformed parishes.[12]

The Dutch, the Huguenots, and the English Calvinists in Bergen were elaborating a New World evangelical pietism. This first became evident at the 1618 Council of Dordrecht (Dort in English) in Holland, where European Protestants in Europe gathered to hammer out a theology that would greatly affect the future of Dutch settlement and the texture of race relations in North America. These European Puritans tried to iron out the contradictions of Christianity and servitude. This council, the last general meeting of Reformed churches, included representatives from the Netherlands, England, Scotland, the German states, and Geneva. It assembled for the purpose of establishing canons of belief that still today form the main part of the Reformed Standards of Unity. The Canons of Dort affirmed predestinarianism, a limited atonement, the irresistibility of grace, and the perseverance of the saints.

An underlying agenda was refutation of the rising power of Armenians, who defended doctrines of free will. Conservatives worried that embrace of free will meant that individuals possessed the power to determine their own salvation, making obsolete the church polity that had been so carefully constructed by John Calvin and enlarged by his zealous followers in the United Provinces. Quickly, the orthodox faction, headed by Professor Franciscus Gomarus and thus known as Gomarians, routed the Arminians and reestablished a hierarchical theological order. The Gomarians condemned the Arminians as heretics and barred ministers and theologians who refused to accept the new orthodoxy.[13]

Decisions made at the Council of Dort strongly affected New Netherlands. Politically, the new orthodoxy was important because the Gomarians favored the emerging plans for a West India Company and a settlement in America.[14] The Council of Dort's orthodoxy confirmed a hierarchical election, predestined by God. Sinners, among whom followers of African beliefs were decidedly the lowest, could be saved only by accepting the will of God—as interpreted by the elect—and by the mystery of the faith. European faiths also had mixed messages. The Dutch republic had only recently separated from Catholic Spain, and the Reformed Church lacked a monopoly on faith. Many settlers in New Netherlands came from Catholic regions.[15] In Dutch colonies, conversion into the Reformed Church became the path to emancipation. Manumission was a meritorious act in the eyes of God. Slaves or servants were encouraged to work out terms of their self-purchase with masters.[16]

The church insisted that masters be responsible for deciding whether their slaves were to be baptized. Like their counterparts in Puritan New England, the Dutch Reformed in New Amsterdam doubted that pagans could be saved in this lifetime, but had to content themselves that "by the same grace of God, they know and feele, that in their hearts they beleeve and loue their Saviour." In short, Africans could never be truly Christian, but could approach grace. Baptism was a first step, but true acceptance was impossible until after death. What was incumbent upon true Christians was offering pagans the means of faith. Because the Council of Dort and the Dutch West India Company were so intertwined, such declarations amounted to government policy; in this way, the Dutch West India Company constructed a paternalist ideology of servitude composed of power, wealth, a desire to convert, and a belief in hierarchy.[17]

Perhaps the Gomarians would have been less supportive had they realized that the Synod actually enhanced Arminian power by publicizing its theology among lay Christians. The cross-fertilization of English, Scottish, and Dutch pietism coalesced in the New World, affirming freedom of choice and individual conversion. These components of pietism stirred significant disagreements between company and settler policies over many issues, including slavery. This conflation of church policy and frontier pietism was strongest in rural areas such as Bergen, where religion was a core means of resistance to the state power of the Dutch company and, later, the English government and church. Believing their brand of Calvinism was the true Reformed Church, pietists in the remote frontier settlement of Bergen emphasized a theology that gave greater power to individual interpretation of religion. Key to this understanding was the right of each master to have the choice whether or not his or her slaves should enter into the Body of Christ through baptism.[18]

The legitimacy of baptism for slaves was a matter of unceasing controversy in North America. Bergen, known as the "Dutch county" was a flash point of resistance to official demands for baptism for the enslaved. The Council of Dort's deliberations on pagan baptism, as Robert C.-H. Shell has noted about South Africa, troubled relations between masters, clerics, and enslaved blacks for the next two centuries. The Synod debated the fundamental question of whether slaves should be baptized, incorporated into the master's family, and then freed. In a signal measure that gave immense power to slave masters, the Synod declared that baptism was a household choice for the Reformed Christian. The Reformed head of household, not the Church or the parents of the child, who could also be unconverted adults, had the primary responsibility for baptizing slaves and heathens. That declaration gave colonial slave holders in the New World patriarchal power over children, servants, and slaves. The fate of African-American souls, indeed of their mortal bodies, was thereby placed in the hands of the family patriarch, who regarded unrelated servants as legally dependent on him. Effectively, the edict created the personality of a pietistic, domineering slave master, male or female, who was expected to fiercely regard governance of slaves as family business.[19]

However problematic those edicts were, a second statement, made by the Swiss theologian, Giovanni Deodatus, was more troubling. Deodatus argued that "those baptized should enjoy right of liberty with all other Christians" and should not be sold. Deodatus's interpretation influenced Dutch opinion and judicial action and effectively disallowed slavery in Holland. Henceforth slave traders and masters customarily understood that slaves brought to the United Provinces of Holland were automatically emancipated. In the New World, there was no timetable for the proper age of baptism, or for freeing a Christianized slave, or for determining how Dutch slave masters would obey church advice. Even if masters refused to baptize their bondspeople, as proved to be the case, enslaved blacks could easily understand the equation between baptism and liberty. In a religious environment in which baptism was analogous to legal enfranchisement, the stakes were immensely high for masters and for slaves. Dutch masters in Bergen obdurately refused to baptize their slaves. This deeply alienated enslaved Africans, who learned of missionary efforts to baptize blacks elsewhere in East Jersey—efforts that created opportunities that were unavailable to them.[20]

Unlike their urban relatives who gradually acceded to English mores in New York City, Dutch pietists in Bergen rejected acculturation and found the deepest source of resistance in their faith. Randall Balmer has provided a useful typology of the pietist character in the Mid Atlantic in the 1690s. Pietists, who were of peripheral social status, had informed, ecstatic religious expression derived from inner light conversion. Proof of conversion was necessary for membership in churches governed autonomously by parishioners who valued charisma over learning and illumination over doctrine. Sacraments were reserved to the faithful, though they were incidental to spirituality. Identity was local and dependent on an "inner elect" who had withdrawn from the outside world. These characteristics matched Reformed behavior in Bergen perfectly and proved helpful in efforts to resist ecclesiastical acculturation from the missionaries of the Church of England. Frontier pietism became more powerful after the Glorious Revolution of 1688 and the local impact of the Leisler Rebellion the following year in New York. After the English government brutally suppressed the rebellion in the 1690s, Leislerians fled westward to Bergen County, where they reaffirmed its pietist culture.[21]

The presence of Leislerians in Bergen County toughened the resistance of local masters to calls by the Church of England to catechize their slaves. Despite passage of a law in 1704 which disconnected holy baptism and emancipation, non-English masters, especially the pietist Dutch, distrusted such legislation and preferred to offer religious instruction in their homes or not at all. The Anglican missionary, Elias Neau, himself a Huguenot, despaired of any success among the rural Dutch. In a report to his superiors, Neau commented: "I have not catechized [in New Jersey] because they are almost all Dutch that live there and are intractable for if they that live in town are afraid that their slaves may demand freedom after baptism, the country people will certainly believe it deprives them of their slaves." Forty years later, the

Swedish botanist Pehr Kalm noted very strong resistance to black cate-
chism among the Bergen Dutch.[22]

Undergirding this culture was the power of Dutch women. Under
the Duke of York's laws of 1664, the Dutch had the right to retain
inheritance customs that differed sharply from English codes of primo-
geniture. According to Dutch custom, widows received the vast bulk of
their deceased husbands' property, even if only to hold it in trust for
the next generation, a practice that allowed mothers to wield power
over their sons and daughters. In 75 percent of 138 wills probated in
Bergen County between 1690 and 1775, the wife inherited slaves.
Compare this to the 52 percent allotment of slaves to widows in English-dominated Middlesex County, and the ability of Dutch women to
influence the course of slavery is apparent. Dutch women, as the
guardians of culture, were likely to prefer the Dutch language to English, to hold Calvinist tenets dear, and to maintain their the households as sanctuaries for Dutch culture. For slaves, this meant that the
Dutch wife could be even more fearsome in her beliefs about baptism
and liberty than her husband, and she was just as likely to be their
master.[23]

Hints of concern about the gender of many slave owners came in the
first full law of slavery in New Jersey. In 1704, New Jersey's legislature created a *code noir* when it passed "An Act for Regulating Negro,
Indian and Mallato Slaves." Two years later, New York enacted similar legislation. The first few clauses reasserted bans on sales to slaves
and made attempts to curtail stray blacks by offering rewards to any
white "so taking [up slaves] and carrying them to be whipped." Black
theft was now threatening enough that slaves convicted of theft were
branded "on the most visible part of the left cheek near the nose, with
the Letter (T) by the constable." Most controversial was the clause in
the New Jersey law that required that black rapists or even fornicators
with white women be "castrated at the care and Charge of his Master
or Mistress." The Privy Council in London quickly disallowed the law.
Despite this negation, New Jersey's citizens, including farmers in
Bergen, had come to regard blacks as permanent chattel, without religious sanction or economic incentive for manumission. Any black
male who crossed the sexual frontier could expect the most brutal
repression.[24]

Having fully embraced slavery as a source of labor, Bergen County
overcame its slow growth in the seventeenth century to prosper in the

next era. Bergen County's white and black populations grew rapidly in the early eighteenth century. New Jersey's first census, in 1726, enumerated 2,673 people in Bergen, of whom 492 (18.4 percent) were black. By the next census, in 1738, the black population had grown at a faster rate than the white population, rising by over 60 percent to 806 (19.7 percent of the total). When Bergen County was partially split to make new counties in the 1740s, its black populace dipped to 616, but actually increased its overall proportion of the whole society to 20.5 percent As was common in rural societies in the Mid-Atlantic, black males predominated over black females. In 1738, for example, there were 443 black males to 363 black females, a ratio of 122:100, high above the norm of 105:100.

What factors promoted the rapid growth of the black population? The answer lies between natural reproduction and the slave trade. Peter Kolchin, in his survey, *American Slavery,* contends that the growth of an American-born class of slave owners and, significantly, a new generation of locally born African-American slaves shaped the contours of the evolution of slavery in the decades before the American Revolution. One key requisite for the emergence of a native-born generation of slaves was a more favorable ratio of men to women.[25] As noted above, as late as 1738, the male population of Bergen was still substantially higher than the female, hampering natural population growth. The number of women and children in the probate inventories of Bergen County slave holders between 1690 and 1775 averaged 38 women and 58 children, or only 1.5 children for each adult female under the best conditions. Such data suggest the difficulty of black family formation in Bergen County.

Hard evidence about the involvement of Bergen County masters in the slave trade is sketchy. Arent Schuyler, the local mine owner, was very active in the burgeoning New York slave trade in the 1730s. Prices for a healthy adult male slave stabilized around £40 during this decade. Bergen County masters, who were notoriously reluctant to partake of the commerce in convicts and indentured servants, undoubtedly were encouraged by lower prices to turn increasingly to the slave trade for labor. One hard fact that survives is the ratio of slaves to free white male laborers in the county at the middle of the eighteenth century. In the tax assessments of 1751, surveyors counted 306 slaves against only 8 single white males; in 1769, the ratio was 422 slaves and servants as compared to 34 single males. Dutch farmers seeking permanent or additional labor turned to slave ownership.[26]

The widening racial chasm in the county was also reflected in housing. By necessity in the first generations during the late seventeenth century, masters, their families, and slaves lived in fairly close proximity. As Dutch families prospered, separation became sharper. White master families added wings to their homes in the 1750s, with separate areas segregated by race. An important architectural symbol of this separation may be seen in the home of the prerevolutionary Abraham Demaree, a Huguenot in Closter. Two doors lead from the main house to the slaves' wing. Cut into the panel of each door is a small square spy-light through which the master could observe his slaves. In other homes, after new wings were built, older parts of the houses were used as combined kitchens and slave quarters. Other slaves lived over ovens, in separate huts and barns, in crude tents, and even in caves.[27]

Slaves on the large plantation and copper mine belonging to the slave trader Arent Schuyler lived "without the gates in quarters." Lieutenant Isaac Bangs, visiting Schuyler's estate in 1776, noted that fifty to sixty slaves worked on the plantation, but: "I never saw more than 2 in the house otherwise than in the kitchen and those were waiters. Those who live in the Out House each have their own particular Department and Regular Hours to work in." Bangs noted that "their Victual is cooked at Certain Hours by their Owne Cooks. The slaves were regularly called to work by a Bell." Intimacy between masters and slaves was thus discouraged. Strict separation between masters' and servants' quarters not only furthered divisions between the cultures, but could prove dangerous.[28] A weak black family structure, frequent new arrivals of young black males via the slave trade, and an increasing reliance by local farmers on slaves characterized this eighteenth-century society, in which little acculturation occurred and separation between the races became ever wider.

One source from which we are able to determine the conditions of slavery are runaway notices, which, though sparse, tell much about the bondsmen's appearances; their possessions; and, occasionally, their personalities. Bergen County slavemasters advertised for runaway slaves only fourteen times in the colonial period. Rather than indicating the slaves were docile, this small number of ads suggests an unwillingness by the Bergen Dutch to use English newspapers, a point that was further strongly demonstrated during the American Revolution when there were virtually no advertisements, although there were over 100 Bergen County runaways. The existing fugitive notices are very revealing.[29]

Few Bergen County slaves escaped with many possessions. In contrast to slaves in other New Jersey counties or in New York, who often left with several changes of their own clothing, or with some enough of their masters' possessions to sell, Bergen County fugitives rarely left with much more than the shirts on their backs. Jacob Powellse of Hackensack ran away from the jail in 1734 wearing only "a yellow coat with old buttons, Holland waistecoat and breeches." A few years later, Robin ran away from John Zabriskie of Hackensack, taking with him but "a linnen jacket, short trowsers and a leather hat."[30] Jack, who left Abraham Van Buskirk of Hackensack in 1751, took with him "a grey, homespun, linsey wollsey coat, a tan shirt and a linnen shirt, three pairs of breeches, white woollen stockings and a leather hat." Peter and York left with more possessions than any other Bergen slaves in the colonial era, but their property consisted only of "several shirts and pairs of breeches . . . new shoes with Brass Buckles, a worsted hat and a Castor hat . . . a dog, a gun and a fiddle."[31] Several fugitives were fiddlers; fiddling was a frequent skill possessed by numerous blacks in colonial America, and was useful in marketplace frolics in New York City.[32]

Bergen County slaves sometimes ran away in small groups. Cuff and Jack fled with a slave from Staten Island in 1756; Peter and York, mentioned above, escaped in 1759. The destinations of these pairs may have been the sea, for their masters warned captains of vessels not to employ them. A similar warning was issued for Nell, the only black woman runaway advertised from Bergen County. Nell was a "tall slim wench, has three diamonds in her face, one on each side and the other on her forehead." She took with her "three petticoats, one is an old quilted one, and the other two homespun, one striped and the other mixed, a blue and white striped short gown, a bluish Homespun Waistcoat and an Ozenbrig shirt, with homespun sleeves, a short blue cloke a new pair of blue stockings, a pair of old brooked shoes and several other things to tedious to mention."[33] Nell, Cuff, York, Jack, and Peter were probably headed for New York City. Another runaway traveled to Perth Amboy, where he was captured and held in jail for his master.[34]

Colonial Black Violence

Unable to seek emancipation, removed from tender family relationships, and working in a pinched economy, enslaved blacks in Bergen sometimes unleashed their frustrations in violent retaliations against their masters. In 1735 a slave named Jack assaulted his master with an ax, beat the man and his son, and then tried to burn his master's house. After his arrest, Jack attempted suicide before being put to death by burning. In 1741 Bergen County blacks supported the larger slave conspiracy across the river in New York City by burning down seven barns. Still a third slave named Jack and his companion, Ben, were tried on May 4, 1741, by five freeholders in Hackensack: "Jack, slave of Albert Van Vorr Hezen and Ben, slave of Derrick Van Horn, the two were convicted and burned at the stake," the next day at Yellow Point along the Hackensack River. Three years later, two men, "Ian and Tom" were convicted of poisoning other slaves and were hanged; the court noted that this was the second case of poisoning in a dozen years. A decade later, several blacks were jailed in Bergen on suspicion of poisoning their masters. After jailing the slaves, magistrates uncovered "some other schemes of Villainy in that neighborhood . . . the Negroes . . . have lately assembled together oftener than usual."[35]

Bergen's slave masters reacted to black crime with ferocity. Dinar of Hackensack was sentenced to thirty lashes on her back for theft. Just before the American Revolution, Pero of Hackensack was sentenced to 500 lashes for theft. Some masters used their own methods to torture recalcitrant slaves, including leaving them bound to trees in the mosquito-ridden swamps near the Palisades.[36]

The most infamous incident occurred in 1767. A white laborer, Lawrence Tuers, and a slave, Harry, both living in the home of Hendrick Christians Zabriskie of Hackensack, quarreled. Later, while Tuers slept, Harry crushed his skull with a cart rung, then drove two small plugs into his ears. After Tuers's body was discovered, Dutch magistrates obtained proof of Harry's guilt by forcing him to stroke the corpse's face. In the sworn testimony of coroner, Johannes Demarest, "Blood immediately ran out of said Tuers nostril." Convicted by this premodern method, Harry was burned at the stake two weeks later. The incident is noteworthy in several ways. First, the method of conviction, known since the Middle Ages, but fallen into disuse in Europe, indicates the highly traditional character of Bergen society. Second, the incident, along with other moments of violence in Bergen, suggests that the enslaved population was desperately angry and that some of its members were prepared to lash out fatally when provoked.[37]

The Black Revolution in Bergen

By the late summer of 1776, the Revolutionary War was ablaze in Bergen County. As white residents acknowledged their own Patriot or Tory sympathies, local African Americans watched for their opportunity to use the conflict for their own advantage. By September 1776, William Howe's British regulars and Hessian troops had swept across Long Island and New York City, and had established a toehold at New Barbadoes Neck. A number of blacks, including a slave named Jack, Thomas Lydecker, and John and Kitty Ryerson of Hackensack, fled from their masters to find freedom and work behind the British lines. Freeborn blacks, including John, Jacob, and Betty Richards of Hackensack, joined the British. Sam Albert, Thomas Lydecker, Peter Jackson, and Jacobus Westervelt of Bergen quickly found work in the Wagon Master General's Department or as woodcutters. Another slave with the common name of Jack became an important spy, working with Ensign Peter Myer. In addition, this Jack was a "cunning man," able to secure obedience from others by use of charms.[38]

With each army positioned for winter, the British commenced raids into the region of Closter, Tenafly, and Tappan, to secure cattle and forage. George Washington first stationed his troops at Hackensack; then, when he retreated in November 1776, he left the town open to British control. The American effort seemed doomed, as old Whigs swore allegiance to the Crown, and Tories who had secretly enlisted in the English Army now proudly paraded their colors.[39]

Though blacks took part in earlier British efforts, the first acknowledgment of their role came on November 23, 1776, when blacks and Tories sacked the homes of Patriots in Schraalenburgh. The destruction of Reverend Dirck Romeyne's and other homes turned up the heat under the cauldron of local hostilities.[40] The British established a wide offensive line stretching down from Tappan to Monmouth County. Until Washington's victories at Trenton and Princeton at the end of December, the Patriot side seemed doomed.

Over the next year, British and American troops took turns occupying and ransacking Bergen County. Residents lost many of their possessions to the foraging armies.[41] Eleven blacks from Hackensack and Tappan used the cover of chaos to go behind the British lines. They found work and security in New York City or in Staten Island, where Nathaniel Greene reported that 800 blacks mustered with the British in late 1776. Richard Varick, writing to his friend Philip Van Rensselaer, echoed many slave masters in Bergen County who felt the loss of slaves: "In the beginning of the war, my father had two middle-aged negroes and wenches—he has lost the wench . . . one negro died and the last wench and one negro left with the enemy to my mother's distress." Not only were blacks leaving their masters, but it was becoming harder to purchase replacements.[42]

Runaway slaves found refuge along the highlands and among the gangs in the blockhouses, who raided Bergen County homes at will in early 1779. Like similar probes occurring in Essex and Monmouth counties, the raids on Closter on March 28, Little Ferry on April 12, and English Neighborhood on April 11, as well as the strong attack on Closter on May 9, 1779, kept the Patriots off their guard and discouraged. The raids were carried out by a combination of Loyalist troops and blacks serving under Tom Ward.[43] Other New Jerseyans worried about a substantial slave plot in Elizabeth-town, promoted by British officers.[44] Bergen residents anxiously wondered whether escaped slaves would return to ravage their property. The constant parade of hungry troops through Tappan, Schraalenburgh, English Neighborhood, and Hackensack deepened these worries.

The activities of Ward's blacks, spies, pilots, and guides sufficiently impressed the English to permit the formal organization of Black Guides and Pioneers and the more partisan Black Brigade. Though denials were occasionally made, the English, especially the Hessian soldiers, welcomed blacks into service throughout the war.[45] The British practice, employed in South Carolina and North Carolina, and Virginia, was to place white officers in charge of black soldiers. Similar appointments were made in New York City, but Colonel Stephen Bleuke, a freeborn black living in New York City, quickly became the open leader of the Black Guides and Pioneers.[46]

The most feared black unit was the Black Brigade. This unit, the last to leave New York in 1783, included four blacks from Bergen County: Close Herring of Tappan; John of Hackensack; and Lewis Freeland of New Barbadoes Neck and his wife, Elizabeth Freeland, a free black from Paramus. Elizabeth's presence demonstrates how the British and Black Loyalists accepted women's contributions in key fighting units. Worried while Americans clearly feared the Black Brigade, Henry Muhlenburg warned, "the worst is to be feared from the irregular

troops whom the so called Tories have assembled from various nationalities—for example, a regiment of Catholics, a regiment of Negroes,
who are fitted for and inclined towards barbarities, are lacking in
human feeling and are familiar with every corner in the country."[47]
Such comments revealed white anxieties about blacks' knowledge of
the terrain and their desire for retribution.

The Black Brigade's knowledge of Bergen County and other New
Jersey counties became essential to the British effort in the winter of 1779
to 1780, which was long remembered as one of the worst periods of the
war. Over seventy-five sleighs were able to cross the ice-bound Hudson
River at one time. Blacks participated in many raiding parties, securing
forage for the British-occupied isolated population of New York City.[48]
Blacks stationed on Staten Island made quick raids into Monmouth
County or Essex County. Others attacked Bergen County from blockhouses along the west side of the Hudson. Blacks immeasurably aided the
British war effort by laboring on fortifications and by ushering runaways
into occupied New York City. The greatest benefit was derived by African Americans themselves, whose bursts to freedom undermined the institution of slavery throughout eastern New Jersey.

The year 1779 saw the greatest number of African Americans en-
gaged in freedom struggles. They were personally invited by Sir William Howe to join the British, in a series of proclamations offering
freedom to *any* blacks who came within the British lines. The "Embarkation List" shows that at least eleven blacks left Tappan, seven left
Hackensack, and four left New Barbadoes Neck. Women, children,
and newborn infants became instantly free. Accordingly, the runaways
included families such as Joseph and Betsy Collins of Hackensack; the
eight-member Van Nostrandt family from New Barbadoes Neck; and
Nicholas and Lena Clause; Sarah Stevens and her son; and John and
Nancy Van Bruyek and their daughter Sarah of Tappan. Single
women, including Susan Herrin and Dinar Blauveldt of Tappan and
Polly Richards of Acquackanonck, left for New York City.[49]

During 1779, the Black Brigade was a key part of British raids on
Bergen County. On May 9, 1779, an interracial force of Van Buskirk's
New Jersey Loyalists and "a party of Negroes" overran the town of
Closter in Bergen County, burning every building they entered, killing
several Patriots, and capturing several others. The attack was part of a
series of such raids occurring in eastern New Jersey from Bergen

County to Monmouth County. In each county gangs of escaped slaves led British and Loyalist forces to their old ex-masters' hidden valuables or livestock, then sacked and burned their property.[50]

Some blacks were swept away by the invading British forces. Information on other escaped blacks can be found on the inventories for damages committed by the British that Americans submitted after the war. Adolph Waldron of Hackensack listed on September 25, 1779, the loss of: "A Negro Man aged fifty years old; one ditto named Liverpool, aged 27." On February 25, "A Negro wench named Isabel, aged 38 years and her 2 year old child, a Negro man named Sango, aged 35 years, a house negro and a cook; a negro man named Jo, aged 40 years and one named Jack, aged 19 and one named Wan," aged twelve, left Waldron.[51] Not all blacks were successful in their bursts to freedom. The Patriots stopped many from reaching British protection at Hoboken and New Barbadoes Neck. On March 22, 1781, Hannah, Job, and Tom from Franklin and Harry from Hackensack were arrested before they could reach Hoboken. Marmeter, a slave of Peter Van Voorst of Harrington, was found with two stolen horses on his way to the British lines at Schraalenburgh.[52]

The waves of arrivals began to disturb the Americans and British. On May 25, 1780, Major General James Patterson wrote the Loyalist ferry master, Abraham Cuyler, that "not only male but female Negroes with their children take advantage of your port in New Jersey to run away from masters and come into the city where they must become a burden to the town. . . . Be so good as to prevent their passing the North [Hudson] River as far as it is in your power to do it." Shortly after Americans warned Bergen and Monmouth residents, "it may be dangerous to the community to permit Negroes to reside near enemy lines . . . remove them to some more remote part of the state." To shore up local defenses, Governor William Livingston declared martial law. Undaunted, in early June 1780, "twenty-nine Negroes of both sexes deserted . . . from Bergen County." Their method was to flee with the interracial, guerrilla bands sent out to forage in Bergen County. Blacks could leave through ferry landings at Fort Lee, Bull's Ferry, and Fort Delancey at New Barbadoes Neck, where blockhouses manned by refugees and black soldiers guarded access to New York City. The blacks could also roll logs down a natural gorge at Weehawken, tie the logs together, tow them across the Hudson River, and travel south to freedom in New York City.[53]

Poised at Bull's Ferry, a group called Ward's Blacks continually raided Schraalenburgh and Tappan and left them devastated. A scourge of Patriots, these black soldiers escorted black brothers and sisters down the roads from Tappan and Hackensack to freedom inside the British lines.[54] Individual Patriots lived in fear of their lives after Ward apparently hired three of the blacks, including "little Will, owned by Van Ryper," to kill a creditor in Bergen. Patriots caught the three blacks and hung them in the swamp north of Brown's Ferry Road; their bodies were left hanging for weeks.[55] The Continental Army attempt in July 1780 to blast the black woodcutters and gangs out of Bull's Ferry met with a crushing defeat.

As free trade resumed between New York and Bergen, Ward and his men became heroes, their successes rivaling the exploits of Colonel Tye, an escaped slave from Shrewsbury, Monmouth County, whose "motley crew," operated an interracial partisan force from "Refugee-town" at Sandy Hook, or of Colonel Stephen Bleuke of the Black Pioneers, who scouted and fought for British forces in Morris County. Inspired by their desires for freedom; possessing boldness, courage, and resources; and with British sponsorship and protection, blacks made life very dangerous for their former masters. In the strife-torn neutral zone, the blacks gained a large degree of civil authority.[56] The British demonstrated approval of their actions with a visit by Prince William Henry, who was the third son of George III, and later became William IV, in September 1781.[57]

As the local war deteriorated into nasty partisan clashes after the defeat of General Charles Cornwallis in the fall of 1781, freer commerce between New York City and Bergen County encouraged Patriot slave masters to reenter the city in search of their bondsmen. Former slave Boston King described the terror of seeing ex-masters from the South, from Philadelphia, and from New Jersey seize their former slaves off the streets.[58] Only the protection of the British Army kept the 3,000–4,000 blacks in New York City safe from their former masters. When British commander-in-chief Guy Carleton determined that blacks who responded to proclamations from the British general before 1782 were free, and were entitled to protection and to be transported to Nova Scotia, he set off a furor which lasted unresolved for thirty years.[59] Despite the British inclination to assist black freedmen, American slave owners persisted in chasing former slaves.

One remarkable incident demonstrates black response. Captain

Hessius from Totowa Falls went into New York City with a Van Houten in early July 1782 to "enquire about some runaway negroes and 'tis said sold a wench of his." On his return, Hessius "was beset and murdered by about 12 or 15 of Wards' Blacks not far from Bergen." Though the writer, Reverend Dirck Romeyn, believed the blacks would be disarmed and transported, the incident demonstrated the militancy with which blacks responded to attempts at reenslavement. The murder of Hessius foreshadowed the black mobs who fought slave owners in the streets of New York City in the 1790s and 1800s. Another Hackensack slave holder seeking the return of his chattel found he "had formed such connections with an important personage that I could no longer look upon him as my own. He told me he was going to Novy Koshee."[60]

While General George Washington and Guy Carleton quarreled about the meaning of clause seven in the peace treaty, which called for the return of all property including slaves, New York City blacks, like their counterparts in Savannah and Charleston, attempted to flee the city before the British evacuation, which was scheduled for November 1783.[61] By June 1783, fifty-four former slaves from Bergen County had set sail for Nova Scotia. They included fifteen single men, nine single women, four couples with no children, two women with a child each, and four couples with a total of eight children. By the end of November 1783, a total of ninety-nine blacks from Bergen County were among those transported to Nova Scotia. The overall proportion (53 percent) of Bergen families leaving New York in family units is just slightly under the average for all evacuated blacks, indicating that black family units flourished in wartime New York City.[62] Despite the hazards of war and exile, these extended black families hung together and negotiated with the English for farmland in Nova Scotia or Sierra Leone.[63] Religious organizations, previously hidden, quickly became apparent during the evacuation when ministers assembled entire congregations to travel to Nova Scotia, and, eventually, to Sierra Leone.[64]

The ninety-nine Bergen County embarkees included at least eight described as "in the possession of," suggesting a continued bondage. The British Loyalists and officers firmly believed in the legality of slavery; thus a number of Bergen County blacks apparently exchanged one master for another. Others were more fortunate. General Samuel Birch, who issued the coveted passes to Nova Scotia, recognized any claims to freedom older than 1782. The declarations made in the spring of 1783 of some escaped slaves indicate how long they eluded their masters. John, for example, a member of the elite Black Brigade, was but 13 when he left his master Jacob Fortune in 1776. Isaac Taylor, another Black Brigade veteran, left John Van Horn in late 1775 at the age of 14. Lewis Freeland left his master in New Barbadoes Neck in 1776 to join his freeborn wife Elizabeth, from Paramus, in New York City.[65]

By November 1783 the Black Brigade was the sole group of blacks left in New York City, though other isolated blacks were present in the war-torn city. An incident that took place in October demonstrates that blacks shared the violent animosities that were still aflame around New York City and New Jersey. The British agreed to officially turn over New York City to the Americans on November 25, 1783. Unquestionably, many Americans, including vengeful slave masters, were unwilling to wait that long. One American ship in the harbor received much of the wrath of the remaining Loyalists. On October 28 the *Pennsylvania Packett* reported that "capt. Steweart's vessel, with the colours of the United States of America flying, was boarded by the Canaille, who, in a riotous manner, torre down and carried through the streets in triumph, attended by a *Chosen group of blacks,* seamen and loyalist leather-aprons."[66] With complete evacuation just weeks away, the Black Brigade's ire was unquenched.

The departure of nearly a hundred Bergen County blacks for Nova Scotia, representing a loss of 12 percent of the county's African Americans, was costly but did not end slavery in Bergen County.[67] Nonetheless, the 1784 tax records show that slavery remained strong in Bergen County and grew in western counties such as Hunterdon and Somerset. When abolitionist measures arose in the state assembly, Bergen County representatives were quick to object. The county remained very sympathetic to the South, and to slavery itself, throughout the antebellum period. For New Jersey's blacks who remained enslaved, some things remained the same but others changed forever and continued to affect relations between slaves and their masters. Other slaves had not only escaped their masters but returned to fight against them. No national group of slave owners was exempt from these events, although the Dutch were harder hit than others. The slave owners' resolve had been met with aggressive force.[68]

In the next twenty years there was a sharp increase in the number of assaults by blacks upon whites. Arson also increased in Bergen County

as free blacks and slaves showed their discontent about the slow movement toward abolition.[69] Black resistance in Bergen County during the
Revolution, as when Wards' Blacks and other black brigades controlled the blockhouses, raided slave masters, and conducted freedom
paths to New York City, created cherished memories for blacks. There
would never again be in Bergen County an opportunity like the one
that occurred in 1776 when the world split open and slaves ran free.
Slavery continued in Bergen County well into the nineteenth century,
but now blacks in the county had the living memory of those who had
left with the British for greater freedom in Nova Scotia, and became
important symbols of black autonomy to a free black identity emerging
in New Jersey after the war. The escapes of these slaves shone bright
as morning stars, giving the remaining slaves hope for alternatives to
slavery.[70]

Bergen County's Resistance to the Abolition of
Slavery After the American Revolution

The American Revolution did not end slavery in Bergen County. As
noted, in fact, the peculiar institution of slavery actually grew in
strength in this county during the postwar years, as it did in other rural
counties in the North. Bergen County was unlike other locales, however, where magistrates were at least considering means of abolishing
slavery. Instead, Bergen County farmers stubbornly refused to enter-
tain any thoughts of black emancipation. Their refusals shed a novel
perspective on historical accounts of the close of slavery after the
American Revolution.

The first modern studies of the abolition of slavery in the North
emphasized the power of ideology. Revolutionary egalitarianism, the
enlightened philosophical ideas behind the Declaration of Independence and the Constitution, made servitude an unacceptable contradic-
tion in the young republic. In New England, where the economic
power of slavery was weak and its place in society was marginal,
slavery died quickly. In Pennsylvania and New York, which had much
larger populations of slaves, elite liberal Episcopalians and Quakers
formed abolition societies and laboriously lobbied for the death of
slavery. Although, as David Brion Davis has contended, the motive of
these northern elites may have been less altruistic than they indicated,
and more inclined toward the introduction of free wage labor, they

were nevertheless able to banish the institution of slavery from their societies in the decades after the American Revolution.[71]

Recent studies have emphasized pragmatic causes for abolition and have demonstrated that emancipation occurred much more slowly in reality than in law. Gary B. Nash and Jean R. Soderlund have noted the increased expense of slave owning for urban artisans, the sharp drop-off in the availability of slaves during and immediately after the American Revolution, the flight of slaves, and the sales of slaves out of state, and have credited the emergence of an African-American middle class in the cities with calls to abolish slavery. In an independent work, Soderlund has contested the image of the Society of Friends as a philanthropically minded, ideologically motivated force to end slavery, and has also shown how Quaker actions differed geographically, a pattern I have noticed just within Monmouth County, New Jersey.[72]

The most recent studies have emphasized the resilient strengths of slavery. For example, Kings County, New York, possessed social characteristics close to those found in Bergen County: intense Dutch ethnicity, rural values, and a powerful adherence to slavery as a social and economic system. In his study of the end of slavery in New York, Shane White offers the closest examination to date of the conditions of servitude in Kings County. He argues that the end of slavery came not from the efforts of the elite but from the growing power of New England farmers in the Hudson Valley and from a crisis within the Dutch community, though he also offers powerful evidence of resistance to emancipation. White has remarked that slavery in rural New York in the early national period did not so much decline as move to the periphery of the state.[73] In my own work, I have found that in Monmouth County, New Jersey, a pluralistic county with sizable English, Dutch, and Huguenot settlements, the non-English farmers rigorously opposed emancipation. Patience Essah and T. Stephen Whitman have discussed the slow pace of abolition farther south in Delaware and in Baltimore.[74]

As the petitions to restore slavery cited at the start of this essay indicate, Bergen County's slave masters lagged far behind the rest of the state in support of the abolition of slavery. One key reason for the lag was economic. Just after the war, tax data indicated sharply different property levels for slave holders and non–slave holders. In 1784, just over 200 slave masters owned farms of slightly less than 150 acres each; in contrast, 1,354 non–slave holders possessed freeholds of just under 56 acres each. The gap widened in subsequent tax records. By 1796, 371 slave-owning freeholders possessed over 160 acres each, with non–slave holders owning just forty acres. By 1802, two years before the advent of gradual emancipation, the number of slave masters grew to over 400, against over 2,000 non–slave holders with but 35 acres per farm. As John Rutherford commented in his famous survey in 1786, ownership of a farm had become distressingly difficult for young men; prices were high, mortgages were nonexistent, and wages were too low to allow accumulation for future purchases. In a county where 90 percent of arable land was cultivated by 1784, ownership of slaves often meant survival for small freeholders.[75]

Few masters in Bergen County allowed post revolutionary liberalism to affect their attitudes about slave ownership. Allocation of slaves by will remained staunchly traditional. Of 182 slaves mentioned in wills in Bergen County between 1783 and 1800, 102 (56 percent) were bequeathed to the widows and another 35 were granted to daughters or other female relatives. The remainder were granted to sons and other male relatives. Only one slave was freed by will during these years.[76]

Undergirding this grim economic determinism was a sharp split over slavery between the urban and the rural Reformed churches. Reform came, however gradually, even in the Dutch Reformed Church. Officially segregated since the 1660s, the New York City Dutch Reformed Church began accepting black communicants soon after the Revolution. The church constitution of 1792 resolved that "no difference exists between bond and free in the Church of Christ; slaves or blacks when admitted to the church possess the same privilege as other members; their infant children are entitled to baptism and ministers who deny them any Christian privilege are to be reprimanded." In the early postrevolutionary years, black members were usually servants or slaves of white worshipers. Several new communicants, however, were free blacks, with certificates of membership from Dutch Reformed parishes in outlying regions. The Dutch Reformed Church also performed marriages either between slaves, between slaves and free blacks, or between free people, and the Dutch Reformed cemetery accepted several black burials. Still, black membership in the Dutch Reformed Church, while far greater than in the colonial era, remained small compared with the number of African Americans owned by the Dutch. Colonial-era splits between rural pietists and urban paternalists affected this reform. The new liberalism was largely confined to the city.[77]

The Rise of a Free Black Class

Any freedom won by blacks in Bergen after the Revolution was hard-earned. The commonest arrangements were made with masters to borrow money or time against bondage. An example was the experience of Jack Earnest, a slave living near Harrington in Bergen County. Born in 1770, Jack was originally a slave of the Gesner family of Lower Closter, near the Palisades. Nicholas Gesner purchased Jack from his father in 1793. A year later Jack "desired a paper to seek a new master," despite Gesner's promises to free him after seven or eight years. A brother-in-law of Gesner's, one Jacob Conklin, promised Jack Earnest freedom and land after seven years. Gesner warned Jack that Conklin was not to be trusted, and Gesner's warnings about Conklin's duplicity eventually proved true, when Jack was denied freedom after the promised seven years. Earnest was freed only after a third white, Peter Willsey, paid Conklin $100 to insure that Jack did not become dependent on county welfare funds. By 1806, Jack Earnest was finally a free man, and he owned over five acres of land near Harrington.[78]

Earnest's land was in the first independent local black community, which was called Skunk Hollow and was located near the New York–New Jersey border in Bergen County. Earnest was followed by thirty or more black families in the next few years. Many of the residents of Skunk Hollow were former slaves in Bergen County, who bore the names of their former masters. As archaeological investigations by Joan Geismar have demonstrated, Skunk Hollow was a below-subsistence community where black farmers barely scraped together a living over several generations before the community failed in the late nineteenth century.[79]

One harsh fact of slave life was that blacks in New Jersey never received any compensation for their labors as slaves. One looks in vain at the probate records of Bergen County for evidence of grants, loans, or gifts given to former slaves, nor was any example of assistance offered to a former bondsperson found. Rather, the probate records through 1830 are a monotonous register of slaves bequeathed to wives, sons, and daughters. The examples are either terse, such as John Van Buskirk's inventory in 1822 of "Slaves . . . $345"; more evocative, such as Adrian Rost's "1 Negro Wench named Masi . . . $25; 1 Negro wench, Flora, $20; 1 negro man named Tom . . . $300"; or a careful calculation of time remaining under the "Abolition Law," such as Jerry

Van Ryper's inventory of 1824. Even as late as 1828, James Outwater measured the next eleven years, the time still owed by his slave, Tom, as worth $100. In the first forty years after the American Revolution, a significant omission from the probate records was the presence of free blacks. Apparently no emancipated blacks in Bergen were able to accumulate enough capital to warrant a legal statement.[80]

Opportunities for legitimate freedom were few and far between. As in the colonial period, blacks showed flashes of anger reflecting their anguish. Penalties were as harsh as in the colonial era. For example, on three different occasions black men assaulted white men between June 1793 and October 1795. In Bergen in January 1801, two slaves, Ned and Pero, were found guilty of larceny and ordered whipped from place to place throughout the county during the course of a month. Each week they were whipped at a new location—the courthouse, Pond's Church, Hoppertown, and New Bridge—for a total of 400 lashes each. Ned died from his whippings. Besides violence and larceny, arson was another weapon blacks used against white society. Three slaves in Bergen burned down the homes of their masters between 1796 and 1801.[81]

Black Culture in Bergen

There was little opportunity in Bergen's tough, rural society to form the middle-class black culture shaping up across the Hudson River in New York City. Lacking records from churches and other institutions, glimpses of black culture in Bergen appear in folklore. For example, much information about black culture can be found in accounts of festivals. Holidays promoted temporary interracial harmony. For *Paas,* or Easter, blacks baked holiday cakes, then competed to see who "could throw the paas-cakes the highest and still catch them." The most important holiday was *Pinkster* (Whitsuntide or Pentecost), a summer frolic of great festivity. Originally Pinkster featured booths selling beer, mead, cider, meat, fish, and cakes; there were gambling, dancing, and parades. These occasions were multiethnic and crossed class barriers. Trusted blacks from Bergen obtained passes. They poured into New York City or retreated to counties in upstate New York to dance to African bands that played fiddles, banjos, drums, pipes, flutes, fifes, and Jew's harps. Black music, with "eel-pots covered with dressed sheepskins," and black dancing became featured activities. Pinkster became a vehicle for Africanity. One observer near Kingston, New York, was relieved to note that a gathering of Negroes at Pinkster was "only to elect their King." At Pinkster, blacks elected noble men, who would "lead the Guinea dance, dressed in Pinkster clothes, in a heat of yellow lace." Never directly confrontational, Pinkster blacks turned the world upside down for a day. Gradually, Pinkster became an entirely black festival.[82]

Other African cultural patterns can be found in blacks' frequent jaunts to the markets in New York City. The frequency with which Bergen County blacks flowed in and out of New York City indicates a slave network, loosely guided by European structures but based upon African traditions. New York City established public markets in the 1670s, at which butchers, bakers, and other regulated tradesmen sold food. The markets quickly attracted, to the dismay of licensed traders, a picaresque array of hucksters, peddlers, and hawkers crying out their products. Many were women, wives of Jersey farmers, accompanied by their slaves, who sold milk, vegetables, and cider to supplement the earnings of their subsistence farms. Others were widows, who were given market licenses to keep them off the public dole; they sold hot chocolate and cakes, and often also fenced stolen goods. A third, prominent presence was blacks hawking vegetables, sweets, firewood, or animal skins. The markets were hot spots for African Americans from all over the New York region. After a day of selling and talking, the night brought dances, music, and gambling. Occasionally, the New York City Common Council would attempt to bar blacks from selling at the markets, but to little avail. On any weekend or holiday, blacks gathered together anything might sell, from roots, berries, and herbs, to birds, fish, clams, and oysters, then rushed off to the markets.[83]

The dance contests seemed to observers to be directly derived from African tradition. At the Catherine Market in post-revolutionary New York City, blacks from Tappan danced for prizes against the champions "Ned," slave of Martin Ryerson, or "Bobolink Bob, from Long Island." Tappan blacks were famous for their suppleness, and for their "plaited forelocks tied up with tea-lead" (an alloy used for lining tea-chests). A butcher would sponsor the initial prize, and the competition was on. Blacks brought their own "shingles," or dancing boards about five to six feet long, of large width, with good spring. First, dancers could be seen "turning around and shying off" around a designed spot; "shake-downs were next." Assistants held down the board while the dancer showed his art accompanied by clapping hands or tapping heels. These dances, practiced at home on a barn door or at frolics, lasted all night. Onlookers urged on the competitors with shouts, much like the African shouts identified in the American South.[84]

Gradual Emancipation in the Antebellum Period

Blacks in Bergen County fled into the city because civil and economic opportunity was so limited at home. The decades after the Gradual Emancipation Act of 1804 saw little improvement in black status in Bergen County. As the first generation of blacks freed under the Gradual Emancipation Act of 1804 reached their times of freedom, Bergen County masters gradually adapted to the new economics. The census of 1830 reveals the aging nature of servitude. Taken three years after New York State finally abolished slavery forever, the census shows that human bondage was still very much a fact of life in Bergen County, just across the river from New York City. In Bergen County, 300 males and 278 females were still enslaved. Nearly all of these were between the ages of twenty-four and fifty-five, which was the latest age at which masters were allowed to emancipate their bondspeople. (This measure was designed to avoid the practice of masters dumping aged slaves onto community support.) The bulk of slaves, then, were still in the prime of life, and their presence indicates that, if Bergen County masters adjusted to the new political realities and freed youthful blacks, they were determined to retain any black born before the date of gradual emancipation in bondage. For the cohort between thirty-six and fifty-five years of age, there was far less chance for legal freedom. Enslaved blacks outnumbered free people in Bergen by 224 to 124.[85]

Remember that land purchase in Bergen had become more and more difficult. The census of 1830 indicates that black freedom in Bergen offered limited opportunities. For most free people, liberty was still restricted by the boundaries of their masters' farms. In 1830, dependent blacks living and working on masters' farms outnumbered free independent blacks by 1,185 to 684. Moreover, Joan Geismar's investigation of Skunk Hollow, where Jack Earnest owned his farm, indicates a terrible poverty. Few black farmers in this isolated black community owned much more than a few cows, a pig, and a tiny amount of household goods.[86]

Only by 1840 could the long-term effects of emancipation be discerned in Bergen. Virtually the only blacks still in bondage were over the age of thirty-six, though, unfortunately, 115 men and 103 women remained enslaved. Independent status rose sharply for blacks. In rural Saddle River, independent black householders outnumbered dependents by 115 to 85, a total qualified by the presence of 19 slaves. The sustained power of slavery was evident in Hackensack, where 50 blacks were enslaved and were lived on their former masters' farms; only 155 blacks were independent.[87]

Even more shocking than the continued dependence of free blacks, a phenomenon evident in Monmouth County with its more liberal Quaker population, was the sudden drop in the number of blacks living in Bergen. Remember that in the colonial period, the black percentage of the county's overall population was usually about 20 percent. By 1820, even though the county's overall population grew only slightly, its black population actually decreased by some 500 people, to just over 15 percent. Although part of Bergen County was industrializing by 1820, most of the land was still used for agriculture. The number of blacks rose a little by 1830, then dropped back in 1840. African-American percentages of the county's total population continued to slide, to 11 percent in 1840 and all the way down to just below 8 percent in 1860.[88]

The flagging percentage of blacks in Bergen County brings us back to the original question regarding the future of slavery in America without Quaker influence. Bergen of course did not exist in a vacuum, and a coalition of philanthropic Friends and liberal Anglo-Americans eventually did convince Jersey legislators to abandon slavery, over the objections of citizens such as the petitioners from Bergen County, who were cited at the beginning of this chapter. The result of emancipation was not, however, a black free wage labor class in Bergen. Rather, as in New York City, where the percentage of African Americans in the overall population dropped precipitously in the antebellum decades, free blacks found very little opportunity in Bergen County and so left if they could. By 1860, as analysis of the manuscript census reveals, blacks, dependent or independent, left Bergen County as soon as they reached adulthood. On the eve of the Civil War, over half of local African Americans were nineteen years old or less. Twenty-two blacks living in Bergen County were still enslaved, almost six decades after passage of the Gradual Emancipation Act. The census also reveals growing segregation. In a few towns, such as Saddle River, Franklin, Union, and Lodi, whites outnumbered blacks by over twenty to one. With no work in sight, African Americans in Bergen simply voted with their feet and left.[89]

Bergen County's contribution to the answer to my counterfactual argument is that slavery would surely have continued without external pressure from the Society of Friends and other abolitionist groups. The ensuing history of racial engagement in Bergen County after the era of Gradual Emancipation tells much about American attitudes in the decades before the Civil War. It is well known that whites moving westward did so in part to escape competition from slavery and to create homogeneous, racially distinct communities.[90]

Within this stultifying social and economic environment, African Americans turned inward and spontaneously recreated African traditions. Grave sites at Gethsemane (formerly the Colored Cemetery) in Little Ferry are covered with pieces of broken white pottery. This is a clear recollection of African religious customs from the region of the Kongo in which the color white symbolize the land of the dead, while the broken pottery was placed to provide the departed with objects of use beyond the grave. On one grave, pipes permit communication between the deceased and the living. Such objects, common in Kongo societies, act, as Robert Farris Thompson has observed, to impose the wisdom of the dead upon the living. The pipes suggest travel underground to the world of the ancestors beneath or beyond the sea. Such tombs, Thompson suggests, become "ritual earthworks, conceptual doors to another universe, an intricate field of mediatory signs." In the same cemetery, trees, each with its own symbolic importance, indicate the strength of the elders' spirits and their resistance to the forces of time. At another grave site, in Bergenfield, huge rocks act as spiritual landmarks. In short, African Americans in Bergen in the tough antebellum years consciously took refuge in the customs of their ancestors. These ceremonies were the last gasps of a dying black presence in Bergen County. After the Civil War, the black presence in Bergen slid lower and lower, reaching a nadir, in percentage of the whole, of 2 percent in 1920, a level it remained at until 1980. Today few Bergen County residents recall hearing about the hard days of enslavement and freedom without compensation.[91]

4

Violence and Religion in the Black American Revolution

For over thirty years Benjamin Quarles's *The Negro in the American Revolution* (1960) has remained the standard account of black participation in the War for Independence. Quarles's detailed achievement culminated black historians' efforts to remind other scholars of the African-American contributions in America's wars. In tightly argued chapters, Quarles revived the forgotten history of Black Patriots and Loyalists, propounded the effect of revolutionary rhetoric on slaves, and outlined the development of a black postrevolutionary consciousness. As Quarles demonstrated fully, many blacks fell victim to British treachery and were resold into slavery in the West Indies. Others, evacuated from New York City in late 1783, went on to freedom in Nova Scotia and Sierra Leone. Despite the disappointment of blacks in postwar America, the resurgence of the plantation system in the South, and the duplicity of the British, Quarles concluded that African Americans benefited from their participation in the war. Their contributions, his argument implicitly stated, merited their greater inclusion in American citizenship.

Since publication of Quarles's masterly work, scholars have generally skirted its findings,[1] discussed blacks in the American Revolution as part of longer studies, or concentrated on discrete aspects.[2] Sylvia Frey's massive study* offers the first book-length extension of Quarles's work. Rather than refute Quarles, she extends and amplifies his arguments and evidence. In a superbly written and edited work, her impressive research and conclusions merit much admiration.

---

*Sylvia R. Frey. *Water from the Rock: Black Resistance in a Revolutionary Age.* Princeton: Princeton University Press, 1991.

Frey employs three major strategies. First, the book begins and concludes with powerful, synthetic discussion on southern African-American
life in the era of the American Revolution. Her daunting, original
research in British military records informs the middle chapters on
blacks in the war itself. Second, eschewing a general approach, Frey
concentrates on economic, legal,and religious factors within an unfolding military experience in specific regions. Although she spends little
time in the North where much fighting occurred, Frey's full coverage
of conflict in the South offers major new perspectives. Third, although
she acknowledges Peter Wood's concept that the revolution was a
triangular war between Patriot, Tory, and black,[3] Frey's study emphasizes the dynamic relationship of black and British.

Frey's carefully drawn introduction places slave resistance and rebellion within the economic and political crisis of the old colonial
empire and the emergence of a new republican order in the Americas
between 1760 and 1790. Partly constructed upon the work of Quarles
and Herbert Aptheker, whose 1944 dissertation remains the foundation
for all subsequent studies of black resistance,[4] she elaborates the meaning of resistance with key questions about its collective and individual
nature, gender, and, importantly, its ideology.

A useful first chapter provides contextual background on the development of the Chesapeake, Carolinas, and Georgia. While Frey does
not initially offer much new evidence, each point is based solidly on
the best scholarship. Fifteen ably written pages covering several prerevolutionary decades describe the creation of slave-based agricultural
systems and the establishment of slave codes, and interpret Anglican
proselytizing of African Americans. Despite the sweeping discussion,
she is always sensitive to regional differences.

The second half of the opening chapter is more revelatory. After
illustrating the emergence of an African-American culture in the prerevolutionary South, Frey shows how patterns of racial demography
created caste similarities among blacks and heightened cultural distances from whites. While acculturation with European society increased over the generations, African retentions were still visible.
While North American slavery dismantled African community systems, African-influenced matriarchal households and polygyny were
present in the South. Intruding into this traditional world were Anglican missionaries and, later, Baptist and Methodist evangelicals. Contact with Christianity did not mean blacks renounced African

cosmology. In burial rituals, Frey demonstrates, blacks retained traditional practices and fostered community. Frey is unconvinced that African Christianization was deeply felt in this period. Yet, at the eve of
the revolution, the dual influences of Anglican literacy and evangelical
faith and salvation prepared southern blacks for the "secular philosophy of Republican ideology" (p. 44) emphasizing liberty and equality
with an accompanying indictment of slavery. Not immediately apparent in the 1760s, the revolution fused this African-American ideology.

Blacks were deeply interested in the ideological furor of the 1770s.
Their physical reactions to the unfolding conflict were rooted in military traditions in Africa, and maroonage and individual flight in the
Americas. As the British paid great heed to slave restiveness, the immediate years before the revolution saw a triangular tension in North
American colonies among Whig, Tory, and African American. Ex-
ploited most in Virginia by Lord Dunmore, the colony's governor,
racial polarization flared throughout the South.

As the book illuminates the revolutionary experience in Georgia, the
Carolinas, and the Chesapeake, Frey's research and analysis is highly
convincing. Centered in her portrayal is black opportunism to enhance
liberty by accepting halting, often slippery, British promises to exchange freedom for military service. The results, she argues, were
uneven. In Georgia, over 5,000, or one-third, of the colony's slaves
quickly left their masters during the British invasion of 1779. As the
colony plunged into chaos, English officers worried that the heavy loss
of bonded labor would collapse Georgia's society and economy. In a
distinction key to her overall reasoning, Frey resists depiction of this
huge flight as a type of slave revolt by noting that the "high incidence
of escapes . . . lessened the possibility of organized rebellion and preventing the revolt from becoming a revolution" (p. 87). As British
officers exerted control over slaves, black aspirations for freedom became secondary to military necessities. Tory and Whig raids caused
misery among blacks and whites. Independent of British channeling,
however, black banditti pursued their own destinies. Her conclusions
about the effect of the revolution on blacks in Georgia are equivocal.
For many, the disruption caused calamity. For those escaping to the
English, "military service was . . . a complex mixture of servitude and
freedom . . . extending the tradition of slave resistance in a new direction" (p. 107).

In South Carolina, theater of a devastating civil war, thousands of blacks flocked to the British after the Phillipsburg Proclamation of 1779. Although some blacks adopted a cautious attitude, those thousands embracing the freedoms promised in the British order quickly overwhelmed authorities. Anxious again about the dimensions of the revolt, British commanders relegated blacks to military use as laborers housed in unsanitary conditions in camps riddled with typhus and smallpox. As in Georgia, Frey concludes, British organization of black refugees nullified potential slave insurrection.

Despite harrowing conditions and British duplicity, over twenty thousand slaves fled their masters in South Carolina. Near the end of the war, British commanders commissioned several black companies and, in 1782, evacuated them with regular troops to safety in New York City. Long after the English departure, African-American guerrilla bands plundered and foraged in the countryside.

In Virginia and Maryland, despite Patriot attempts to secure slaves well behind the battle lines, blacks were again able to flock to the British lines. Virtually every slaveowning family lost bondspeople. Frey's evidence of these movements is impeccable and assured. Less convincing is a static argument that "thousands of other slaves . . . chose to wait out the war quietly on the plantation" (p. 169). In a work marked by extraordinary research, one could hardly ask Frey for deeper investigation into the black disaffected, but this unsubstantiated assertion lacks conviction.

After Cornwallis's defeat at Yorktown in 1781, tens of thousands of blacks awaited British rulings whether to honor the promises made in battle or abandon them to their American slavemasters. In the lower South, the English left thousands of black refugees behind, sold others into slavery in the West Indies or retained them as servants. Dunmore, once liberator of slaves, condemned his former allies to servitude in the Bahamas. Perhaps the most famous evacuation of former slaves was from New York City to Nova Scotia. Over the vehement objections of George Washington, Sir Guy Carleton, commander of British forces, declared free all blacks who joined His Majesty's forces before 1782. Over three thousand black men, women, and children packed transport ships en route to a new life in Nova Scotia and New Brunswick. Hampered by Loyalist racism and burdened by economic hardship in the chilly maritime provinces, these refugees were still the most successful of the black revolutionaries. In a highly original insight, Frey detects an African-American variety of republicanism. In Nova

Scotia, and, later, in Sierra Leone, to which over one thousand jour-
neyed in 1791, the Black Loyalists "viewed themselves as heirs of the
revolution" (p. 197). Like their Patriot counterparts, the black refugees
sought land, security from racial intolerance, limits to arbitrary authority and burdensome taxes, and freedom of religious expression. Frey's
deft account of the origins of black republicanism offers pregnant possibilities for a racial synthesis of early American ideology. Undergirding this black republicanism was an insurgent evangelicalism. Black
Methodist and Baptist preachers and congregations sprouted in Nova
Scotia and intensified in Sierra Leone, often with strong nationalist and
antislavery messages.

Frey's account of the Nova Scotians prompts questions about her
general portrait. Much of her analysis of the black military experience
accentuates the callous judgments of British commanders. Substanti-
ated by her thorough research in military sources, she is undeniably
correct in her assessments of the British. Yet these sources slant her
cautious conclusions of the results of black flight to the English lines.
Throughout the key chapters on the revolution, British commanders
hold deterministic power over African-American motivations. Yet in
Nova Scotia, black ideology and evangelical, religious liberty appear,
doubtless products of the colonial and revolutionary experiences. To
be sure, black aspirations were thwarted elsewhere, but the Nova Sco-
tian republicanism is the model for African-American freedom struggles Frey uncovers in postrevolutionary America. To this reader, such
evidence suggests that British ideological and military control over
blacks may have been less hegemonic than indicated.

The aftermath of the war in the southern United States saw a weakened slavocracy. The loss of one hundred thousand slaves caused high
prices and scarcity of bonded labor. Frey uses excellent demographic
and econometric analysis to render the slow recovery in the South.
Amid the destruction of the war, black maroons, slave plots, and insurrections revealed a heightened black consciousness. Revolutionary
ideas prevalent in society "were powerful catalysts in moving slave
resistance beyond these inchoate forms of violent resistance" (p. 226).
Frightened by persistent outbreaks and horrified by the Haitian Revolution, state assemblies and courts mercilessly reified popular fantasies of
the dangerous black into laws and horrific punishments. The net effect
of these sections is forcibly to remind readers of the enormous influence
slave rebelliousness had upon lawmakers in the constitutional period.

Using Eugene Genovese's theory of paternalism, Frey shows how southerners adapted evangelical religion to pacify rebellious slaves. A chapter on the reformulation of the Christian social order recounts in detail how Methodists gradually abandoned their antislavery rhetoric in the South. While much of this is familiar to scholars of early national religion, Frey enlightens with classic tales of backwoods intimidation of Methodist itinerants. For example, Thomas Coke, a distinguished cleric, naively exhorted Virginians to emancipate their slaves in 1784 and was nearly assassinated.

If Methodists learned to be discreet in their sermons, blacks transformed the denomination for their own purposes. Frey skillfully mixes the work of Genovese and Margaret Washington Creel to delineate the rise of African-American churches. Black Christianity, she asserts, was a product of white Protestantism. Within Protestant structures, however, "blacks created their own institutions," with a subculture arming them with the "psychological and moral resources necessary to withstand slavery" (p. 284). If whites used religion for social control, blacks created in city and countryside churches replete with Africanized cemeteries and burial societies, benefit societies, and bible schools. It is within the Christianization of African Americans that Frey finds the true legacy of the American Revolution. The ability of African-American Christians to resist the accommodation of white Protestantism contributed significantly to the "racially distinct value systems and cultural communities" (p. 329) which came to characterize southern society.

Frey also chronicles an effective, militant black leadership shaped by the Haitian Revolution. Gabriel's Revolt in 1800 and the Vesey Revolt in 1822 were the most famous of these rebellions. While Frey credits these insurrections as legacies of the revolution, she discovers the majority of African Americans found cultural assertiveness in the church. The moral qualities and egalitarian sentiments in black churches, she concludes, were "the most effective challenges to the ideological superstructure of slavery" (p. 329). Gabriel Prosser and Denmark Vesey, however, like the tens of thousands of African Americans whose revolutionary militancy she documents, fought for their freedom. After reading Frey's magnificent and powerfully documented narrative of the revolution, this reviewer questions if her evidence of black rebelliousness, alienation from Whig America, and cooperation with British does not point equally to an alloy of religion and violence as the true black heritage of an incomplete revolution.

5

Black Revolt in New York City and the Neutral Zone, 1775–1783

The Year of Jubilee is Time
Return ye Ransomed Sinners Home.[1]

On 30 November 1783, a few days after the official evacuation day of British forces from New York City, the H.M.S. *L'Abondance* departed from Staten Island on its way to Port Mallton in the province of Nova Scotia. On board was the Black Brigade, the last of the estimated four thousand black refugees leaving behind servitude for a new life of freedom. Unlike the shiploads of escaped slaves and freeborn Afro-Americans who had departed from New York on such voyages since mid-March 1783 accompanied by masters or sponsors, the Black Brigade sailed alone. The brigade was the remnant of the several regiments of escaped slaves and freeborn blacks who fought for the British in Virginia, South Carolina, and around New York City during the American Revolution.[2]

The brigade contained a small community of forty-seven men, thirty-seven women, and sixteen children. It included escaped slaves and freeborn and emancipated blacks from nearly every colony. Several examples illustrate the experience and variety of individuals who composed the Black Brigade. Cato Winslow, a forty-seven-year-old escaped slave from New York City, left his master to fight for Lord

Dunmore in mid-1775; his wife, Rose, a "likely wench of forty years," left her master in Boston in the same year along with her son, Toby, aged eleven. The couple's daughter, Hannah, an infant of one year, was "born free within the British lines." From Virginia to New York City in 1779 came Peter Harding, aged twenty-eight. In New York City he married Kate, aged forty. Soon the couple had a daughter Eliza, "born free within the British lines." On board the *L'Abondance* was a group of freeborn women from Newark, New Jersey, including Mary Thompson, aged fifty-four, her daughter May, twenty-five, another daughter, Polly, ten, and two small children, Rachell, three years old, and Sally, one. Another couple, John and Hannah Jackson, left different masters in Morristown, New Jersey, in 1776, "in response to the [Dunmore] Proclamation." One veteran, Toby Castington, aged thirty-three, an escaped slave from Kent County, Virginia, came north with Lord Dunmore when the Governor of Virginia fled the colony in 1776. Accompanying Castington was his wife, Chloe, and daughter Betsy, "born free within the British lines." These members of the Black Brigade arrived in New York City during different periods of the American Revolution. In New York they became a cohesive military force.[3]

The Black Brigade were participants in the largest slave revolt in the New York and Eastern New Jersey area during the eighteenth century. "A desire of obtaining freedom unhappily reigns throughout the generality of slaves at present," complained the *New York Weekly Mercury* on 27 November 1780. Unlike the suppressed uprisings of 1712 and 1741, the black revolt that coincided with the American Revolution succeeded for nearly eight years, ending only with the defeat of the British and the subsequent removal of thousands of slaves from North America. Before that event, African Americans established a community in New York City that included elements of religious and secular society. Their example demonstrates how blacks worked within the social fissures created by the American Revolution to develop their own institutions. After their escape to Nova Scotia, black churches, schools, and political organizations emerged from the experiences of the American Revolution in New York.

The black rebellion that accompanied the American Revolution in New York and New Jersey is a major exception to current scholarly theories of slave rebellion. That scholarship emphasized several factors. There must be an absentee and impersonal master class, economic distress, and famine. Slaveholding units must approach an average of 100 to 200 slaves, far more than in the slave South and infinitely greater than the small masters of New York and New Jersey afforded. Blacks must outnumber whites, with African-born slaves in the majority. The ruling classes must be split, preferably by war. A successful slave revolt required a favorable terrain for escape and formation of maroon colonies. importantly, the slave-holding regime must permit the emergence of an autonomous black leadership. Finally, true success lay only in political overthrow of slavery. By this standard, revolts before 1792 were "restorationist" or sought escape from slavery into freedom. After the Haitian Revolution, slave revolts with political leaders became truly revolutionary and sought overthrow of the slaveocracy.[4]

Some but not all of these conditions could apply to the urban/small farm slave system operating in colonial New York City and its hinterlands. The lack of these conditions, however, should not undercut the importance of black efforts towards freedom, community, and political power during the American Revolution. The Black Revolt in New York City between 1775 and 1783 was characterized by a conscious choice of alliance with the British who offered personal freedom and the potential for development of a black community. The revolt was fueled by a desire to avenge past wrongs against blacks and to earn new status as soldiers, and even military leaders.

This black slave revolt occurred in New York City and the surrounding "neutral zone," which included Long Island, Staten Island, and Westchester County, New York, and the eastern counties of New Jersey—Bergen, Somerset, Essex, and Monmouth. Several factors besides British support for black resistance made the revolt possible. First was ready access to the city. There were over eighteen thousand slaves within thirty miles of lower Manhattan; mobile, rural slaves were continually filtering into the city on errands, visits, or escapes on foot, by horse, and boat. Second, many of these slaves were skilled and experienced; some were literate, especially those who had learned reading and writing from the Society for the Propagation of the Gospel in Foreign Parts. Those slaves gained visions of equality and freedom through their educations. A third source of resistance was the formative elements of black community. Hampered by the small farm/urban system of slavery in and around New York City during the colonial period, slaves nonetheless created a fluid culture in taverns, at dances, funerals, and executions, along the docks, and in the streets and roads. Extended slave families became the center of African American society. The last and most persistent source was the tradition of violent resistance, collective and individual.

None of these conditions, however, would have activated a black revolt had not the British army occupied New York City for most of the American Revolution. The British were the blacks' most consistent allies. Black Americans, desiring what Boston King described as "the happiness of liberty, of which I knew nothing before,"[5] chose to side with the Crown either for protection from bondage or, frequently, to fight against the Patriots in an effort to end slavery, despite the obstacles of British racism, deception, and support for slavery.

The Patriots recognized the black preferences. Henry M. Muhlenberg realized early in the war that the Negroes "secretly wished the British army might win, for then all Negro slaves will gain their freedom. It is said that this sentiment is universal amongst all the Negroes in America." Muhlenberg complained that "Barbarous Indians & Negroes are being enticed by the so-called Christians with gifts and promises."[6] As the first year of the war unfolded, Patriots worried about a full-scale black revolution. In early 1776, Charles Lee wrote of the need to impose military order over the black population of Virginia. He noted, "dominion over the black is based on opinion, loose that and authority will fall."[7]

Choosing Loyalism did not mean that blacks blindly followed British instruction. Blacks watched the unfolding conflict carefully, choosing sides according to their best interests, and were less pro-British than pro-black. In their guarantees of liberty the British were quite capable of deception and brutal fraud. Nonetheless, the proclamations by Lord Dunmore, Lord William Howe, and Sir Henry Clinton were calls to action received by a highly restive, rebellion-prone black society.[8]

Freedom inside the British lines meant a number of things. Freedom allowed the right to marry and live with one's spouse and to have children, "born free." It allowed blacks to work for wages and to live in integrated housing in previously segregated New York City. During the American Revolution in New York blacks enjoyed the support and membership in a receptive religion, Anglicanism, which offered religious consolation and education. Anglicanism made New York City more than just a hospitable refuge for escaped slaves; it provided them with support to establish a black community.

The choice of Loyalism permitted legal revenge against an American population that not only enslaved blacks but also terrorized them with a patrol system legally enforced by constables, justices of the peace, and minutemen, and a judicial system that employed quick execution for minor crimes. Capital punishment frequently included atrocities such as hanging in chains, burning at the stake, and posting heads after punishments forcibly attended by the area's black population. More blacks were put to death during the colonial period in New York than in any other northern colony. New Jersey was a close second.[9]

Freedom meant becoming a soldier, a prospect more attractive than the whip. Many blacks escaped to become servants of British soldiers. While nominally still enslaved, these blacks did so with the promise of freedom upon British victory, a frequent method of recruitment. Black pilots, guides, and soldiers were aware of the profits of plunder and the potential of rewards for special feats. The Black Brigade, particularly the thirty members from New Jersey, knew the homes of Patriots and could easily raid throughout the neutral zone. For this reason, Patriots feared the Black Brigade more than the regular British army. Henry Muhlenberg warned, "the worst is to be feared from the irregular troops whom the so-called Tories have assembled from various nationalities—for example, a regiment of Catholics, a regiment of Negroes, who are fitted for and inclined towards barbarities, are lacking in human feeling and are familiar with every corner of the country."[10]

The Black Brigade and the Black Pioneers and Guides were invaluable to the British forces. New York City was the most important British holding in North America before and throughout the Revolutionary War. Its protection was fundamental to any British success. Eastern New Jersey, although not always controlled by British forces, was a rich source of agricultural products, cattle, and firewood. The Black Brigade, particularly under the leadership of Colonel Tye, played a key role in protecting vulnerable New York from Patriot incursions. Colonel Tye and the Black Brigade were masters of guerrilla warfare. The Black Brigade, an adjunct force attached first to Banastre Tarleton's regiment, which later worked with General John Graves Simcoe's Queens Rangers, was quite effective in raids on New Jersey and Westchester County. These raids softened up local militias, captured key officers, and acquired valuable livestock and forage for the British forces and loyalists in New York City. They also ushered escaping slaves to their freedom inside British lines, and eventual transportation to new lives in Nova Scotia.[11]

The roots of the revolutionary black experience lie in the context of slave resistance during the colonial period. Blacks historically responded to their enslavement by conspiracy, revolt, and escape. The slave conspiracies of 1712 and 1741 were but the largest of a continuing series of violent confrontations between whites and blacks that spread across the two colonies. In each instance the slave planned to rise up, burn houses and buildings and, while the whites were distracted, murder and pillage before making their flight. In 1712 the slaves first enacted an African brotherhood ritual before the insurrection in which they succeeded in murdering a number of whites. This incident, coupled with murders in 1708 by slaves in Hallet's Cove, Long Island, worsened white fears and resulted in harsher and more restrictive laws.[12] In 1734 New Jerseyans were shocked by a well-developed conspiracy in Somerset County that endangered the lives of all whites living there. The same decade saw a series of grisly murders by slaves. Using axes and poisons, the bondsmen dispatched their masters despite the grim threat of punishment by burning and hanging. The Slave Conspiracy of 1741 spread terror from Long Island to West Jersey. Each of these revolts included careful planning, a willingness to massacre whites, and a desire to create a black state.[13]

To confront their bondsmen's threats, New York and New Jersey whites instituted the largest and harshest slave system north of the Chesapeake, circumscribing blacks' legal, political, and economic lives. An expanding slave trade managed by New York's most successful merchants was complemented by numerous private transfers by slaveowners. Yet the growth of the slave trade in the 1750s caused some northerners concern. Quaker Anthony Benezet feared that rising percentages of blacks in the North could create a rebellious situation akin to the American South, the West Indies, and Surinam. In a letter to Englishman David Barclay, Benezet, the leading American abolitionist, anxiously requested that certain British antislavery pamphlets not be distributed in America, "as this was thought to be of too tender a nature to be exposed to view, in places where it might fall into the hands of the Negroes."[14] As black percentages of New York and New Jersey populations rose above fourteen percent, reaching a high of 18,000 slaves by 1771, white repression grew more brutal with each threat of slave resistance.

Black resistance to slavery remained an underlying current throughout the colonial period. The proximity of the frontier enabled runaway slaves to join Indians warring on the English, escape to Canada, or form maroon societies on Long Island or the Ramapo Mountains. Some ex-slaves organized tough gangs on the New York City waterfront, mixing freedom with vandalism. Despite heavy penalties and an efficient patrol system, northern slaves continued to flee throughout the colonial period.[15]

Slaves also used religion to question slavery. Under the Dutch there was some ambiguity over the status of Christian Blacks. Even during the earliest years of English rule, blacks employed Christianity as an avenue to escape from bondage. During the eighteenth century, the Anglican church, as a part of its missionary activity, worked to convert blacks and initiated an important alliance. Anglican missionaries, in their efforts to save black souls, taught slaves the important tools of reading and writing, and, in sermon and classroom, espoused doctrines of spiritual and intellectual equality.[16]

Slaveowners regarded Anglican instruction of blacks with suspicion. Not only did such education distract blacks from their labors, and implant dangerous ideas of equality, but it permitted emergence of a literate leadership. Many New Jersey runaway notices mentioned slave literacy. Black preachers, capable of reading and circulating political arguments about liberty, were a natural consequence of "such indulgence." In 1774, for example, Major Prevost of Bergen County, New Jersey, announced the escape of his slave Mark. Prevost described Mark as "serious, civil, slow of speech, rather low in stature, reads well, is a preacher among the Negroes, about 40 years of age." Accompanying him was his wife, who was "smart, active and handy, rather lusty, has bad teeth and a small cast in one eye; she is likely to look upon, reads and writes well and is about 36 years of age." They were headed for New York City, where during the American Revolution they would be joined by other black religious leaders. There, together, these blacks created an ethos of egalitarianism and salvation, both personal and racial.[17]

New York City was always a magnet for freedom-bound blacks. There were many black females in the city, increasing the possibility of family life. Jobs were available to runaways, either as domestics or as hired hands along the docks. Although colonial law attempted to prohibit sea masters from hiring blacks without proper passes, by the 1770s, New York's docks were filled with black laborers and mariners. The assertive, often skilled, finely dressed, independent, and scarcely deferential New York City blacks appeared as a beacon to their country cousins, beckoning them to join the ranks of the free, or at least emulate the city black in style and behavior.[18]

It is against this background of long-standing opposition to slavery during the colonial period, and the intensifying disorder created in the mid-1770s, that we must view the black revolt of 1775 to 1783 in New York City and the neutral zone. This revolt took on three related dimensions. First was the continuation of waves of conspiracy spilling over from the colonial era. Second was the large number of runaways who flooded the Loyalist lines. Third were those blacks who took up arms to fight for their liberty in the service of King George. Such blacks often formed opportunistic gangs that looted and burned Patriot property for their own gain. These forms of revolt frequently merged.[19]

The years just before the American Revolution were filled with threats of conspiracy from the more than eighteen thousand slaves living either in or close to New York City. In 1772, as Somerset County, New Jersey, slaveowners considered seriously proposals for an African colonization movement, they also fretted over reports of mass meetings of slaves. Owners were shocked by two slaves' retorts that: "it was not necessary to please their masters, for they should not have their masters long." Somerset County slavemasters found themselves unable to keep their bondspeople home after nine o'clock in the evening. Slaves stole liquor, "fowls," and other food. Some stole their masters' horses to ride to late-night meetings. For example, George Van Nest charged his slave Tom with theft and "riding horses three nights after midnight." The bad consciences of Perth Amboy residents in 1774 caused them to beseech the New Jersey Assembly not to consider any more manumission proposals because the "slaves are a very bad and dangerous people."[20] In 1775, as American eyes uneasily considered the unfolding drama of Lord Dunmore's conflict with Virginia planters, a dispute that would result in the governor's famous Proclamation freeing all "indented servants and slaves" willing to fight for the Crown, New Jerseyans and New Yorkers worried about a "wave of revolt." Somerset County was racked by rumors of associations of blacks and disaffected whites, urged on by British soldiers. A report to the Continental Congress asserted that "the story of the Negroes may be depended upon, so far . . . at least to their arming or attempting to form themselves, particularly in Somerset County. Our militia are gone off in such numbers that we hardly have Men in

Armes enough left in those parts which are affected to the cause." There were numerous and ominous reports coming from New York as well. In the city, "two Tory Negroes" were hanged for "engaging to murder their masters who were supporters of liberty." On Long Island Patriots burned Dunmore in effigy and worried about slaves "being too fond of the British troops."[21] One prominent Monmouth County Patriot noted with displeasure the union of slaves and refugee whites, pointing out that he had previously employed a number of the Tories and blacks as wheelwrights. These now were "the very fellows who tried to take my Father prisoner and perhaps kill him."[22]

Anguished by reports from near and far in late 1775, the Committee of Safety in Shrewsbury Township, Monmouth County, ordered search parties to stop "meetings of servants Negroes and other disorderly persons as they are attended with great mischief." Reports from Monmouth indicated that blacks were taking advantage of the political splits among whites to engage in practices legally forbidden, particularly night meetings and carousing at taverns. On 11 and 16 October 1775 the committee ordered "Colonel Breeze to secure the Negroes," and cease "Riotous and numerous meetings of Negroes at unlicensed houses." The committee ordered all guns and ammunition taken from blacks "until the present Troubles are setled." Later the committee resolved that all "Slaves, Negroes and Mollattos found off their master's premises shall be arrested."[23] The fears of the slaveholders were more than paranoia; they were a recognition that their bondsmen were preparing for a move.

As in previous decades, escape was the principal means of black revolt. Despite harsh penalties and constant surveillance, black runaways were a persistent and expensive problem.[24] During the American Revolution the number of runaways was nearly four times the amount known in the previous seventy years in New Jersey; in New York City and on Long Island, far more slaves fled their masters than at any previous time. Using newspaper advertisements and the embarkation list of blacks leaving New York City with the British in 1783, it is possible to identify 516 slaves who escaped from their masters in New Jersey and New York Provinces between 1775 and 1783.

The most convenient sources enabling historians to identify runaways are newspaper advertisements. However, New Jersey slaveowners gave notice of only 80 of 308 or 29 percent of runaways during the American Revolution. The remainder may be found in the embarkation list.[25] Runaway notices represented more than an effort to help masters recapture their bondsmen, a method that rarely worked. They also freed the master of any obligations or damages incurred by their slaves. During the war notices acted as warnings to other Patriots of slave intentions, especially "joining the ministerial army," as many planned.[26]

Runaway advertisements provide the clearest available images of individual slaves. Not only do they inform us of the intentions of many to join the British army or of plots by whites, free blacks, and slaves to help free bondsmen, but the notices include detailed information about physical features and clothing. Masters described slaves with limps, severe scars, small-pox scars, and bashful looks. They were "likely, comely, short, tall," in poor health or lusty. Hairstyles were often "bushy," or on occasion, cut in the fashionable "macaroni" style, indicating the spread of urban fashions into the provinces.[27]

Slaves frequently took not only their own belongings, but an assortment of their master's clothing to keep warm in the harsh winters or to barter in the used clothing markets of New York City. Sam, who ran away from Colonel John Reid in New York City in 1776, took with him "a tight-bodied blue cloth livery coat with red cuffs and a collar and red lining," as well as six pairs of breeches, vests, six pairs of shoes, and numerous stockings. Reverend Smith identified his runaway Michael Hoy as probably wearing "a suit of superfine mixt broad cloth, a red new great coat, white stockings, halfboots, a blue velvet stock and a beaver hat, but littleworn." Hoy also took with him "a dark bay horse . . . a natural trotter."[28] While many slaves stole fine clothes, their own possessions appear to have been more modest. Sixteen wore buckskin breeches; five wore handmade bearskin coats. Beaver hats were very popular as were regimental garb. Women were often dressed in petticoats, jackets, stockings, flat shoes, and bonnets. Although they tried to take extra clothes with them, there is little indication that the women were as successful as males.[29]

Much information about black families is contained in the "Book of Negroes," the ledger kept by the British of departing slaves in 1783. Almost sixty percent of blacks leaving New York City at the end of the war did so in family units. The evidence about New Jersey slaves provides proof of a powerful and opportunistic drive by blacks to take advantage of the war and unite in New York City. Cornelius Van Sayl, thirty years old, escaped from John Lloyd of Monmouth

County in 1778; he took with him his wife, Catherine, and his daughter Mary, both of whom formerly belonged to John Vander Veer of Monmouth County. The couple gave birth to Peter in New York City and were joined there by Peter Van Sayl, Cornelius's brother from Tom's River. Joseph Collins, aged thirty, escaped from John Kipp of New York City after his master sold him to Dr. Van Buren of Hackensack. In New Jersey he met his wife, Betsy, slave of Nicholas Terhune; together they escaped to New York in 1779. Brothers sometimes escaped together such as Harry and Vaughn Couwenhoven, who formerly belonged to Peter Couwenhoven of Middletown, New Jersey. Some masters lost several slaves. John Sipe of Acquakanonck lost Susan Van Ryper, Polly Richards, Dianah Kingsland, her son, Caesar, and a young daughter, all in 1779. The Van Rypers of Bergen County, New Jersey, lost nine slaves over the course of the revolution. In all, Bergen County masters lost at least 90 slaves, a comparable number probably escaped from Monmouth County slaveowners.[30]

Runaways were not the only Afro-Americans who departed from New York City in 1783. In addition to the 516 fugitive slaves leaving New York City, there were forty-three freeborn blacks from New Jersey and forty-nine from New York. There were also thirty-two blacks from New York and eighteen from New Jersey who were freed by their masters after death through manumission, personal grants, or simple abandonment.[31] For example, Colonel Stephen Bleuke, later commander of the Black Pioneers and Guides, was freeborn in Barbados; in New York City he met his wife, Margaret, who was "born free in Mr. Coventry's house in New York City." Margaret was probably a black indentured servant because Stephen was forced to purchase her freedom in 1770. The couple also purchased Isabel Gibbon from Coventry's daughter. Isabel, twenty years of age, was probably Margaret Bleuke's daughter. Another slave who purchased his family's freedom was Joseph Paul, thirty years, who bought his freedom from Lawrence Kortwright of New York City. He also paid William Brown of New York City to free his wife, Susannah Paul, aged thirty, and their three children.[32]

Some former slaves gained their freedom by manumission from religious whites who scrupled at holding slaves. Isaac Corlies, twenty-seven, gained his freedom from Will Mott, a Quaker from Great Neck, Long Island. His wife, Hagar Corlies, twenty-two, also became free by manumission from Quaker Joseph Hewlett of Great Neck. Peter Johnson, thirty-five, gained his freedom from a Quaker, Silvestre Brinoly of New Jersey, and moved to New York City in response to General Howe's Proclamation in 1778.[33] The frequent necessity of free blacks to serve some time with white masters may be seen in the case of Charity Morris, twenty-eight, freeborn in Long Island but who completed an apprenticeship with Jonathan Mills at age eighteen. Charity Morris, and her children, Issac, nine, Edward, five, and daughter, Mary Ann, one year, traveled with her husband, Ned Morris, and escaped slave from Fairfield, Connecticut.[34]

Despite the American hope that free blacks and slaves would have little social contact, the case of Prince suggests otherwise. Prince, fifty-three, formerly slave to Abraham Peers of Second River, New Jersey, negotiated a deal with a new master, Joseph Stokes of New Jersey, and purchased his freedom for forty-five pounds. Margaret, his wife, was freeborn in Bergen County, New Jersey, but left with her husband and son, Mintard, for New York City in 1780. There they joined their daughter, Elizabeth, twenty, her small child, and husband, Samuel Van Nostrandt of Acquackanonck, who escaped from his master in 1779.[35]

Once inside the British lines, blacks became valuable recruits to the English army. As the conflict unfolded, blacks declared their willingness to fight with either side, but met with sharply different reactions from Patriots and Tories. The Whigs were generally negative. Not only was there danger of revolt, but slaves were valuable property, made more so by the absence of white laborers in the army. Further there were ideological problems. American revolutionaries were apprehensive that the British wished to reduce white colonials to the levels of black slaves. Patriots firmly believed that they were engaged in the conflict to avoid English enslavement of the colonies. Such talk of liberty was dangerous if heard by America's true slaves.[36]

Throughout the war, however, blacks served in military roles for the revolutionaries. Some Patriots used their slaves as replacement substitutes for their own military service. In smaller states such as Rhode Island and Connecticut blacks made up significant portions of the regiments. Even though most Americans rejected Henry Laurens's proposal that the Continental Congress purchase slaves from their masters and then draft them, blacks continued to filter into the American forces.[37]

In contrast, the British openly enlisted blacks in their army. Blacks aided the British cause around New York in several ways. One hundred and twenty blacks worked as laborers in the Quarter Master General's Department, for the Wagonmaster, or in the Forage and Provision Departments of the Army around New York City. While the British paid these laborers less than white Loyalists, several occupations filled by Loyalist blacks such as cartman, wagon driver, and carpenter had been rigidly segregated in New York City before the war. Now the black Loyalists were given an opportunity to work at whole new occupations. As the labor shortage worsened, blacks were able to command the same inflationary wages as whites.[38] Tory blacks served as personal servants. For an escaped slave, offering one's services to a British officer was a good way to avoid detection. Unskilled labor and personal service have customarily been viewed as the sum of black activity in the American Revolution. Except for the few who filled the ranks in a handful of cases, most blacks were, according to historians, the "men behind the men with the guns."[39]

Recently, however, scholars are uncovering not just individual black participation in the Revolution, but whole units of black soldiers fighting for the British. The Black Guides and Pioneers in North Carolina and Pennsylvania, the Ethiopian Regiment fighting in Virginia, New York, and South Carolina, and the Black Brigade of New York City were not exceptions but were parts of an important, sustained black participation in the British and Loyalist efforts.[40]

General Sir Henry Clinton commissioned the first Black Pioneer company on 2 April 1776 in New York. Similar companies existed in the Carolinas, Virginia, and Pennsylvania. Each had two white officers, a lieutenant and an ensign. The rest of the company usually consisted of sixty to seventy black recruits including three sergeants, three corporals, and thirty-two privates. Pay was the same as for white infantrymen, a shilling a day for a sergeant, eightpence for a corporal, and sixpence for a private.[41]

The British swore blacks into the Pioneer company with a simple oath. The oath briefly noted that volunteers entered the Black Pioneer company without compulsion and that applicants would faithfully serve the British army. Thomas Peters recalled being sworn in on 14 November 1776 by Alderman William Waddell in New York City. His captain, George Martin, was, like other officers commanding the Black Pioneers, a member of the Queen's Rangers. Peters remembered promises from the officers that after the war, he would be "at our own liberty to do & provide for ourselves."[42]

The British quickly put black fugitives to work in paramilitary ways. The "Black Pioneers" performed paramilitary services as guards, pilots, spies, interpreters with Indians; performed executions; and were able horsemen, hunters, and drummers. The British richly rewarded one black guide for informing them of a prospective Patriot attack on New York City in 1779.[43]

The British frequently used Black Pioneers as spies. The roster of "Capt. Martin's Company" gave the names of blacks, their geographic origin, and their knowledge of specific areas. One example was Benjamin Whitecuff, freeborn on Long Island. At the beginning of the war, Whitecuff first joined the Americans to become a sergeant. Whitecuff joined the British forces on Staten Island in 1776 and worked for General Sir Henry Clinton as a spy for two years, earning over fifteen guineas in that time. Caught by the Patriots near Cranbury, New Jersey, Whitecuff was hanged. The Americans left him dangling and a few minutes later he was rescued by an English regiment. Whitecuff proceeded to Staten Island then went to Virginia. Captured by the Americans, Whitecuff was again condemned to be hanged in Boston. Fortunately for him the British recaptured him a second time and brought him to England for refuge. Later he served in the Siege of Gibraltar as a regular British soldier.[44]

The Black Pioneers were officially part of the British army from the earliest years of the war. Less recognized, but equally valuable, were the many blacks termed loosely "followers of the Army and Flag." These were escaped slaves and free blacks expert in guerrilla warfare and very useful for softening up Patriot militias with nighttime raids or securing valuable livestock for the English garrison in New York City. At first the British used "followers of the Army and Flag" opportunistically. By the close of the war, however, the British recognized the importance of their service by formally organizing them into the Black Brigade.[45]

The Black Brigade resembled several historic British formations of slaves. First were "Black Shot" organizations of whole units of slaves, armed for military action. Used in Jamaica in the 1740s and again in the 1780s, the Black Shot was usually a one-time temporary military system. A second type were "Black Corps," which were special military units of free blacks, mulattos, and recently freed slaves. "Black Corps" could be auxiliaries to other fighting units added to the militia or created as units of black rangers that could be transferred between colonies to meet special crises.[46]

Volunteers for these units came largely from fugitive slaves attracted by British proclamations offering freedom to those willing to serve in the King's Army. For example, in 1779 General Sir Henry Clinton issued a proclamation promising to "every Negro who shall desert the Rebell Standdard full security to follow within these lines any Occupation which he shall think Proper."[47] The American reaction to this invitation was racist ridicule. A New Jersey poet wrote:

> A proclamation oft of late he sends
> To thieves and rogues who are only his friends
> Those he invites; all colours he attacks
> But deference pays to *Ethiopian Blacks*.[48]

Clinton's promise of sanctuary, widely circulated in Loyalist newspapers, set off a rush of black enlistments as buglers, drummers, and common soldiers. According to their own testimony inscribed in the "Book of Negroes" in 1783, hundreds heard Clinton's proclamation and left their masters for freedom in Philadelphia and New York City. There they joined with family and friends and formed their own communities.

Blacks in New York City lived in "Negro barracks" at 18 Broadway, 10 Church Street, and other locations. The quality of such housing may be inferred from the grousing of Thomas A. Jones, the Loyalist historian, that excellent housing was being wasted upon refugee blacks that could have been rented to deserving white Loyalists with the profits to be used to support the war effort. Jones's attitude was not uncommon among American Tories, many of whom felt the British commanders were unduly concerned about the former slaves. New York was the scene of "Ethiopian Balls" in which Afro-Americans and British officers and soldiers freely mingled to the music of black fiddlers and banjo players. Black tavern life, no longer restricted by law, flourished. Afro-Americans joined British soldiers, if comments about their fraternization may be credited, in various sports, especially horse racing, which enlivened occupied New York life.[49] The size of this community at times frightened the British and they attempted to limit its further growth. The British asked the ferrymen along the Hudson River to refuse passage to escaping blacks desirous of entering New York. However, the British ambivalence could not stem the tide of freedom-seeking blacks. In this light Clinton's proclamation not only allowed the general to fill important manpower needs, a problem for both sides as the war wore on, but offered a positive method of dealing with the hundreds of young blacks, eager to fight against the Americans and who could have easily become rebellious if not allowed to fulfill their desires. The British were able to channel the black revolt for their own purposes, yet in return for military service had to recognize black demands.

One of the most important "followers of the Army and Flag" was Colonel Tye, who escaped from John Corlies, a prosperous Quaker farmer from Colt's Neck, New Jersey. Corlies's farm was located along the Navesink River, which stretched along sandy beaches and wooded inlets until it emptied into the Atlantic Ocean. On the Navesink Tye mastered river piloting and learned about Corlies's property as well as that of his neighbors.[50] Fearful Patriots knew that Tye could provide the British with information on their homes, wealth in livestock, plate, and other valuable commodities. Monmouth's Patriots were especially vulnerable. Located directly across a narrow strip of water from Staten Island, the headquarters of British regular and irregular forces, Monmouth was an easy and profitable prey. In the nearby Bay of New York, British warships offered protection for periodic raids on Patriot towns. To add to Patriot difficulties, Monmouth was not only geographically impossible to defend, but many residents were sympathetic to the English cause. Part of the militia was suspected of working openly with the British; others engaged in lucrative smuggling along the coast. Much of Monmouth's population was disaffected, many by religious conviction. Anglicans were openly Tory while Quakers, who constituted twenty percent of Monmouth's population, remained at least neutral, and in the eyes of many Patriots, hostile to their efforts. A few Friends were willing to sign loyalty oaths to the new government, but as the war progressed, the Shrewsbury Meeting expelled members with any contact with either army. Worse, there was the continual problem of Tye and other refugee blacks.[51]

Tye's first known military venture was during the Battle of Monmouth in 1777. Elisha Shepard, a captain in the Monmouth Militia, recalled his capture and transfer by "Captain Tye" to the Sugar House in New York City. That Tye should assume first the title of captain and later of colonel, was, if unusual, not without precedent, as the British army often granted such titles out of respect, particularly in Jamaica and other West Indian islands. Tye not only commanded blacks but directed whites as well.[52]

Tye's next recorded appearance came in the summer of 1779. During a period of intense racial anxiety in New Jersey aggravated by reports of an anticipated massacre of whites by blacks in Elizabethtown, Tye and his men, accompanied by the fierce Loyalist John Moody, began a series of raids against Monmouth's Patriots. On 15 July 1779, "about fifty negroes and refugees landed at Shrewsbury and plundered the inhabitants of near 80 head of horned cattle, about 20 horses and a quantity of wearing apparel and household furniture. They also took off William Brindley and Elisha Cook, two of the inhabitants."[53]

This combined force of black and white Loyalists was the military arm of a plan sponsored by the erstwhile New Jersey governor, William Franklin, to employ the bitter anger of Loyalists against Monmouth's Patriots. For the first years of the war, British commanders chose the cream of New Jersey's Loyalists as officers, enlisted a few others, but largely ignored the common Loyalist. Made unhappy by Patriot sales of their confiscated property, New Jersey's pro-British citizens were infuriated by the revolutionaries' summary executions of Loyalists. Whigs hanged several captured Loyalists under the vigilante law that governed Monmouth after early 1779. "A Loyal Refugee," demanded immediate retaliation in the *Royal Gazette* of 5 June 1779.[54]

Tye's July 1779 raid established a pattern that continued for over a year. These raids were a combination of banditry, marronage, and commissioned assistance to the British army. All three aspects, moreover, were conscious methods of rebellion, often aimed directly at former masters and their friends. Tye and his men, at times aided by white refugees known as "cow-boys," would surprise Patriots in their homes, kidnap soldiers and officers, carry off plate, clothing, and other valuables, and secure badly needed cattle for British troops in Staten Island and New York City. For these accomplishments, Tye and his men were paid handsomely. Tye's deep knowledge of Monmouth's swamps, rivers, and inlets made his presence undetectable until it was too late. After a raid, Tye and his "motley crew" would return to Refugeetown at Sandy Hook, headquarters for maroon activity, or hide in nearby swamps.

The fall and winter of 1779–1780 were filled with raids from Sandy Hook and Staten Island. The planting season of 1779 was "unfavorable to crops" and although farmers preferred selling food to the British for gold than to Americans for paper money, food, hay, and firewood were scarce. One Loyalist in New York City contented himself with green twigs for firewood. That winter was unusually harsh, and the ice-bound Hudson River made the British apprehensive about protecting New York City. The combined forces of the Queen's Rangers and the Black Brigade enabled the British to both protect the city and send out exploratory raids to secure food and fuel.[55]

On 30 March 1780 Tye and his men captured a Captain Warner, who purchased his freedom; less lucky were Captain James Green and Ensign John Morris, whom Tye took to Refugeetown at Sandy Hook en route to imprisonment in the Sugar House in New York City. In the same raid Tye and his men looted and burned the home of John Russell, a fierce Patriot associated with raids on Staten Island, before killing him and wounding his young son. Three weeks later a band of refugees and blacks captured Matthias Halsted at his home near Newark and plundered the house of "bed, bedding, family wearing apparel and 7–8 head of creature [cattle]."[56]

These attacks came during a period of rising concern about Patriot prospects in New Jersey. Governor William Livingston, who two years before on the advice of Samuel Allinson, had attempted to abolish slavery in New Jersey, now wrote fearfully of Lord Dunmore's effect upon local blacks. The borders between New York and New Jersey were flooded with black refugees bound for sanctuary with the British. Loyalists in New York, eager to organize against Livingston's government, were encouraged by reports that George Washington's army was down to 1,600 men. As part of the concern over black runaways to New York City, New Jersey slaveholders were urged to remove their slaves "to some more remote or interior parts of the state."[57]

On 9 June 1780 Colonel Tye and his men murdered Private Joseph Murray of the Monmouth County militia at his home in Colt's Neck. Murray was a nemesis of local Tories and had been personally responsible for several executions.[58] This was the first of several such retaliatory assaults in the month of June 1780. On 12 June Colonel Tye commanded a large band of slaves and refugee whites in a daring attack on the home of Barnes Smock of the Monmouth militia while the main body of British troops attacked Washington's forces. Smock, a horse trader and a promoter of local thoroughbred races, was the leader of Patriot resistance in Monmouth County. Using a six-pound cannon to warn residents of the raid, Smock summoned a number of men around his house to fight Tye. After a stiff battle, Tye and his men captured Smock and twelve other Patriots, disabling much of the leadership of Monmouth's militia and preventing them from aiding Washington's troops. The victors captured valuable livestock and looted Smock's home. Tye spiked Smock's cannon, a symbolically disheartening action. Tye and his men then spirited their prisoners back to the Loyalist stronghold at Refugeetown before sending them on to imprisonment at the Sugar House in New York City. Immediately local Patriots wrote anguished letters to Governor William Livingston, begging for help against the ravages of Colonel Tye. In response to Tye's attacks of 8, 9, and 12 June 1780, Governor William Livingston ordered martial law effective in Monmouth County. But many farmers ordinarily warm to the Patriot cause were in the middle of the planting season and Livingston openly despaired of supplying Washington with a full complement of troops from Monmouth County because of the farmer's needs. While the New Jersey Patriots were distracted by Tye and his men, other blacks took advantage. The *New Jersey Journal* noted that "twenty-nine Negroes of both sexes deserted from Bergen County in early June, 1780."[59]

Tye's June incursions caused great fear among New Jerseyans. In one week Tye carried off much of the officer corps of the Monmouth militia, destroyed their cannon, and demonstrated his ability to strike at will against a weakened Patriot population. If before he was a banditti in service to the British, he now became an important military force. There were more attacks to come. On 22 June 1780 "Tye with thirty blacks, thirty-six Queen's Rangers and thirty refugees landed at Conascung, New Jersey." The invaders slipped undetected past Patriot scouts and captured James Mott, Second Major of the Second Regiment of the Monmouth militia. Tye's men sacked and destroyed Mott's and "several Neighbor's" homes. Tye's troops also captured Captain James Johnson of the Hunterdon militia, and six privates.[60]

It was a stunning blow to the Patriot side. Tye captured eight men, plundered their homes, and then took the captives to New York. Despite the martial law and the presence of several militias, Tye and his men escaped without any reported casualties. Although the notorious Tory John G. Simcoe, commander of the Queen's Rangers, was present, Tye received credit for the raid in newspapers. Throughout the summer of 1780 Tye led his "motley band" on raids into Monmouth

County burning barns and looting farms. On one such raid in late August, Tye and his men captured Hendrick and John Smock, brothers of Barnes, and sent them to join the latter in prison in New York City.[61]

On 1 September 1780 Tye attempted his greatest feat. For years Loyalists had tried to capture Captain Josiah Huddy who was famed for his leadership in raids on British positions in Staten Island and Sandy Hook and much hated for his quick executions of captured Loyalists. Colonel Tye led a small army of blacks, refugees, and Queen's Rangers against Huddy's home in Tom's River. Normally the center of Patriot activity in the area, Huddy's house was occupied only by its owner and a female friend, Lucretia Emmons. As Tye's men attacked, Huddy ran from room to room, firing muskets, which Miss Emmons quickly reloaded, creating an illusion that Patriots filled the house. After a two-hour battle Tye set fire to the house and flushed out Huddy. During the battle, Tye was shot in the wrist. The fighting attracted the attention of other Patriots and, as Tye was leading Huddy back to Refugeetown, the militia intercepted his band. During the ensuing skirmish, Huddy escaped by jumping overboard and swimming to his rescuers, shouting, "I am Huddy."[62]

Tye's wound proved more serious than originally thought. Within days lockjaw set in and, without proper medical attention, shortly killed him. Though Tye's exploits ended in this savage encounter, his memory was avenged when Huddy, captured nearly two years later, was snatched by Loyalists from a British prison ship on a pretext and hanged on the shore of Monmouth County. A black man performed Huddy's execution. This arbitrary justice, occurring after Cornwallis's surrender at Yorktown and as peace negotiations were underway, caused an international furor and threatened to affect peace terms between the Americans and the British. Its effect was to deepen local animosities between Patriots and Loyalists.[63]

Colonel Stephen Bleuke of the Black Pioneers replaced Tye as the leader of black raiders in the New York area, but Tye's memory lived on. Patriots remembered Tye's revolutionary activities with admiration in contrast to their hatred of white Loyalists. Even during the angry dispute over Huddy's execution, Americans recalled Tye as a "brave and courageous man whose generous actions placed him well above his white counterparts." Despite his opposition to the American side, Patriots admired his military skill and argued that had Tye been enlisted in the American forces the war would have been won much sooner. Such sentiment remained common in New Jersey through the antebellum period.[64]

As the war continued in the early 1780s, Bleuke and the Black Pioneers and the Black Brigade propped up the fading hopes of local Loyalists. Despite Cornwallis's defeat in 1781, Loyalists refused to accept the inevitable, and raided Long Island and New Jersey constantly. On 5 June 1782 forty whites and forty blacks landed at Forked River, New Jersey, plundered Patriot homes, and burned a number of salt works, to the great anger of New Jersey's Patriots.[65] Such actions, combined with the constant runaway problems, indicate that despite the British defeat at Yorktown, slaves continued their revolt by any means possible.

The close of the war in November 1783 found racial relations between whites and blacks in New York and New Jersey permanently altered. The slave populations of Monmouth and Bergen Counties in New Jersey and Westchester County and Long Island in New York were significantly reduced. Both states began a long-drawn out debate over the abolition of slavery. The debate's tenor was far less egalitarian than in Pennsylvania or New England. Rather, the two largest slave states north of the Chesapeake desired to acquire more white immigrants, which they hoped would be a more loyal and less contentious labor force.[66]

One institution remained open to blacks. Trinity Church, composed of many conservative Whigs and leaders of the New York City government, opened its doors to blacks. Within a few years Anglicans held an average of forty black marriages a year in Trinity, including many between slaves and the free. Trinity Church members were prominent in the New York Manumission Society, founded in 1785 to combat the institution of slavery and, most immediately, to confront slavecatchers who attempted to re-enslave the free blacks living in the city. In 1787 Trinity reopened its African Free School after a hiatus of four years.[67]

The 4,000 blacks who sailed to Nova Scotia in 1783 faced an uncertain future. Colonel Stephen Bleuke led his regiment of Pioneers and Guides to a remote area where they founded Birchtown, named after the commanding general in New York City who had given them their passport to freedom. Bleuke thrived in his new environment and over the years became a school teacher, politician, and wealthy landowner. Others such as Thomas Peters found the British to be deceptive and soon sought to leave. By 1790 Peters negotiated with John Clarkson of the English Manumission Society for over one thousand refugee blacks to leave for Sierra Leone where Peters, along with becoming a landowner, ran into his own father after a thirty-year absence. Still other blacks went to London where they became impoverished; eventually a few declared their intention to return to America.[68]

The overall effect of the American Revolution upon Afro-Americans has yet to be written. In the nineteenth century many black scholars and citizens concentrated on the achievements of Patriots such as Crispus Attucks in an effort to insure that black contributions to the War for Independence were not completely disregarded by white scholars and citizens. At the same time, an underground perception of the revolution emerged. David Walker in his profoundly revolutionary *Appeal,* written in 1829, sought to rouse his fellow blacks into open rebellion against their slavemasters. As part of that effort he reminded his black readers that during the American Revolution the British were "our real friends and benefactors."[69]

6

Gabriel's Republican Rebellion

Several years ago, a panel of distinguished scholars convened at Monticello to discuss the turbulent topic of Thomas Jefferson and race. Comments ranged from defensive explanations of the racial attitudes of our third president to the irreconcilable question of his relationship with Sally Hemmings. Never during the two-hour exchange did any expert question if Jefferson's slaves, or any other Virginia blacks, ever *comprehended* his egalitarian ideology. This singular oversight continues in a recent, highly critical collection of essays, aptly entitled *Jeffersonian Legacies*.[1] Similarly, though Jefferson's influence on the formation of working-class radicalism is now well understood, no scholar has heretofore systematically connected artisan republicanism with the aspirations of free or enslaved blacks in the early republic.

Using the lessons of artisan republicanism to explain African American history is but one of the many virtues in Douglas Egerton's incisive analysis of Gabriel's Rebellion of 1800,* and its aftermath two years later. Since Herbert Aptheker first pointed attention to the political tenor of Gabriel's calls for slave revolt, few studies of slave conspiracies have failed to mention Gabriel's partisan appeals.[2] Egerton is the first to apply theoretically consistent microhistory to this conspiracy. In his sinewy narrative, Gabriel emerges as an assertive, literate artisan, fully aware of other insurrections around the Atlantic basin. The slave blacksmith shared with white artisans a small producer ideology and trusted that white mechanics would support his struggle for

---

*Douglas R. Egerton. *Gabriel's Rebellion: The Virginia Slave Conspiracies of 1800 and 1802.* Chapel Hill: University of North Carolina Press, 1993.

liberty. That Gabriel failed to understand racial barriers to revolutionary unity does not undermine the significance of his attempt.

Egerton's book is precisely organized. Historical articulation of rebellion demands an engaging narrative style, so Egerton eschews problem-solving on the surface of his story, preferring to debate other interpretations in his introduction and extensive notes. The introduction also serves to correct historical misperceptions of Gabriel's name, hair-style, and, importantly, religious motivations. The body of the book begins with a contextual account of the immediate effect of the American Revolution and its aftermath on servile systems in Virginia, followed by a vivid re-creation of the conspiracy. Part 2 reports the multiple trials of Gabriel and his fellow conspirators; these trial scenarios, informed by deep reading of the voluminous trial records in the Virginia State Library, constitute one of Egerton's strongest heuristic achievements. Egerton completes his study with an account of Sancho's conspiracy of 1802 and Virginia authorities' ensuing crackdown on postrevolutionary black freedoms. Useful appendixes discuss Gabriel's religion, his French confederates, and a careful tabulation of executed slaves.

Gabriel's artisan republicanism arose from the ashes of black insurrections during the American Revolution in Virginia. Recently charted by Sylvia Frey,[3] black responses to Lord Dunmore's famous proclamation revealed deepening African American demands for liberty. Although slavery survived postwar abolitionism, its existence was insecure. Economic change mixed with postwar egalitarianism, flavored by evangelical religion, prompted slave masters to award emancipation to over ten thousand black Virginians after 1782. When a fearful Virginia legislature quickly tabled St. George Tucker's 1796 plan for gradual abolition, and moved to curtail the numbers of free blacks, literate black artisans like Gabriel prepared to revolt.

Born of slave parents at the Prosser plantation in Henrico County, Virginia, a few miles outside of Richmond, Gabriel experienced life in ways easily comprehensible to a white artisan. Literate and skilled, Gabriel was frequently hired out by his master, Thomas Prosser, a process which gradually made Gabriel think like a free wage laborer. While Prosser gained the bulk of the profits, cash in Gabriel's pockets brought him self-assertion, nominal independence, and a propensity to work for artisans sympathetic to abolitionism. His status allowed Gabriel greater freedom to consort in urban taverns, where he met other discontented blacks and whites more angry about class inequalities than split by racial animosities. Egerton's fine evocation of Gabriel's political education within Richmond's tavern culture demonstrates how barrooms offered heady draughts of conspiracy and intrigue in addition to liquor and common gambols. Like a white artisan defiant of social betters demanding deference, Gabriel ran afoul of the law during a pig-stealing incident. Discovered taking the pig by a former overseer, Gabriel bit off part of the man's ear. Convicted and facing a death penalty, Gabriel's literacy warranted "benefit of the clergy." Clemency was limited and Gabriel was jailed, then branded. Thomas Prosser was forced to post a one thousand dollar bond for a year to assure the nervous overseer against any future violence by the giant slave. In Egerton's estimation, the branding, imprisonment, and stigma tilted Gabriel toward a rebellious mentality.

Eugene Genovese and Barry Gaspar have noted that slaves seized opportunities to rebel when the white power structure seemed in disarray.[4] In turn-of-the-century Virginia, newspapers abetted by a local grapevine shared by slaves and artisans reported angry words in Congress over the XYZ Affair, Alien and Sedition Acts, and the conflict over the French Revolution. Most intoxicating for Gabriel was the successful black insurrection in San Domingue which he learned about from a radical Frenchman named Charles Quersey, and refugee blacks. Egerton argues that whether Gabriel correctly understood that Quersey's extreme radicalism did not represent North American republicanism is not significant. These reports, combined with his own punishment, helped Gabriel attain a "psychological autonomy that empowered him to break free from what he had borne for so long" (p. 48).

Now free of servile inhibitions, Gabriel initiated plans for a November surprise to coincide with the elections. Egerton compares Gabriel's hopes to achieve freedom through insurrection with those of urban mobs in the North, who would rise up, not "in protest over a single practice" (p. 49), but to enforce a political presence. Gabriel planned to gather one thousand urban slaves to take Richmond. He designed a banner inscribed "death or Liberty," reversing Patrick Henry's famous plea and reminding other bondsmen of Dunmore's Ethiopian Regiment. However, Egerton argues that Gabriel failed critically to attract evangelical whites, blacks who combined New Light with African faiths, and women. Gabriel turned instead to artisans, haranguing them at Saturday frolics. As Gabriel recruited a chain of skilled slaves in towns and plantations, the conspiracy grew in numbers and spun out of control. Inevitably, the plot attracted a traitor, Pharaoh, a slave with materialist ties to his master and willing to trade his soul for temporal freedom. Warned, determined whites quickly rounded up the rebels. Word of discovery sent blacks fleeing across the countryside, soaked by a thunderstorm. Rumors that slaves planned to rape white women exacerbated white anger. Although there was no evidence to support these racist fantasies, sexual paranoia gave whites further impetus to deal harshly with the conspiracy.

Egerton handles the ensuing show trials very effectively. Since Thomas J. Davis's remarkable reconstruction of the slave conspiracy in New York City of 1741, historians have treated slave testimony with greater respect. Once dismissed as desperate pleading, bondsmen's evidence in conspiracy proceedings is now accepted as serious narrative.[5] Egerton's research is especially deep in his accounts of each conspirator's defense, trial, and inexorably, execution. His narrative of the failed dreams of these black martyrs contains marked respect for their courage and faith. Quotes demonstrate slave faith in the pursuit of liberty. One insurgent testified that "I have nothing more to offer than what General Washington would have ... had he been taken by the British and put to trial." The slave continued: "I have adventured my life in endeavoring to obtain the liberty of my countrymen, and am a willing sacrifice in their cause" (p. 102).

Gabriel was still at large. Harbored by a sympathetic sea captain, Gabriel was turned in by a slave eager for the reward. In court, other slaves testified against him; Gabriel's stony response to conviction was a request to hang alongside other condemned conspirators. As in New York City sixty years before, the leader's courage and resolution in the face of death insured the spiritual success of the rebellion. As trials rushed past and the grisly toll mounted, Virginia lawmakers nervously noted the costs of executions. Required to compensate slave masters for twenty-seven executed bondsmen and pay the militia, Governor James Monroe faced financial fees of over thirteen thousand dollars. Gabriel's execution had satiated an angry public; future convictions would result only in transportation.

Little time passed before Gabriel's example inspired a second insurrection. Sancho, a ferryman, designed an insurrection in Halifax, Virginia in 1802. Again, work experience offered the conspirators common ground. Undeterred by the massive blood-letting two years before, Sancho and his men planned a holiday uprising of anarchic killing, followed by negotiations with a wounded white populace. Sancho placed much of his faith in other watermen; unfortunately for his hopes, as the conspiracy spread, he lost control, and a slave informant stepped forth. Monroe's government swept the plotters into jail, and pondered their fate.

This time, Monroe and President Thomas Jefferson had little appetite for a massive round of executions. Transporting the arrested seemed plausible, but Jefferson preferred a new destination. Jefferson observed how the British liberals convinced Black Loyalists to migrate to Sierra Leone, ridding England and Nova Scotia of the republican-minded blacks, and enabling Britain to establish a colonial beachhead on West Africa. Colonization, in the air in America, was favored by such eminent blacks as Paul Cuffe and Peter Williams, Jr. Unhappily, the Virginians learned that English governors, already beset by unceasing demands from black Nova Scotians and, lately, from rebellious Jamaican maroons, had no stomach for seventeen rebels from America. The Spanish West Indies also closed their doors, fearful of the spread of black revolt in the Caribbean. The sole option was to sell the imprisoned slaves to a dealer, at a discount.

Egerton's concluding chapter focuses on the passage of new laws by the fearful Virginia legislature. Intent on crushing black autonomy, abetted by the disappearance of white guilt over slavery, new codes outlawed black liberties. Virginia's woes affected national policies. Thomas Jefferson and James Monroe used the local turmoil to renew hostility toward the black government in San Domingue. Virginia's new police statutes curtailing black movements were, according to Egerton, especially brutal. Egerton's analysis of the legal ramifications of the two revolts rings true on one level. Virginia lawmakers aimed restrictions on slave nighttime activities and curtailed work permits to free blacks.

Were Virginia's blacks cowed by these new rounds of repressive new legislation? It is doubtful that slave frolics ended for very long and use of blacks as watermen was an entrenched tradition. Moreover, had Egerton pushed his chronology a bit further we might have learned if the memory of Gabriel inspired the hundreds of slaves who fled Virginia with the British for Nova Scotia during the War of 1812. Unlike their black republican predecessors who left New York City in 1783, this group has attracted little notice save for some dismissive comments by Robin Winks in his history of blacks in Canada.[6] As nearly 2,400 of the refugees came from Virginia and Maryland, it is not too great a plunge to argue that Gabriel was a living memory to many.

Is this the definitive account of Gabriel's rebellion? Egerton's search into the trial records and his synthetic re-creation of postrevolutionary Virginia are both exhaustive. Egerton's disavowal of Gabriel's evangelical roots will bother scholars who find revolutionary roots in religion. Still, Egerton's powerful synthesis of artisan republicanism with black revolutionary activity in Jefferson's Virginia sustains a badly needed union between the political hopes of white and black laborers during the age of revolution. In so doing, Egerton offers a solution for a disturbing cul de sac within early American labor historiography. Rather than passively point at the racism of artisans and founding fathers, Egerton has reconstructed a world in which the deferred dreams of white and black workers merged, if only for a moment.

7

Reconstructing
Black Women's History in
the Caribbean

These three trim books* offer excellent introductions to the vast, emerging history of black Caribbean women and stand as challenges to North American social historians to match their efforts. Despite the recent flood of literary and sociological studies on African-American women, social, feminist and ethnic historians have neglected this fruitful subject. Those wishing to learn more about black women in early America, for example, must rely on very few books and articles.[1] The simultaneous arrival of three solid books on Caribbean women provides a major step forward for West Indian historiography and offers important lessons for North American scholars.

The three books are quite similar in intent and approach. Hilary Beckles, responding to the demands of female graduate students, attempts to expand existing conceptual and methodological approaches in order to provide a labor history of black women in Barbados. Barbara Bush's concentration is primarily on Jamaica and other Anglophone colonies after the close of the slave trade in 1807. With skill and originality she emphasizes the power of sexual dynamics in the slave system and its resulting coloring of historical perceptions of

---

*Hilary McD. Beckles. *Natural Rebels: A History of Enslaved Black Women in Barbados*. New Brunswick, NJ: Rutgers University Press, 1989.

Barbara Bush. *Slave Women in Caribbean Society, 1650–1838*. Bloomington: Indiana University Press, 1990.

Marietta Morrissey. *Slave Women in the New World: Gender Stratification in the Caribbean*. Lawrence: University Press of Kansas, 1989.

black women. Marietta Morrissey ambitiously seeks to analyze the slave woman's experience in British, Dutch, French, Spanish and Danish West Indies from a broad Marxist perspective to determine whether or not gender defined slave status. As she is making a large geographical survey, her findings speak to either Frank Tannenbaums's "terms of the religious and cultural variations of slavery or to the stages of capitalist development suggested by his critics" p. 15). Second, gender study addresses for Morrissey the issue of the economic basis of Caribbean slavery. As might be surmised, Morrissey uses a materialist strategy, acknowledging slaves' economic motives rather than an unequal structuralist explanation or study of slave culture. The latter she regards as unwarranted, exaggerated claims based on emotion and political intention. This final point sharply separates Morrissey from Beckles and Bush. Yet, because they agree that gender is the most prominent variable, the three authors assert that the slave woman's history is sufficiently divergent from the male's to require reassessment of Caribbean history.

On the surface, the three works are quite similar in approach. The authors weave chapters on domestic slavery, field work and garden plots, discussions of fertility and child-bearing, and family structure towards goals of explaining the prevalence of women's resistance to slavery in the Caribbean. Although each offers some new evidence, their principal approaches are to reinterpret existing research in order to provide new frameworks for analysis rather than to introduce major new areas of evidence. These goals provide a firm platform on which future efforts can stand. As the organization, evidence and, often, conclusions of the three books are frequently close, this review concentrates on areas of agreement and contention in key methods and points of analysis.

The first important subject is the demography of Caribbean slave women. Hilary Beckles contends that female laborers were the majority of Barbados's black population after 1715. Even though seventeenth-century African slave traders were reluctant to supply women to the Royal African Company and the majority of slaves brought to the Caribbean were male, he argues that by "the early 18th century, the ratio had settled down to about 48% male to 52% female" p. 9). This important statement, however, leans on a single, secondary source and lacks the fuller documentation he provides for later periods or for the white population, where females were also in the majority. Beckles is firmest in his demonstrations that black females outnumbered males in the cities. Bush, looking at the remainder of Anglophone West Indies, is in substantial agreement. She notes in passing the black female majority on West Indian plantations. Slaveowners gave little allowance for fertility or immunity from punishment for women before 1807, when the slave trade ended. Morrissey adds that pursuit of short-term profits in the Spanish West Indies set the tone for the treatment of black women and the devaluation of their fertility throughout the Caribbean. As slavery intensified in Cuba during the early nineteenth century, birth rates and natural increases declined. Overall, the authors skim the ramifications of this important section, which seems crucial to their arguments and which has significant application to North American cities and gender analysis.

Black women, like men, were brought to the Caribbean to work. Field labor was the most universal experience for black women. The three authors agree that black women were not spared the heaviest forms of labor, especially at crop time, and were not spared cruel punishments. Monocultural crops produced the most intensive labor. Morrissey's argument that black women, working in a three-tiered gang system on plantations, gradually suffered a decrease in conditions, providing more and more of the unskilled labor, is the most fully developed. Morrissey's finding that, over time, labor intensification created harsher labor and longer workdays mirrors evidence Lois Carr and Lorena Walsh have found in the Chesapeake.[2]

The second important occupation for black women was domestic labor. Beckles' finding that women comprised the majority of the white population in Barbados accentuates the significance of such work. About one-quarter of slaves in Barbados were employed in the domestic service. As he notes, domestics received the highest material rewards, social status and human rights. At the same time domestics had little additional value and but faint hopes for manumission. Nannies were expected to be pro-slavery and educate their children to support the institution. Beckles emphasizes the immense variety of human experience for domestics and argues that sexual liaisons with white masters were among the most reliable forms of mobility. Using the Elizabeth Fenwick diary, Beckles illuminates the psychological warfare between mistress and slave. Poisoning was a common form of retaliation for frequent use of the lash. Bush does not separate the domestic experience from her general history though she is in substantial agreement with much of Beckles' conclusions about the relationship of mistresses and slaves. Morrissey conflates domestic labor with other types of work and, like Bush and Beckles, acknowledges that female slaves sought close contact with slave masters for hopes of freedom. Observing that women were generally barred from artisanal occupations, she argues that domestic labor was perhaps the best vehicle toward female manumission. None of the authors, however, discusses the possibilities for emancipation from female mistresses, an area of some controversy in North America.[3]

Bush and Morrissey tie domestic labor with provision grounds, an important area of female autonomy. Formally, women had Saturday afternoon and Sunday to cultivate their own crops on "po-links," or provision grounds. Bush describes how women expended amazing energy growing food for their own consumption or sale at the markets. Using African-based methods, black women regarded food production and sales from these plots as virtual rights. Morrissey illuminates the difference between kitchen gardens—collectively cultivated, estate-supervised provision grounds—and individualized provision plots. Morrissey, however, concludes that males still held principal control of lands and the means of production, diminishing female power. She does confirm that women held sway over marketing.

Surprisingly, neither Bush nor Morrissey gives much room to female hucksters. Beckles, who covers provision grounds in passing, allots an entire chapter to marketing. Despite constant attempts to curb female hucksters, their activities became institutionalized by the eighteenth century. Here, as Beckles notes, poor whites and black slaves intermingled and practiced legitimate and illicit commerce. Beckles distinguishes various types of female hucksters in Barbados from plantation women who sold garden foods "on their own account" p. 79) or on their masters'. Beckles' conclusion that huckster markets were "the cornerstone of survival strategies for most households" p. 87), only partly covers the story. Markets were major operations for resistance, whether petty or major, as reference to Daniel Horsmanden's account of the 1741 slave conspiracy in New York will indicate.[4]

The three books offer extended comment on women and the family. Bush emphasizes the matrifocal family as the fundamental social unit and urges historians to use flexibility in defining the various forms families took in the Caribbean.[5] She cautions historians who would regard the matrifocal family as pathological and contends that the family was the crucible for resistance. Morrissey regards this assertion as too sweeping, commenting that "a more critical perspective is that slave women's affection and love for their families was functional to slavery" p. 98). At the same time she acknowledges that slave enterprises and activities closely tied to kinship were disruptive to slavery and, second, that families could be the locus of conspiracy. Her preference is that families "sometimes formed and in specific ways contributed to tensions and contradictions in slavery" (p. 98). Beckles' contribution to this debate is an historical overview of the slave family in Barbados. He delineates three family patterns. From 1627 to 1720 African-born slaves were in the majority and polygamous structures and strong tribal consciousness were dominant. The second stage from 1720 to 1780 saw a rapid creolization of the population, a pro-reproduction planter policy and continued polygamy. Only in the third stage, from 1780 to 1834, as planters supported family integration did the nuclear marriage become common and motherhood recognized in custom and law. Implicitly, Beckles, by emphasizing African survivals in Barbadian slave families, agrees with Bush. A corollary to this argument is Beckles' tough analysis of the relationship of black motherhood and the rise of free coloured elites. Free coloured elites defended slavery and white supremacy with the same passion as did whites during the 1816 slave revolt.

Inextricably linked to the history of the family is the study of childbearing and nurturings. One of the most significant comments on the dark history of slavery in the Caribbean is the decline in female fertility, a focus of innumerable historical studies in recent times.[6] It is generally recognized that despite female majorities and planter amelioration policies after the close of the slave trade in 1807, worsening physical conditions in field work caused high mortality rates and declines in fertility. Beckles and Bush, concentrating on the British Caribbean, study the effect of planter pro-natal, amelioration policies aimed at maintaining a supply of labor after 1807. Beckles comments on the paradox of pro-natalist attitudes against an ever-growing need to purchase more slave women amidst continued high mortality rates. Even though pro-natalism meant ameliorative policies such as childbearing assistance, task reduction and recognition of slave marriage, population growth was halting. Morrissey, looking at the entire region, cites Barbados as the exception in the region and blames low fertility rates on venereal disease, poor diet, lack of slave-owner interest and long-term illness. Although Morrissey acknowledges that African women in the New World used abortifacients and infanticide, she disagrees with Bush over the effectiveness of such methods. Morrissey finds that women had an economic incentive to have as many children as possible, regardless of levels of infant mortality. In line with her argument about female fertility, Bush sees little incentive for black women to have children, despite the significant importance of childbearing in African culture. In this light Bush comes close to the provocative arguments Albert Hurtado has made about California Native American women. Hurtado, citing the psychological impact of interracial rape, a crime all too frequent in the Caribbean, concludes that Indian women prevented pregnancy with emotional as well as physical contraceptives. Bush's discussion bolsters her argument about the nature of female resistance.[7]

The debate over fertility leads to one of the sharpest areas of disagreement in the three books. Slave polygamy, seldom mentioned in North American works, takes on special importance in the three studies. Beckles finds polygamy customary in Barbados, despite harsh criticism from Anglican clerics. Planter amelioration policies after 1807 even condoned the practice. Bush emphasizes African models of polygamy, with husbands and wives often coming from the same ethnic group. Morrissey disagrees strongly with this position, arguing that population density discouraged African polygamy, with its emphasis on bride wealth. Caribbean men rarely, she concludes, had the means to afford multiple wives.

Related to the subject of polygamy is prostitution. Beckles ably describes the secular culture centered around taverns, bars, and whorehouses in the port city of Bridgetown. Prostitutes could earn money to purchase manumission or gain male allies. A fascinating practice was that of white mistresses leasing out their female slaves as prostitutes for sailors. Beckles argues that prostitution, while harmful, was also a means to power and prosperity. In contrast, Bush, who devotes an entire chapter to European stereotypes of African-American sexual immorality, distances herself from this perception, clearly regarding much of interracial sex as exploitation. She acknowledges that black concubinage was "inextricably woven into the social fabric" p. 111) but emphasizes the physical power white males held over black females. Morrissey, though she lists prostitution as one of four areas of female livelihood, barely discusses the occupation.

Each of these patterns in the mosaic of female life in some way touched upon the spirit of resistance. Morrissey, after a review of white physical oppression of black females, offers but three pages to protest. She cites the political presence of the Jamaican obeah women Nanny as the only female Maroon leader and concludes that such rebellions were primarily male. Beckles, whose book title announces his perception, gives a skillful typology of Barbadian revolt. Slaves, he argues, could resist through violent revolt, Marronage, nonviolent protest and Constitutional Civil Rights Action. He contends that the "heterogeneity of slave action was probably the most outstanding characteristic of anti-slavery resistance" p. 157). While armed rebellions were the rarest, women did kill, burn and plunder. Women could resist through labor withdrawal, flight and in collective bargaining over conditions. He offers evocative evidence of petitions presented by slave women to their masters to improve their work lives and to obtain freedom. Bush also accentuates day-to-day resistance and contends that women were very difficult to manage. She cites punishment books to show frequent use of the whip on women and cites the notorious insolence of female servants. In contrast to Beckles and Morrissey, Bush argues that African women held considerable political power, which translated into important positions within slave revolts. In addition, rather than viewing Marronage as exclusively a male activity, she cites female gardening as an essential factor sustaining the Maroon communities.

Morrissey's conclusion that "slave women, along with children and other slaves, were generally more vulnerable to hegemonic institutions than bondmen" p. 166) conflicts with the other two studies. Bush's description of black female life as a "unity of misery" p. 163) evokes well the sense of self-worth and the spirit and struggle of freedom found in the Caribbean. Beckles, too, articulates a vision of survival in which resistance was a central part of everyday behavior and pervaded every known sphere of existence—work, sexual relations, leisure activity and family life. All three books modestly call for further research. Whatever direction scholars of the Caribbean will take, they will benefit from these efforts. Scholars of North American slavery and gender and race relations should read and weigh these presentations carefully. How one accepts the findings of these authors depends ultimately on where one stands on the issue of culture and class.

8

Flaneurs, Prostitutes, and Historians

Sexual Commerce and Representation in the Nineteenth-Century Metropolis

In Edgar Allan Poe's short story, "The Man of the Crowd," the narrator pursues a jaded demon on a relentless nocturnal tour of London. On the second night, he finally confronts his quarry, only to realize that he did "not permit [him]self to be read."[1] Squalid urban night life, the subject of Poe's investigation, has inspired generations of novelists and poets, but has confounded historians. Even in the last decade, inquiries into the denizens of the night have focused on the policing and reform of sunless practices. The three books under review are major advances toward understanding two key activities after dark, prostitution and sexual murders, within the context of evolving class and gender formation in New York and London.[2]

Investigation of prostitution and sexual violence presents significant problems for historical analysis. Evanescent by nature, the work of prostitutes and sexual criminals appears largely in police records, sensational novels, tabloids, and moralistic tracts, all burdened by built-in biases and confused by multivocal evidence.[3] Historical perceptions change frequently. Were prostitutes fallen women, victims of poverty and predatory males, or were they, as Charles Baudelaire suggested in his 1863 essay, *La Peintre de la vie Moderne,* "women in revolt?" Such relationships complicate understanding of the men who purchased their time or attacked them violently. As Baudelaire compiled his taxonomy of prostitutes, courtesans, and actresses, he styled himself as a *flaneur,* or man-of-the-crowd, who mixed incognito through Parisian streets, sketching the manners of the immoral poor.[4] Baudelaire's characterization of the flaneur is now a staple vehicle for historians peering into the darkest corners of the nineteenth-century city. Similarly, Judith Walkowitz points out that each generation revises the image of Jack the Ripper.

Given the dearth of locally focused studies of urban American prostitutes, it is noteworthy that two major books have appeared targeting love for sale in Victorian New York City.* In the third work,** Judith Walkowitz, author of a pioneering study of prostitutes, turns her gaze on Jack the Ripper's savage murders of prostitutes, which are among the most sensational, yet misunderstood, crimes in Anglo-American urban history. To avoid repetition, I review first Gilfoyle and Hill's common grounds, interspersing analysis of significant differences. Because Gilfoyle's study spans a longer period than Hill's, his work provides a bridge to our analysis of Walkowitz's study, planted in the late nineteenth century.

The studies by Timothy Gilfoyle and Marilyn Wood Hill on New York City's nineteenth-century prostitutes appear similar at first, but have significant differences in approach and conclusions. In brief, Timothy Gilfoyle examines prostitution as an economic process. At the onset of the century, Gilfoyle argues, prostitution was geographically marginalized and socially isolated. After 1820, sexuality was increasingly organized around and by market forces, located at the core of city social life. After 1900, prostitution declined and sexuality became more exclusive, monogamous, and restricted (p. 313). Marilyn Hill concentrates largely on the prostitute's gendered history during the middle of the nineteenth century. While she shares much of Gilfoyle's interest in the geography of prostitution in New York, her real aim targets the lives of prostitutes.

Gilfoyle's brief overview of prostitution in colonial and early national New York uncovers little evidence of harlotry in the postrevo-

---

*Timothy J. Gilfoyle. *City of Eros: New York City, Prostitution, and the Commercialization of Sex, 1790–1920.* New York: Norton, 1992.

Marilyn Wood Hill, *Their Sisters' Keepers: Prostitution in New York City, 1830–1870.* Berkeley: University of California Press, 1993.

**Judith R. Walkowitz. *City of Dreadful Delight: Narratives of Sexual Danger in Late-Victorian London.* Chicago: University of Chicago Press, 1992.

lutionary era. Still, his succinct appraisal introduces his methodology, which identifies prostitution by neighborhood and patronage. Gilfoyle maps pockets of prostitution sprouting within the newly developed Trinity Church Farm neighborhood along the Hudson River and on George Street near City Hall Park, and further north on East George Street close to the East River wharves. Gilfoyle argues that prostitution was confined during this period to a few disorderly blocks, particularly to the dock areas, and was generally restricted to transients and local poor. This observer is unconvinced of the paucity of prostitution before 1800. For example, the Five Points, the site of notorious interracial taverns and brothels in the nineteenth century, was but the latest in a series of such black and tan areas dating back as far as the 1670s. Similarly, it would be highly unusual if New York's dock areas, like those of West Indian ports, did not employ prostitutes much earlier than Gilfoyle suggests.[5]

Gilfoyle and Hill concentrate the bulk of their studies between 1830 and 1870. These decades saw the blossoming of sex districts and public, bawdy revels in the Five Points, slightly northeast of City Hall, on the West Side near the Astor Hotel, along Water and Cherry Street, and in the Corlears Hook slums up the East River. The Five Points was especially notorious for its interracial dives, where Charles Dickens and a generation of flaneurs, accompanied by policemen, observed the creation of modern popular music in gritty brothels and taverns.

Gilfoyle and Hill differ over why the "whorearchy" developed. Gilfoyle argues that Manhattan's rapid demographic and real estate expansion after 1820 spurred prostitution's entry into public life. Using real estate records, Gilfoyle establishes that prominent families eager to reap profits from whorehouses owned much of the Sixth Ward slum district. This point helps Gilfoyle build a pyramid of interest from the cheapest, most competitive brothels along Corlears Hook, to houses of prostitution near expensive hotels, ascending to the profit-taking landlords at the peak. His economic architecture of prostitution agrees with Elizabeth Blackmar's investigations of slum ownership in the booming real estate market of antebellum New York.[6] In contrast, Hill relegates such gentry proprietorship to a footnote (p. 292, n. 21), emphasizing instead the internal management of prostitution.

How widespread was prostitution in Victorian New York? Hill and

Gilfoyle use two yardsticks. First, they analyze estimates of nine-teenth-century reformers that broadly claimed the participation of 10,000 to 50,000 women; the latter figure engulfed over seventy per-cent of New York's young female population. In fact, Gilfoyle and Hill both contend the number was much lower. Generally, they find that five percent of urban women between fifteen and thirty years old en-gaged at least in occasional prostitution; hard times propelled the total to ten percent. Hill lists a high mark of just under ten thousand prosti-tutes in 1870. The two scholars agree that depressed economic condi-tions and broken families pushed women into brothels and street-walking. Low wages among milliners, servants, chambermaids, and laundresses enhanced prostitution's allure. Using House of Refuge admission transcripts, Gilfoyle and Hill concur that the death of a father often predicated a girl's career in prostitution. Although fallen women were generally young adults, children were also vulnerable, partly because of the myth that intercourse with a virgin cured venereal diseases. While contemporary observers claimed that immigration fos-tered prostitution, Gilfoyle and Hill find that most prostitutes came from the northeastern states.

Prostitutes seemed by definition beyond the protection of the law. Suffering from venereal diseases, unwanted pregnancies, alcoholism, and drug abuse, they were also vulnerable to the rampages of young, working-class males. As Paul Gilje has shown, houses of ill-fame were targets of mobs well back into the eighteenth century. Gangs with political connections occasionally sacked brothels, especially in the 1830s.[7] At the same time, using police and court records, Hill and Gilfoyle show how prostitutes sought and obtained protection against boisterous clients and unruly mobs while trading evidence of criminal activities to the authorities. During the halcyon days of the 1850s, prosecution of brothels virtually vanished. Prostitutes also used the courtrooms and media to humiliate their foes. In one sensational in-stance, Hill describes how prostitute Kate Hastings publicly mortified novelist E.Z.C. Judson (Ned Buntline), using a tart tongue and beauty to advance her case.

Gilfoyle and Hill offer evidence that pushes the boundaries of sexu-ality. They uncover instances of lesbian relationships among prosti-tutes and cite sex shows featuring "unnatural love." Their evidence of homosexuality was not exclusively female, as the example of Peter

Sewally, a black transvestite employed in brothels, indicates. Although these instances are fragments of Hill and Gilfoyle's larger arguments, they offer tantalizing evidence of public homosexual behavior well before the twentieth century, when historians believe public gay practices commenced.[8]

Differences again arise as Gilfoyle and Hill turn their attention to the prostitutes' workplaces. We have already noted their geographies of urban sexual commerce. The authors do concur that the workplaces for prostitutes included the third tiers of theaters; public houses with large, residential populations; and smaller parlors or private houses for exclusive forms of commercial sex. Beyond that, their emphases diverge. Gilfoyle points to the first large-scale sex district around the Bowery by 1850. Gilfoyle sees the importance of brothels as symbols of commercialized sex, as profitable subleasing of apartments, to whores who integrated prostitution into the city's tax and property structures. The rise of a sporting literature and "gay guides" helped knowledgeable New Yorkers identify brothels. By mid-nineteenth century, commercial sex's economy and the subculture of prostitutes and "shoulder-hitters," or sporting men, fixated American perceptions of New York City. Accurately pointing out that antebellum New York housed a classless male culture composed of sailors, clerks, Bowery B'hoys, and dandies in search of rough amusements, Gilfoyle establishes that prostitution was the sexual norm for these young males. This male subculture challenged bourgeois conventions about sex. Gilfoyle's analysis, based on earlier findings by Gilje and Richard Stott, offers an important connection between middle-class morality and laboring-class customs.[9]

In contrast, Hill contends that by midcentury, houses of prostitution appeared in virtually every neighborhood. New Yorkers were very flexible and tolerant about prostitution. While Hill acknowledges the economic importance of brothels, she accentuates how prostitutes and moral citizens lived and worked amicably. In a major point, Hill maintains that for a brief time, prostitutes were able to work in an atmosphere far superior to that of thousands of working-class sisters, and considered themselves moving up or down the social ladder according to their profits, comforts, and sense of security. The person who held the key to this self-conscious pursuit was the madam, who used charm, wit, and business skills to own and manage brothels. Using census and real estate records, Hill and Gilfoyle establish that by 1850, New York City boasted a well-developed network of female brothel proprietors. Hill's evidence about madams' ownership of brothels supports her assertion that prostitution was a viable alternative to pain-wracked factory and domestic work.

Hill also differs from Gilfoyle in her coverage of prostitutes' relations with men. Acknowledging rough treatment by mob bullies, Hill points to sympathetic relations between men and women. Brothels functioned as men's clubs; while males held financial strings, prostitutes knew more about sex and wielded exposure as a club over unruly patrons. Hill's significant research into the prostitute Helen Jewitt's correspondence with her customers reveals relationships bordering on love and respect. Customers became lovers after a liaison of several months; some became legitimate husbands. Even then, prostitutes drifted in and out of the life, at times even supported by their husbands.

Hill expands the empathetic world of prostitutes by examining their relations with other women. Although prostitutes were unable to form relationships with "respectable women," among themselves, as Hill substantiates through Helen Jewitt's letters, affection developed within the sisterhood. Further, using House of Refuge papers, Hill finds that friendships were crucial in the profession. Prostitutes toured the town together and gathered in theaters. Other relations mirrored mainstream family life. Parents assisted the careers of young prostitutes; their children lived in brothels, Cousins and sisters remained the best friends of prostitutes. Such relationships undercut, in Hill's view, the presumption that prostitution damaged families.

Hill concludes her work by observing that prostitutes existed in a variety of possibilities and responses. While beset by problems and difficulties, they also found opportunities advancing their occupation and their status as women. While her evidence supports such conclusions, Hill cautions against romanticizing the prostitute. Rather, she urges that for a brief moment in time around midcentury, prostitution and its historical conditions offered a "significant degree of autonomy and control in their professional lives" (p. 324). These gains were fleeting, as pimps and geographic segregation emerged in the late nineteenth century. While Hill's conclusions are prudent, her evidence greatly enlarges our understanding of the inner society of urban prostitution.

Hill closes her work around 1870; Gilfoyle charts the ensuing experience of prostitutes. He revisits the sex districts and finds that despite the efforts of moral reformers, the city's march uptown carried prostitution along. The new center for commercial sex was the Tenderloin, the entertainment district that sported houses of prostitution on every Broadway block between 23rd and 42nd Streets. On Seventh Avenue, known as African Broadway, black and tan bars were, in Gilfoyle's eyes, the sole violators of New York's racial moral economy.

Gilfoyle's survey of commercial sex in the 1880s bolsters Hill's earlier conclusions about the widespread phenomena of prostitution in the city. By 1880, Gilfoyle finds that prostitution flourished around Union Square, on Bleecker Street near Washington Square, in the Lower East Side tenements, below Canal Street, and above 59th Street and in the outer boroughs. This public dispersal of sexuality fostered a new, erotically charged form of prostitution, the French Ball. In this masquerade, spouses of all kinds hit the bordellos for merrymaking. These balls were not exclusively heterosexual, as gays also attended.[10]

French Balls represented, in Gilfoyle's portrayal, universal sexual license, made possible by police tolerance and de facto regulation of prostitution. Whorehouses operated close to precinct houses, as police considered prostitution fatalistically or as a source of profit. Tammany's attitude toward brothels depended on location. Underground syndicates emulated official corruption. In the Lower East Side, the Independent Benevolent Association organized prostitution and contacted syndicates in Europe, South America, South Africa, and in other American cities. Prostitution remained a profitable investment. Gilfoyle presents evidence from real estate records that once again the wealthiest families profited from ownership of bordellos. Gilfoyle pieces together such evidence to make an important conclusion: The absence of legal prostitution and formal structures of regulation led to entrepreneurial methods by the close of the nineteenth century.

The twentieth century found prostitution in transition. In real life, competition intensified, conditions worsened, and careers were shortened. Intellectual perceptions of prostitutes changed. The image of prostitutes transformed from "fallen woman" into the "white slave." Social scientists influenced by Sigmund Freud and Havelock Ellis challenged older moral condemnation of prostitutes by insisting on the primacy of environment. Such views encouraged ambitious politicians to focus campaigns against prostitution. Charles Parkhurst's crusade pushed prostitution underground. Other factors ending the century of prostitution included the replacement of residential buildings in the Tenderloin with skyscrapers and high-rise apartments. The Immigration Acts of the 1920s and the Prohibition Era made prostitution more furtive. Although a few madams continued to manage prosperous brothels, fewer young women entered the field. Better wages and working conditions gave women new avenues of employment. Similarly, the sporting male declined as male heterosexual behavior underwent significant changes, as an increase in premarital sex and earlier years of marriage weakened prostitution's attractiveness. After 1910, Gilfoyle concludes, the steady decline of prostitution and the ensuing romance of marriage demonstrate the "resacralization" of sexuality (p. 313).

Gilfoyle's careful portrayal of the transition of sexuality from the external world of prostitution to privatization in the family is sensible within his argument, but seems overstated in the 1990s, when, even after the AIDS epidemic, sexual commerce in New York City remains wide open. His conclusion, however, provides a connection to Judith Walkowitz's analysis of how sexuality in late-Victorian London became the core of a private identity. Walkowitz uses two accounts that scrutinize Jack the Ripper to frame five chapters assaying middle-class conceptual reordering of sexuality in the metropolis.

After the introduction on the exploits of Jack the Ripper, Walkowitz's first chapter is a cogent analysis of the transition of the flaneur from urban spectator to intellectual mediator of sexuality. Early in the century, Pierce Egan's Tom and Jerry epitomized the night walkers who wandered city streets for fun. Gradually, urban investigators such as Frederick Engels, Charles Dickens, and Henry Mayhew wrote travel accounts that were a mixture of fact and fancy, a melange of moralisms and religious sentiments couched with anthropology. In such a world the prostitute was the quintessential public symbol of vice. By the 1880s, Dickens, Mayhew, Gustave Dore, and later, Charles Booth imaginatively remapped London as an immense world-city, with a modern landscape in the West End overshadowed by representations of urban pathology and decline in the East.

Walkowitz's characterization of these early sociologists as flaneurs has drawn comment elsewhere.[11] My difficulty lies partly in Walkowitz's portrayal of female reformers who braved public harassment to claim their places in the city streets at this time, a public crusade vividly described in Chapter 2. As remarkable as their explorations were, they were resisted and taunted by working-class women (pp. 70–71), who wondered why these "glorified spinsters" (Walkowitz's term) were missing their opportunities at finding a man. Walkowitz makes an essentialist argument about the relative beneficence of female charity workers, whose class antagonism with their working-class sisters was evident, by elevating them above such "flaneurs" as Booth and George Sims. While I admire greatly Walkowitz's examination of the flaneur, she is somewhat unkind in her portrayal. Here, it is useful to use the example of Baudelaire, who invented the term. Recall that Baudelaire committed his love and life to his black mistress, the actress and prostitute, Jeanne Duval.[12] When rendering her portraits of male and female social investigators, it is far better, I think, for Walkowitz to be honest about class mutuality.

Walkowitz moves from the street to the copy room in Chapters 3 and 4 with her reenactment of W.T. Stead's "Maiden Tribute," which appeared in the Pall Mall Gazette in 1885. Walkowitz offers a captivating account of Stead's portrait of white slaves in London. Attempting to rouse the nation by constructing sexual danger as a political issue, Stead employed a melodramatic device bordering on pornography. Along the way, Stead tried to verify his findings by purchasing a young virgin female. Intending to compel vigorous enforcement of prostitution, Stead found himself charged and convicted of procurement. Walkowitz expertly guides the amazed reader through the thickets of this case. While Stead failed to create prostitution's Uncle Tom's Cabin, he did initiate an era of media scandals around sexual violence.

Walkowitz next shifts from steamy journalism to sexuality in middle-class drawing rooms. Ensuing chapters present fascinating case studies of contemporary sexual relations. In the first instance, Karl Pearson, socialist and future eugenicist, founded the Men and Women's Club to provide bourgeois radicals, liberals, socialists, and feminists with a forum to discuss sexual relations. Walkowitz examines the voluminous archives of the organization's brief existence to portray a gendered battleground where club rules privileged a patriarchal Darwinism over "female subjectivist experience" (p. 147). Women were objects of study rather than equal partners while the group spent an entire year on the study of the relation of the state to the sexual question. The club divided by gender over such issues as regulation of prostitution, coercive marital sex, and female emancipation.

An important subtext was a secret love affair between Pearson and a feminist leader of the club, author Maria Sharpe. When the club disbanded, Pearson immediately proposed marriage to Sharpe, who accepted, withdrew, then married him in 1890. Dominated intellectually by Pearson, Sharpe had three eugenically fit children and withdrew from sexual politics.

Evidence of similar repression for middle-class feminists appears in the cause célèbre of Georgiana Weldon, whose husband conspired to commit her to an asylum for spiritualist practices to revenge a messy and costly separation. Walkowitz's eye for fascinating detail is especially sharp in this chapter. Her handling of Weldon's voluminous career and narrow escape from incarceration makes for a very good story. Covered widely in the press, Weldon's case included her imprisonment for libel, a successful suit against her husband, his conversion to her side, and, finally, her emergence from jail to become an advertising star. She was eclipsed only by the arrival of Jack the Ripper.

As Walkowitz demonstrates in her useful introduction, each generation's revision of the Ripper's identity blurred and altered the facts of the case. What is certain is that five prostitutes were murdered between August 31 and November 9, 1888, in Whitechapel, a London neighborhood of miserable squalor. The mysterious murders evoked in the press demands for law and order and further repression of street prostitutes. From police, newspaper, and middle-class anxieties, Walkowitz argues that the Ripper case "established a common vocabulary and iconography for forms of male violence which permeated society, obscuring material divisions that provoked sexual antagonisms in different classes" (p. 220). The Ripper murders were never solved, but came to symbolize the sexual vulnerability of women of all classes across the next century.

The epilogue is an explicit feminist answer to gendered representation. Between 1975 and 1981, Peter Sutcliffe murdered thirteen women around Leeds and Bradford. After his seizure, feminists marched in protest and convened meetings about rape and pornography. As the Ripper case in 1888 initiated twentieth-century fantasies of female vulnerability, so the Sutcliffe murders of the late 1970s propelled contemporary feminists to initiate a political offensive against sexual crime.

Walkowitz's method will disconcert readers lulled by the straightforward narratives of Gilfoyle and Hill. Influenced by Foucault's dissection of sexual power, Walkowitz eschews chronology, preferring a multilayered discourse with poststructuralism to demonstrate that sexuality was a contested site for struggles of class, gender, and race. My first pass at the book left me somewhat disordered by Walkowitz's design; subsequent readings left me dazzled at her intellectual accomplishments. Gilfoyle and Hill's heuristic achievements are deeply informative; Walkowitz deconstructs the characters and forces who shaped the patterns made visible in the other books.

9

The Decline and Fall of Artisan Republicanism in Antebellum New York City

Views from the Street and Workshop

These two excellent works[*] are further explorations into the social history of early New York City. Although offering different perspectives, both are heavily influenced by the new cultural labor history. Paul Gilje's *Road to Mobocracy* is the most comprehensive history available of mob actions, one of the commonest areas of evidence in studies of revolutionary and Jacksonian urban political culture. Richard Stott's intention is to expand our knowledge of the urban working classes by a close analysis of the experiences of immigrant workers. While Stott's primary construction is economic, he includes solid sections on working-class culture. Both works are especially strong in organization, research, and argument.

Gilje's work begins in 1763, much earlier than Stott's. *The Road to Mobocracy* is divided into three discreet sections, partitioned by the election of 1800 and the 1834 riots. The first section, covering the colonial through constitutional periods, discusses mob action within the context of community and commonwealth traditions. The second section covers the declension of community with careful study of eth-

---

*Paul A. Gilje. *The Road to Mobocracy: Popular Disorder in New York City, 1763–1834.* Chapel Hill: University of North Carolina Press, 1987.

Richard B. Stott. *Workers in the Metropolis: Class, Ethnicity, and Youth in Antebellum New York City.* Ithaca, NY: Cornell University Press, 1990.

nic and racial political disturbances. The third part expands these developments and argues that the final cleavage of New York City's revolutionary consensus can be found in middle-class rejection of riots and lower-class retention of communal violence. An afterword discusses the Draft Riots of 1863 in terms of final political rupture between poor and elite.

Each section has decided merits. In the revolutionary period, mobs acted as an external political force. Guided by George Rude, E.P. Thompson, and Gordon Wood, Gilje effectively argues that mobs acted within a political framework that tolerated mob behavior as a safety valve. At the same time, mobs alerted politicians to the spreading boundaries of revolutionary discourse. One significant example was the transformation of the popular ritual of Guy Fawkes Day into triumphant and politically symbolic reenactments of the Stamp Act Riots.[1]

A common pitfall among recent historians has been to idealize mobs as nonviolent demonstrators restricting their anger toward the homes and carriages of prominent British sympathizers. Violence was limited to "tar and feathering." While he provides a very useful enumeration of every known example of such crowd behavior, Gilje avoids an overly rosy picture by careful study of the 1741 slave conspiracy and its bloody aftermath and by original research into the anti-Semitic riots later that decade. A second effect of these interpretations is to signal that not all New Yorkers were considered part of the community.

Gilje's political analysis of mob behavior fits well into prevailing perceptions of the role of the common man in the revolutionary period. His work is part of the overall historical thrust to include fully the common man into the discourse on the revolutionary crisis. The rediscovery of the role of mechanics in the revolution and definition of artisan republicanism have been major theoretical goals of historians combining urban and labor histories in the past twenty years. Gilje adds greatly to the discussion, however, by astute reading of the complexity of the community. While the community he cites as the underpinning of mob action, however, is predominantly artisan, that is to say, middling-class white males, his research and analysis uncovers republican traditions among other groups, most notably, blacks.

Gilje makes a second major historiographic contribution toward the close of the first section. Elsewhere, Edward Countryman has argued that the late 1780s saw inclusion of artisan radicals into the political processes wrought by statehood and the national constitution.[2] This inclusion meant, Countryman argues, that older forms of artisan protest, most notably, mob actions, fell into disuse. In contrast, Gilje offers, through his analysis of the Doctor's Riot of 1788, the protests against William A. Duer's defalcation in 1792, the Jay Treaty Riots, and the Keteltas Affair of 1797, very strong evidence that artisans and other workers took to the streets whenever they felt political grievances. Rather than becoming obsolete, as Countryman has argued, laboring-class perceptions of proper political behavior in the postrevolutionary period favored mob actions.

Gilje uses his careful analysis of these riots as a linchpin into discussion of the early decades of the nineteenth century. His findings are most cogent in the chapters on Irish Catholic and African-American rioting. These chapters are among the highlights of the book because of their thorough, enlightening research and absorbing conclusions.

Gilje is perhaps the first scholar to research thoroughly the early records of New York City's District Attorney Indictment Records at the Municipal Archives. He is also the first historian to analyze a fascinating, lengthy document describing every arrest in New York County between 1784 and 1820. As a result, he gives the most detailed and comprehensive analysis of Irish rioting and of African-American resistance against slave catchers.

Gilje sympathetically discusses Irish resistance against ethnic discrimination in the crafts and in politics. Irish traditions of resistance conflicted with deep-seated anti-papism among New York's working classes. Holidays such as Saint Patrick's Day, Christmas, and the anniversary of the Battle of Boyne became the occasion of pitched battles between the Catholic Irish immigrants and native-born, usually Protestant, New York laborers. As Gilje charts the action, nearly every year, street fights broke out between the warring sides over major religious issues or in brawls sparked by hostile words at taverns. Ethnic riots, Gilje concludes, impressed the local government that riots were a "threat to the workings of both the political apparatus and the marketplace" (p. 135). Indeed, Gilje's research shows that unlike the colonial rioters, who might include promising political activists and middle-class tradesmen, with the important exception of the 1834 election riot, new street brawlers were most likely to come from the bottom of society. Ethnicity mixed with class tensions produced continual rioting.

Racial animosities also sparked the tinder of riots. Gilje first focuses on black defense of community and liberty. For example, he shows how black Haitian émigrés to New York City angrily protested the plans of a white Haitian woman to sell her slaves out of state. In a furious street fight on August 10, 1801, about twenty "French negroes" tried to stop this sale and threatened to "burn the house, murder all the white people in it and take away a number of the black slaves." Similar street protests against slave sales or the return of fugitive slaves occurred in 1819, 1826, and 1832. Gilje's portrayal of these violent black acts of resistance against slave catchers and government authority in New York City offers important evidence against the prevalent historical visions of black passivity during this period.

In contrast to the prevailing paradigm that accents white racism imposing narrow limits on a virtually passive black community, Gilje's research shows powerful currents of resistance by black mobs intent on securing freedom for their brethren. Gilje's contribution could have been even stronger had he connected these mob actions with the legacy of the American Revolution. He limits his analysis to an appropriate description of these mob actions as "testament to the emergent sense of community shared by blacks—a sense of community that contrasted and conflicted with white society and the ideal of order and propriety espoused by the self-proclaimed leaders of New York's larger community" (p. 153). Here Gilje does make clear the fracture of revolutionary consensus over issues of race. Unlike other observers of artisan republicanism who virtually ignore this uncomfortable subject, Gilje provides a full, balanced portrayal of black riots, riots against African-American institutions, and the fearsome 1834 riot.

The "larger community" sponsored violent attacks against the black community. Using original evidence supporting more familiar views of racial relations, Gilje describes riots in the early 1800s against black churches, theaters, and entrepreneurs. Each discussion is heavily detailed and employs a combination of established secondary readings and previously unused legal and newspaper sources.

This important chapter on race culminates appropriately with the 1834 street riot. In early July 1834, mobs of white laborers aided by an occasional elite citizen, ransacked black churches, schools, and homes in the city. Several historians have argued that the conflagration demonstrated white fears over amalgamation or labor competition from recently freed slaves. Overshadowing both issues, Gilje comments, was a desire by lower-class whites to destroy the emergent black community. The intensity of attacks on black institutions shows a new "pattern of nineteenth century popular disturbances" (p. 167).

This is a powerful concept. Rather than discuss the July 1834 riots in terms of the white community, Gilje analyzes the violence as representative of a community warring against itself. Thus Gilje fuses African-American and labor history as no other urban historian has done. Historical analysis of artisan republicanism has been one of the most fertile areas of urban and labor historiography in the past twenty years. Discussion of racial conflict has been one of the weakest aspects of this methodology. One only wishes that Gilje had followed this important point with discussion of the black radical David Ruggles's Committee of Resistance organized in response to the 1834 riots. The committee continued street-level opposition to slave catchers in the antebellum period.

After covering ethnic and racial unrest, Gilje next uncovers fertile examples of class unrest. Historical analysis of mobs during the transition to industrial capitalism has been a staple of labor histories in recent years. However, Gilje initially concentrates on the labor actions of seamen and dockworkers. Unable to rely on a monopoly of skill and thus kept from striking, such semiskilled laborers relied heavily upon eighteenth-century traditions of collective action to enforce their wishes. Gilje emphasizes the transition of the behavior of these workers from "deferential patterns of crowd behavior to collective bargaining by riot" (p. 178) as a major manifestation in patterns of popular disorder. Gilje analyzes with precision eleven important laborers' riots between 1811 and 1828 to prove his assertions. His contentions that by the 1820s, "the chasm between the merchants, businessmen, and magistrates on one side and the seamen, dockworkers, and laborers on the other had widened" (p. 187) give fruitful parallel insights to the standard arguments about declensions in the craft trades. Gilje's evidence of the declension in the crafts supports the findings of Sean Wilentz.[3] What Gilje offers in addition is nuanced comparison of the degree of violence and class hostility among semiskilled and skilled laborers. As social divisions widened, discontented journeymen began using the violent methods of stonecutters, sailors, and dockworkers. Ideological change came from below and was driven by sharper class antagonisms.

This argument is bolstered by the presence of unskilled and semiskilled in many riots. Throughout the book Gilje identifies the participants of important riots. His data show that as the nineteenth century wore on, mobs increasingly were from the bottom of society, not from "Gentlemen of Property and Standing," as Leonard Richards has claimed.[4]

Gilje's thesis that over time the elite and middling classes rejected the mob's political legitimacy gains support in his portrayal of class tensions outside the work arena. Middle-class New Yorkers desired to clean up New York City by banning hogs and stray dogs, sparking angry confrontations between magistrates and irate, poor citizens. Plebeian urbanites also showed disdain for religious hypocrisy. Gilje's discussion of the case of Amos Broad is particularly insightful. Broad, an upholsterer, was convicted in 1809 of cruelty toward his female slaves. As a result, the slaves were freed, and Broad and his wife were fined and sentenced to two months in jail. In prison, Broad discovered God and upon release opened a storefront church. His past sins, however, attracted unruly worshipers who gave "loud plaudits of huzzaing, clapping of hands and stamping of feet" (p. 215). Outside the church, mobs, led by Betty, his abused ex-slave, shouted obscenities, banged at the door, and threw mud, sticks, stones, and excrement at the door of the church. Eventually the mob invaded Broad's church and sacked it. A young black boy preached a sermon while the crowd destroyed the sanctuary and organ. While Gilje interprets this as a role reversal reminiscent of eighteenth-century riots, this reader sees the incident as a useful synthesis of the racial, ethnic, and class factors that Gilje's arduous research has uncovered.

Class, race, and ethnicity are easily comprehensible variables. Often historians use them anachronistically and discard evidence that does not fit easily into their theoretical constructions. Gilje's expansive canvas permits inclusion of mob behavior not easily subsumed into these classifications. Such is his discussion of "the disordered society" of the 1820s and 1830s. Gilje's broad analysis of community declension takes his narrative into previously untreated areas of unruly behavior. Much of this is disconnected from political interpretation. Tavern riots, youth gangs, and "Callithumpian New Year's celebrations," demonstrated the potency of street culture and spurred middle-class demands for better police.

Gilje has been criticized for tacking on a discussion of the Draft Riots to demonstrate finally the gulf between middle and lower classes. Gilje does avoid sanitizing the draft rioters and his connection of their actions with earlier disorders stems directly from the major themes of the book. The Draft Riots did show, as Gilje notes, the powerful currents of violence within the city. Recent work by Robert Fogleson supports Gilje's thesis of middle-class horror of the volcano under the city.[5]

Gilje's principal contribution beyond his exacting and detailed enumeration of all kinds of riots is his exploration of the varying strains of republican ideology among the lowest classes of New York City society. His research illuminates neglected areas of study and greatly expands the discourse on the nature of urban political culture.

Richard Stott is also concerned with the utility of artisan republicanism in the political culture of antebellum New York City. Stott, however, is less convinced of republicanism's attraction for the industrial working classes upon which he focuses. Stott's analysis departs from two important works of the new labor history: Bruce Laurie's *Working People of Philadelphia, 1800–1850,* and of immediate concern, Sean Wilentz, *Chants Democratic: New York City and the Rise of the American Working Class, 1787–1850.* Laurie and Wilentz identified the origins of working-class political behavior in an artisan republicanism descended from the lesson of the American Revolution and from the devastating impact of the declension of craft solidarity into industrial capitalism. Stott, by contrast, cites Amy Bridges's important comments that few of the American working class had artisan origins, and most were foreign born and youthful.[6] Accepting Wilentz's conclusion that the working class was made in the 1830s, Stott asserts it was remade in the late 1840s and early 1850s (p. 3). Although Stott does not directly challenge him, it must be noted that Wilentz argues that in the 1850s New York's industrial laborers were the most radical in America.[7] Stott by contrast asserts that the republican language of "virtue" and "independence" had little meaning for the German and Irish immigrants who peopled New York's factories (p. 3).

To support his points, Stott spends the first three chapters on context, tracing the city's industrial development and changing demography. In the second part of the book, Stott concentrates on the social experience of working-class life. He devotes chapters to family structure, gender, and the labor market. Another chapter offers a close look at the workplace of manual laborers; another on their diet and living standards. The last three chapters discuss the creation of working-class neighborhoods, leisure activities, and finally the "remade working class culture of the 1850s" (p. 6).

The contextual chapters are packed with information about changes in the demography of industries in New York City from 1820 to 1870. Stott finds that the large, land-extensive, heavily capitalized industries departed for New Jersey whenever possible. The most dynamic industrial growth in Manhattan came from those shops that were not transport sensitive, required little land, were seasonal, and demanded only a secondary labor force. This analysis further extends Sean Wilentz's descriptions of "bastard workshops." By 1850, Stott asserts, a bifurcated industrial system developed in the New York region with "manufacturing in the core . . . typically seasonal, labor-intensive, unmechanized and carried on in the home or small shop" (p. 24). Larger, more mechanized, less seasonal industries migrated to the belt areas outside the city.

Stott does not restrict his analysis to industrializing trades but gives succinct commentary on unskilled dockworkers and female domestics. Primarily female, domestics constituted "the largest single occupation in the city" (p. 61). Moreover, although domestics earned only seven dollars a month, the addition of room and board made the job attractive, especially to Irish women. important to Stott's thesis is his observation that Irish women did not share the dislike for service held by native-born women. A major problem with Stott's overall analysis appears in this brief section on women. He asserts, without substantial proof, that domestics were predominantly Irish. While it is true that the proportion of Irish substantially increased in the antebellum period, it was also an important source of employment for African-American women. Since the 1740s New York City's middle-classes either owned or employed female blacks as servants. As Robert Ernst noted in his seminal *Immigrant Life in New York* over forty years ago, domestic service was by far the largest area of work for blacks in the city.[8] Even though the percentage of blacks in this job declined between 1820 and 1855, that does not lessen their importance to Stott's analysis. After all, this decline was not offset by rapid black employment in another sector. Rather, it was a result of increased racism in home and employment, a factor Stott chooses not to discuss.

For new immigrants, however, New York City was a place of opportunity. Stott demonstrates how the diversity of industrialism in the city and the trend toward semiskilled labor expanded employment possibilities and even increased potentials for worker proprietorship. Nor did skilled laborers suffer as the greater number of semiskilled workers opened slots for foremen. If there was a decline in worker status as a whole in the antebellum period, individual skilled workers stayed in the industry at a higher rank.

Irish and German immigrants peopled the rise in semiskilled laborers. Offering valuable research, Stott shows that the typical immigrant was a young male, from the "middling rank of peasant" (p. 75), who came from Europe to escape low economic conditions in hopes of a better material life in the United States. These immigrants had precise goals that were formulated in family decisions back home. Their experiences were the pragmatic evidence for a family determination about migration to the United States. Stott argues that these assessments held true even during the Irish migration of the late 1840s. These characteristics, he maintains, make the immigrant experience essential to understanding the history of workers in the antebellum city. Although this conflicts directly with Wilentz's class-specific analysis, Stott does not say so. Additionally, while gender is carefully treated as a variable, race, again, is left out.

For immigrants, coming to New York was initially a good idea. Wages were high in the region. The frame of reference for Stott's analysis is the family. Flowing from his contentions in the previous chapter, his argument that work in antebellum New York was a family affair generally broadens our understanding of the urban household economy. He charts carefully the seasonal changes for each level of the family and skill. If work for men slipped, their wives stepped in. Higher wages made children more assertive and independent.

Changes in the family power structure were mirrored by the transformation at the job. Work in America was far faster than in Europe. Division of labor became standard by the Civil War. Turnover in the trades was extraordinarily high. The success of the temperance movement made drink the enemy of productive labor. It was replaced by coffee, a stimulant more conducive to the accelerated work pace. Such managerial changes were accompanied by ethnic acculturation. Although diversity brought tensions, strains lessened through humor. In this section, Stott comes to grips with the problem of race. Racial tension, he argues, did not exist in workshops, "for the simple reason that blacks were almost totally excluded from city manufacturing" (p. 145). Stott acknowledges that "city workers were notoriously racist," but drops the matter without further investigation (p. 145). It is not that he should have further argued a well-established point, but the absence of a racial variable in a city where blacks were prominent workers dating back to the 1630s weakens his thesis that the immigrant work experience was most typical.

Similarly controversial are Stott's arguments about unionization. After reviewing the evidence about organization and historical experience, Stott concludes that "unions in this period had too ephemeral an existence to have a major impact on workers' daily lives" (p. 159). He notes that few union halls had permanent headquarters and that even in good times, only a minority of the city's male workers were unionized and strikes often failed to achieve their objectives. For these and other reasons, Stott believes, by the 1850s the Anglo-American artisanal tradition was "virtually dead" (p. 158). This interpretation collides directly with Sean Wilentz's description of the city in 1850 as "the most radical city in America" because of the strength of a labor movement inspired by the lessons of the American and European revolutions. One major reason for the difference in their conclusions is that Wilentz sees the wave of strikes in 1850s as presaging decades of union organization and power, while Stott, looking directly at worker experiences, finds answers more in the relative prosperity of New York's youthful laborers compared to their European counterparts.[9]

That relative comfort was found in other material ways. In succeeding chapters, Stott shows how although crammed into boardinghouses charging high rents, New York's immigrant youth wore better clothing, ate more meat and white bred, grew taller, and lived longer than their European counterparts. Stott provides excellent data on working-class neighborhood development in antebellum New York. He visits with profit such working-class community institutions as the saloon and theater and events such as prizefights and political rallies. Stott makes distinctions in the important area of urban politics between the social demands of artisan republicanism and the new politics of the 1840s. Immigrants, Stott argues, were not attuned to the meaning and significance of American revolutionary concepts and heeded more carefully to the "personal qualities of political leaders" (p. 236) such as Mike Walsh and Captain Isaiah Rynders. Political hegemony depended not only past rituals but on contemporary ability at prizefights. Pugilists were working-class heroes. Saloons were their headquarters. How this sharply diverges from artisan republicanism with its devotion to blood sports and the tavern is not clear.

Stott next turns to working-class religion and here is on stronger ground. Most antebellum immigrants were Roman Catholic, a creed anathema to artisan republicans. However, Stott finds, even with the widespread construction of churches, religion was "not strong enough to challenge the Bowery milieu" (p. 242). Indeed, he asserts, religion was probably not that important to most youthful workers.

What was of the greatest impact was culture. Even though immigration undermined the artisanal society, the youth culture of the Bowery developed rapidly in its stead. Stott concentrates on cultural style. The ideal worker style showed vigor, generosity, a propensity to rowdiness, and loyalty to the "fair fight." "Mose," the archetype for Stott and Wilentz, was highly masculine. Stott furthers our knowledge of working-class culture with superb research on vernacular speech and songs, all described with sensitivity to gender and class. The main book ends abruptly without a conclusion or afterward. Stott does offer, however, highly useful appendixes, including a very valuable survey of working-class autobiographies.

Stott's work, like Gilje's, is thorough, painstakingly researched, and smoothly written. I have noted previously my concern about the monoracial quality of his analysis, but this fault is hardly Stott's alone. Gilje's book is perhaps unique in confronting the racial conflict that racked antebellum New York City and deeply affected labor relations. Regardless, both books renew the great promise of social history in New York City and are major steps toward understanding the urban workers on their own terms.

10

"Desirable Companions and Lovers"

Irish and African Americans in the Sixth Ward of New York City, 1830–1870

In 1850, George Foster, while guiding his readers through a midnight tour of the infamous Five Points, reflected on the frequency of intermarriage among African American males and Irish women, who, Foster believed, regarded their husbands as "desirable companions and lovers."[1] Foster's observations fall sharply apart from historical perceptions of the relationships between Irish and African Americans in antebellum New York City. Pointing to an Irish embrace of pro-slavery ideology, opposition to black suffrage, antagonism over work, and periodic Irish violence toward blacks, historians have constructed a paradigm of irreconcilable racial conflict.[2] A second, related approach emphasizes Irish acculturation through embrace of American racism. Designed to explain the role of race in working-class culture, this perspective, emphasizing the environmental and historical context of racial conflict, explains how the Irish earned "the wages of whiteness" to grasp a tenuous foothold in the American working class.[3]

In numbers and commonality of experience, the lives of Irish and African Americans epitomize the experiences of ordinary New Yorkers in the burgeoning nineteenth-century metropolis. By adding consideration of the gender and racial contexts of their relationships, it is possible to move beyond the fractured paradigm of class that pervades historical discussion of the antebellum working class in New York. Despite the extraordinary importance of the semiskilled Irish and black laborers in New York during the antebellum years, historians have little close description or succinct analysis of their work or culture.[4] One reason is that historians of the antebellum working class have studied industrial laborers primarily as prototypes of the modern, class-conscious proletarian or as pursuers of the American dream, seekers of middle-class fortunes inaccessible in Ireland.[5]

There is, it should be admitted, evidence of racial animosity over work even before the notorious Draft Riots of 1863. In one incident, in 1855, after white stevedores struck for higher wages, blacks replaced them. Fighting soon erupted between the discharged Irish and blacks. After the strike was settled, white longshoremen supplanted the blacks.[6] However many disturbing examples one may find of contention between the Irish and African Americans, there are some countervailing examples of cooperation. In 1853 black waiters agitated for higher wages and won pay of $16 a month to the white waiter's $12. A black man attending a later meeting of white waiters advised them to go for even higher wages. On March 31, 1853, the *New York Times* reported that black and Irish waiters had formed a union and gone on strike. On this occasion, the Irish and African Americans, often portrayed as irreconcilably hostile in the workplace, shared goals including wage protection and reduction of hours.[7]

There are additional problems, beyond those tantalizing fragments, to historical visions of irreconcilable racism. Scant attention is given to variations within the Irish populace itself, which, by virtue of more than 1.1 million immigrants arriving at the port of New York between 1847 and 1860, amounted to one in four New Yorkers by the onset of the Civil War. Some of the divisions among the Irish dated back to their home towns. Within the Sixth Ward, County Sligo men and women gravitated to upper Mulberry Street, Corkonians to the lower part of Mulberry, and Kerryonians to nearby Orange (later Baxter) Street.[8] Although the growth of the Irish populace dwarfed the African American population of the city, concentrations of blacks in certain wards ensured daily contact between the two groups.

This chapter is about the complexity of Irish and African American relations in the New York City's turbulent Sixth Ward between 1830 and 1870. This ward was the crucible of Irish-black relations. African Americans had lived in the area since the 1640s and later shared it with republican-minded journeymen and carters. The remnants of the Negro Burying Ground was near, sustaining a spiritual sense of place among blacks, a trait noticed by George Foster in 1850. Known for decades as the Cartman's Ward, the neighborhood boasted a powerful tradition of assertive trade solidarity. Another force was immigration. By 1810, immigrants and blacks attracted by cheap rents accounted for one-fourth of the ward's population, the highest such percentage in the city. The ward was home for 31 percent of all aliens in the city, primarily the Irish.[9]

Although conflict was present, so was a surprising degree of community, shared work experience, affection, and family building. In many ways, the relationships of Irish and African Americans resembled the spontaneous "communitas" described by Victor Turner in which daily relationships shaped their lives and added symbolic meaning to pedestrian occurrences. This relationship becomes clearer when one examines the demographics of the ward, the effects of rioting and crime on the ward, of race and gender within racially integrated occupations, and of occupation and neighborhood on laborers' culture in the Sixth Ward. In a significant departure from other scholars, I have deemphasized industrial occupations, which included very few blacks, concentrating instead on three groups: laborers and domestics; city-licensed, semi-skilled wage earners, comprised of cartmen, porters, grocers, tavern and porterhouse keepers, butchers, junk and rag dealers; and the "useless trades" of prostitutes and petty criminals.[10] These three groups of workers provide considerable insight into the daily interplay of gender, class, and race among Irish and African Americans.

Each of these occupational groups was extremely important in the Irish experience in New York City. In 1855 the two largest occupations for Irish immigrants were laborers and domestic servants, with 17,426 in the former category and 23,386 in the latter. Together, these 40,812 workers constituted 46 percent of the 88,480 Irish immigrants gainfully employed in the city. These citywide patterns were amplified in the Sixth Ward, where 53 percent of Irish workers were unskilled laborers or service workers. About 12 percent had a permanent status as a carter, porter, or hackman.[11]

Other laborers sustained a tenuous relationship within the skilled trades in New York. As craft skills declined, small shops still dominated the industrial sector in the antebellum period. Although journeymen and unskilled workers made occasional efforts to join forces, laborers generally formed their own unions.[12] Laborers' unions were the largest in the city and the Irish made up the largest portions of the memberships. In the early 1850s, the 3,000–man Laborers' Union used strikes and closed shops to protect standard wages of $1.50 per day and push for a 10–hour work day. The Laborers' Union also boasted successful benevolent societies, associations, and cooperatives.[13]

Irish women crowded into domestic work, an arena once controlled exclusively by blacks. By 1855, over 45 percent of Irish females under the age of 50 in the Sixth Ward worked as domestics: as hotel maids, waitresses, and cooks, as well as personal servants, housekeepers, nurses, and washerwomen. Older Irish women took in boarders, an ancillary occupation to domestic work. Seniority did not insulate a woman from domestic service. Almost 30 percent of Irish females over the age of 50 in the ward worked as domestics.[14]

The semiskilled trades were also open to Irish and black men and women. For example, tavernkeepers and grocers opened their doors to all. Similarly, crime had no gender or racial boundaries. The fleeting nature of prostitution and other minor crime hampers any exact count of these occupations, though census takers did visit the Tombs to list inmates.

As table 10.1 indicates, the proportion of Irish and African Americans in the population of the Sixth Ward was about equal until 1845, accounting for 44 percent in that census. After that the Irish proportion soared while the African American declined precipitously. Although the numbers in the Sixth Ward did not increase dramatically between 1830 and 1870—rising to a zenith of 25,000 in 1855, then falling back to 21,000 by 1870—the size of the Irish population jumped fivefold. The decline of African Americans in the neighborhood may be construed as evidence that the beleaguered minority fled under the oppression of hostile immigrants. Although the Irish eventually accounted for one in four residents of the ward, they still shared the neighborhood with African Americans, Germans, Italians, Chinese, and multinational sailors. Furthermore, although the number of blacks dropped precipitously after the Fugitive Slave Act of 1850, black churches and schools remained in the ward until much later and local blacks held prominent, not furtive roles in the district's picaresque street life.

A tour around the ward in 1850 reveals several distinct neighborhoods. Its southern border was City Hall, with its adjacent row of lawyers' offices on City Hall Place. To the west was Broadway, studded by commercial buildings packed with small businesses ranging from fancy and dry goods to daguerrotypists and book dealers. The

Table 10.1

Irish and African American Populations of New York City and Sixth Ward, 1830-1870

Year		New York City	Sixth Ward
1830	Total	197,112	13,570
	All Aliens	17,773	2,306
	African American	13,976	1,878
1835	Total	268,089	14,827
	All Aliens	27,669	2,026
	African American	15,061	1,797
1840	Total	312,710	17,198
	Irish		2,026
	African American	16,358	1,812
1845	Total	371,223	19,343
	Irish	96,581	7,552
	African American	12,913	1,073
1850	Total	515,547	24,698
	Irish*	133,730,	
	African American	13,815	991
1855	Total	629,547	25,562
	Irish	175,735	10,845
	African American	11,840	545
1860	Total	813,669	26,696
	Irish	203,740,	
	African American	12,574	334
1865	Total	726,386	19,754
	Irish		7,211
	African American	9,943	289
1870	Total	942,292	21,153
	Irish	201,999	11,709
	African American	13,093	203

Sources: Fifth Census, or, Enumeration of the Inhabitants of the United States, as Corrected at the Department of State in 1830 . . . Washington, D.C., 1830; *Census of the State of New York for 1835* . . . Albany, 1837; *Sixth Census, or, Enumeration of the Inhabitants of the United States, as Corrected at the Department of State in 1840* . . . Washington, D.C., 1840; *Census of the State of New York for 1845* . . . Albany, 1847; *J.D. Debow, The Seventh Census of the United States: 1850* . . . Washington, D.C., 1850; *Census of the State of New York for 1855* . . . Albany, 1857; *Joseph C.G. Kennedy, Population of the United States in 1860* . . . *The Eighth Census* . . . Washington, D.C., 1864; *Franklin B. Hough, ed.; Census of the State of New York for 1865* . . . Albany, 1867; *Francis A. Walker, ed., Ninth Census, Vol. 1 The Statistics of the Population of the United States* . . . Washington, D.C., 1872.

*Includes Great Britain and all possessions.

ward's northern perimeter was Canal Street, a composite of stables, porterhouses, pawnbrokers, and boardinghouses. This ambiance flowed into the Bowery, the eastern limits of the ward, where oysterhouses, taverns, and working-class theaters vied for attention with dentists, blacksmiths, junk dealers, and assorted small manufactories. One tabulator found more than 240 trades in a few blocks of lower Bowery.[15] On the side streets between Broadway and the Bowery were clusters of boardinghouses that varied greatly in quality and purpose, produced by a combination of soaring property values and a transient, immigrant work force. Operated by a keeper of either gender, on property usually owned by a businessman, boardinghouses were older homes chopped into single rooms, or, tenements of four and five stories crammed with sailors, laborers, cartmen, domestics, and seamstresses.[16]

A number of institutions anchored the ward. On the east was the Bowery Theater, the home of working-class melodrama. The St. Andrew's and Transfiguration churches served Irish Roman Catholics. A map of the ward in 1846 clearly shows the Abyssinian Baptist Church at 44 Anthony and St. Philip's African Episcopal Church at 85 Centre, both repaired after the 1834 riots. Public schools for whites were located at Mott near Cross and Elm near Leonard; nearby were schools for blacks at 145 Mulberry and 161 Duane. The Tombs glowered over the neighborhood on a block bordered by Franklin, Leonard, Centre and Elm Streets. By 1851 the Five Points Mission had replaced the Old Brewery with a House of Industry.[17]

What accounts for the ward's notoriety was the carnivalesque Five Points, which excited and appalled moralistic New Yorkers. The triangular Paradise Square, the center of the Five Points, was located a scant fifth of a mile from City Hall. Here Little Water, Cross, Anthony, Orange, and Mulberry Streets entered, like rivers emptying themselves into a bay. Early in the century, Mulberry and Orange Streets became centers for laboring and immigrant boardinghouses, surrounded by dozens of groceries selling liquor and by porterhouses and dancing halls.[18]

George Foster's midnight tour at the Five Points highlighted local landmarks. Standing under a gaslamp next to a policeman, Foster drew attention first to the Old Brewery, erected in 1797, and transformed into a residence in 1837, into which were crammed several hundred black and Irish men, women, and children. The Old Brewery, as Foster informed his breathless readers, housed countless prostitutes, many of

Sixth Ward and Vicinity, New York City, 1846

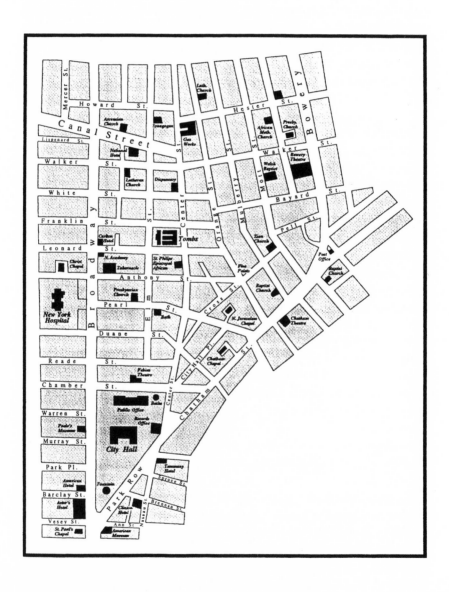

whom, Foster claimed, practiced their trade in rooms shared with their children. Crowded around the brewery, demolished soon after Foster's description, were taverns, oyster cellars, and brothels. Patrons of the bars were "mostly sailors, negroes, and the worst of loafers and vagabonds." Every saloon employed a black fiddler, "ready to tune up his villainous squeaking for sixpence a piece and a treat at the end." The oyster saloons were open all night and served a motley clientele of pickpockets, cardsharps, counterfeiters, gamblers, and thugs.

According to Foster, the brothels employed young, rural women, who, repressed by severe parents, came to the city with desperation in their hearts. Arrival proved their undoing when "either murdering their infants" upon birth, or abandoning them on a doorstep, they prepared for "any course of crime that will procure a living." Foster romanticized the reality of their origins, but was correct about the prevalence of prostitution and pornography in the ward. Middle-class tourists found all the vices ready in another hot spot. Peter Williams' dance hall, immortalized by Charles Dickens, had become a successful tourist attraction. Gleanings from contemporary observers suggest that the Five Points was an early version of the Black and Tan bars in Harlem in the 1920s, around Times Square in the 1950s, and later in the East Village. Like their descendants, the Five Pointers were ripe for casual violence, carousing, and open love-making. Many of the players in these daily human melodramas were black and Irish men and women.[19]

In a neighborhood where shared experiences surmounted racial differences and people were identified more by work than ethnicity, blacks and Irish brushed regularly against each other. By 1820, the greatest concentrations of blacks and Irish in the city lived along Cross Street between Augustus and Duane, in the heart of the Five Points.[20] Thirty years later, blacks and whites still coexisted. Moving up Orange Street, a main street of the Sixth Ward, Doggett's 1851 Street Directory points out Gilbert Palmer, an Irish liquor dealer; then Levi Marks, a Jewish used-clothing dealer; and Anaste Plete, a black barber from Trinidad. Plete's neighbor was Edward McDaniel, an Irish shoemaker, followed by Henry Mathews, a black porter from Maryland. Such random ethnicity continued throughout the principal streets of the ward.[21] Since most activities were public, it is not surprising to read in John D. Vose's tour of New York after dark of "gangs of negroes, Irish, and sailors," standing around "discussing matters . . . [in] their line of conversation." Unrelated Irish and blacks lived together. In the early nineteenth century, a black recorded living in the home of a white was invariably a servant or a slave. By midcentury, around the Five Points, necessity obliterated racial differences. George Washington, one of three black men in the city named after the first president, lived with his black wife, Adelaide, another black woman, Harriet Morris, and an Irish woman, Joanna Cosgrove. The 1860 census reveals Moses Downey, a 43–year-old black musician renting space in his home to James and Mary Gallagher, an Irish printer and his wife.[22]

Often these ties developed early in life as the agencies of social reform pressed many Irish and blacks together. Through fiction, song, melodrama, and folk tale, a secularized version of *Pilgrim's Progress* chronicled the lives of local Irish and African Americans. Sadly, unlike John Bunyan's hero, few of the residents of the Sixth Ward achieved any earthly sanction and were dubious candidates for immortal bliss. Still, missionary and charitable organizations labored to reform the Five Pointers. For troubled Irish and black children, reformation began with enforced training at the House of Refuge, New York's juvenile reform school. Irish and African American teenage boys and girls were commonly taken into the school after committing a petty crime in New York or for simply being poor and orphaned. Irish children constituted 40 percent of the inmates at the House of Refuge while 11 percent were black. After a period of education and training, Irish and black youths were bound out together. Boys were most frequently sent to work on farms or to the sea; girls invariably were sent "into service."[23] Even then, their lives seldom improved. After returning to the neighborhood, some must have felt nostalgia for the rural institutions. Health officials noted that Sixth Ward blacks and Irish lived in disease-ridden, overcrowded hovels. In a letter published in 1845, Dr. B.W. McCready described conditions for typhus patients in "a covered alley-way" on Elizabeth Street just off the Five Points. The three-story building stood in the center of a yard surrounded by pig sties and stables. Animal filth made the ground impassable, so boards covered the yard. The part decayed boards, when pushed, yielded up a "thick greenish fluid" through the crevices.[24]

As adults, African Americans and Irish in New York City suffered under the implacable hands of charity and correction. The Five Points Mission House of Industry tore down the Old Brewery in 1851 and offered shelter and hope in the form of schools and references. The numbers of needy were sufficiently great to garner a clientele, but the

Catholic Irish and the Protestant missionary women were fundamentally opposed. With the loss of temporal salvation, Irish and black New Yorkers suffered from earthly purgatories. In New York City in the 1850s, the Irish accounted for 60 percent of the almshouse population, 70 percent of the recipients of charity, and more than half of those arrested for drunkenness. The "Bloody Ould Sixth" represented the deadly effects of poverty on Irish and African American New Yorkers. By 1855 the Sixth Ward had the highest death rate in the city. Pulmonary diseases including tuberculosis, pleurisy, pneumonia, and hemorrhage of the lungs were the leading causes of death among the young. Intemperance devastated the Irish and black populations equally. Laudanum and opium were favored drugs for suicide for black and Irish women. Children died from neglect, convulsions, and suffocation. Such abysmal statistics reveal shared hardship.[25]

To contemporaries, the Sixth Ward, and the Five Points in particular, epitomized crime. By modern standards, individual attacks on persons were rare. There were only 13 convictions for murder in the entire city between 1838 and 1851, a figure matched in the next three years. Many New Yorkers blamed the increase on conditions in the Five Points.[26] This perception of a violent Sixth Ward was enhanced by the rise of Irish gangs, immortalized by historians in their chronicles of the Forty Thieves, the Kerryonians, the Chichesters, Roach Guards, Plug Uglies, Shirt Tails, and Dead Rabbits. The stalwarts of the gangs were the clientele for the bars and brothels around the Five Points, bringing them into everyday contact with black men and women.

Fist-fights often elevated into riots. Historians cite Irish participation in street battles as overwhelming proof of their hatred of the city's African Americans. In the 1830s, rioting changed from an acceptable mode of political discourse to an unruly, dangerous expression of class, ethnic, and racial antagonism. The government's inability to control rioters deepened the widespread despair about the city's future and heightened the calls for a professional police force.[27]

The July 1834 riots were the largest single action against African Americans before the Civil War years. Rioters, angered by reports of interracial marriage and assertions of racial equality, rampaged through the Sixth Ward for three days and demolished the venerable St. Philip's African Episcopal Church on Centre Street. The riots went beyond past harassment of black churches with frightening intensity and marked an attempt to drive the established black community out of the city. The *Commercial Advertiser,* blaming abolitionists for the riots, reported that "whenever a colored person appeared, it was a signal of combat, fight, and riot." The rioters included professional and commercial men, skilled laborers and tradesmen, and a scattering of semiskilled and unskilled workers. Sixteen percent of those arrested came from the Sixth Ward, while others came from wards with equal concentrations of African Americans. Significantly, most rioters came from established New York families, and only a few of those detained were Irish. On the third day, rioters targeted both the Irish and the abolitionists. As the mob charged down the streets of the ward, it attacked in random sequence black homes and churches and Irish bars. Although African Americans were the chief victims, the Irish were not exempt from the rage of the mob.[28]

This animosity became plain a year later when the Irish battled "Americans" for five days around the Sixth Ward. Stemming from a dispute between an Irish man and a native-born apple vendor, a riot quickly roiled the streets of the Five Points. Newspapers reported an ethnic texture to the fighting. During an initial night of fisticuffs between "citizens and foreigners," bystanders exhorted the brawlers by shouting, "Well-done Americans," or "Irishmen." The danger in these melees can be seen in one report of policemen arresting Irishman Edward Lynch for wielding a "wooden pallisade" studded with nails. Newspapers circulated rumors that Irish gangs were organizing an Irish guerrilla militia. The ethnic nature of the conflict continued in the next few days as squads of native-born rioters ransacked the homes of Irish Five Pointers, destroyed brothels frequented by Irishmen, and wrecked a Bowery tavern, the Green Dragon, also attacked in the riots a year before. Two people were killed, an English piano forte maker and a doctor. Virtually all of those arrested were Irish residents of the Sixth Ward.[29]

In the aftermath, the *New York Sun* blamed its fellow newspapers for the riot, contending the city was suffering from irresponsible journalism practiced the year before by the *Courier and Enquirer,* the *Times,* and the *Commercial Advertiser.* Maintaining that civic authorities neglected to condemn mob violence, allowing the "spirit" of riot to remain respectable, the paper pronounced the city would now "reap the whirlwind." What is significant here is that a popular newspaper equated treatment of the Irish in 1835 with the attack on African Americans the previous year. Reflecting this mutual insecurity, radical

Democrat Gilbert Vale editorialized in 1840 that rioters in the Sixth Ward attacked blacks "for no other reason except the incitation of a brutal editor of a party newspaper." Vale added that in 1835 a mob attacked the Irish "because they were Irish."[30]

Although the ward was the scene of innumerable riots in subsequent years, strikingly little violence occurred between Irish and blacks. Even though interracial lovers, black churches, and abolitionists remained in the ward amidst an escalating Irish population, its residents did not participate in future riots against blacks. In 1849 the *Irish-American* congratulated the Sixth Ward for not brawling during the elections. In the worst incident of rioting before the Draft Riots, at least seven Irish laborers were among the 22 people killed in the bloody fighting at Astor Place in May 1849. In the greatest battle between the gangs, the Dead Rabbit Riots of 1857, there was not mention of abuse of African Americans or their institutions. And while the rest of the city was aflame, during the infamous Draft Riots of 1863, the ward was quiet.[31]

As the Irish battled against perceived grievances, African Americans displayed open hostility against slavery. In 1837 blacks formed a committee of vigilance that confronted slave catchers in the streets. Tugs of war over fugitives often broke into violence. Policeman William H. Bell recorded one such confrontation in early 1851. Angered by the city marshal's determination to return a fugitive slave to his master in Virginia, a crowd of blacks and whites surrounded a "Southern Gentleman" in City Hall Park in the lower part of the ward. Before the police could get to him, the angry mob beat the Southerner in retaliation for the forced return of the fugitive. Such black assertiveness did not provoke violence among Irish residents.[32]

Perhaps the Irish were content with their enormous political superiority. Organized political behavior clearly favored the Irish, who participated in the emerging working-class politics of the 1840s in two ways. They shared with blacks the opprobrium of nativist politics and evangelical crusading. On occasion, Irish newspapers even showed glimmers of sympathy for the slave. Early in the century, the Federalist *Political Bulletin and Miscellaneous Repository,* aimed at an Irish audience, published a number of abolitionist articles. Gilbert Vale, the radical equal rights editor of the *Diamond* in the early 1840s, promoted opposition to slavery, though he argued that wage slavery was much worse. The *Irish-American* disavowed any support for slavery and

commended Irish reformer priest Father Theobald Mathew for his abolitionist efforts, but condemned black activist Frederick Douglass as a
"sworn enemy of republican institutions" and offered support to the
American Colonization Society.[33]

In truth, the Irish had nothing to fear politically from African
Americans. Emancipation from slavery in 1827 in the state of New
York brought a long-awaited, but very limited, civil freedom to blacks.
The end of slavery did not offer economic, political, or social equality
to blacks. Their declining numbers and the unshakable racism of the
political parties doomed the valiant efforts of black clergy and activists
to regain the vote for blacks. New York remained intransigent toward
black citizenship. Voting restrictions limited the ballot to blacks worth
more than $250 under the constitution of 1821. There were six quali-
fied black voters in a population of 1,073 in the Sixth Ward in
1845. Full black male suffrage did not arrive in New York until the
passage of the Reconstruction Amendments in the middle 1860s.[34]

Unlike African Americans, however, the Irish reaped many gains
from political allegiance. Two major legislative drives propelled Irish
citizenship and with it, access to government patronage and work in
the licensed trades. Nativism spurred the initial reform that emanated
from a dispute between native-born carters and butchers and the mayor
over licenses awarded to "aliens" during the War of 1812. This frac-
tious quarrel culminated in legislation in 1826 restricting permits to
citizens. Although this legislation applied primarily to cartmen, it soon
extended to all licensed workers. Unintentionally, the legislation
greatly increased the value of citizenship to Irish aliens.[35]

Believing erroneously that their monopolies were spared, the nativ-
ist-licensed trades faced more opposition in 1829 from the
Workingmen's Movement, which attacked their privileges as authori-
tarian relics of English rule. The Workingmen's Petition sought abolition of all licenses, a position supported by the Irish and blacks. After
the initial hubbub, the issue lay dormant for several years. In 1836 the
Loco-Foco movement, a radical spur of the Democratic Party, made
equal access to licenses its chief political goal. As the Democratic
Party gradually accepted Loco-Foco reforms, it massively enfranchised
the Irish, qualifying them for licenses. Swapping licenses for votes
enabled the Democratic Party to sweep the Sixth War for decades. This
neat exchange further encouraged municipal reformers to loosen regulations in the 1840s, creating structures mixing mercantile and capital-

ist allotments of patronage. Politically, this meant that the Democratic Party could advertise itself as the "true home of the working classes" while favoring the Irish. The Democrats adapted the rhetoric of the American Revolution to fit the rise of symbolic leaders like Mike Walsh, and, most importantly, the spread of patronage throughout the burgeoning public sector. In addition, the Democratic Party rewarded Irish support with appointments to the ranks of police, fire, sanitation, and minor city officials.[36] The explosion in patronage intensified the political weaknesses of blacks. The Democrats refused blacks access to patronage and Whigs rarely mounted sincere efforts for their African American constituents. In short, Irish adoption of what has been called the "wages of whiteness" came not from any innate prejudice, but rather from cooperation with the existing political system.[37]

To gain a toehold in society, Sixth Ward Irishmen poured into carting, Thomas Mooney, in his famous guide for arriving Irish immigrants, described the conditions of carting to aspiring immigrants as the "road to success . . . common to all." The task always earned "advanced wages," provided good connections for future mobility, and was a good "business connection." Carting, noted Mooney, cost little to set up; a horse, cart, and harness cost about $150. Upkeep was minimal. Empty lots served as stables; horses could be fed for $1.50 per week, the carter for $2.50; "cab-tax, horse-shoes, and wear and tear" amounted to half a dollar for a total of $5 per week, an outlay costing little compared with the benefits of the trade.[38]

Mooney misled his compatriots somewhat. When licensed carters gained the right to "horse-hire" their carts, by employing day laborers as drivers in 1844, they expanded their holdings into fleets. Such growth required more stableroom. Virtually all the owners of cart fleets listed in the superintendent's roster of licensed drivers in the 1850s lived in the northern wards of the city. Few of the nearly six hundred Irish cartmen living in the Sixth Ward owned their carts. These transformations instituted a class division among carters. Ownership of a fleet, or even a good wagon placed one carter above another.[39]

This division resolved the issue of race within the trade. There had been periodic African American attempts to integrate the trade before 1840, but mayors cited custom and law as excuses to decline licenses to blacks. By 1850 black carters are listed in the census, although they could not obtain licenses until the mayoralty of Fernando Wood. The few black carters working in the 1850s were harbingers of future changes. By 1900, more than 1,400 blacks drove public carts in the city. The class divisions and racial integration of carting meant that Irish and black carters as wage laborers had more in common than the monopolistic master carters. In addition, both Irish and blacks worked as porters, the simplest form of transport worker. In both trades, black and Irish laborers shared work experiences and philosophies.[40]

Loosened government control allowed Irish and blacks access to other licensed trades. The minor trades of pawnbrokers, intelligence officers (job referral services), and rag and junk dealers lining the blocks of the Bowery and Orange and Centre Streets were of mixed ethnicity. Equal rights logic demanded licenses for all, and the city awarded individual franchises to a host of Irish and black petty entrepreneurs. By 1854 there were 32 licensed junk shop dealers on Orange Street alone. Although displaying gratuitous anti-Semitism, George Foster slurred these entrepreneurs as "jews of course," the diary of William Bell, a policeman patrolling the Sixth Ward in 1850, lists many unlicensed Irish and black peddlers. Dealing in clothing, furniture, junk, and jobs, these brokers reflected the surface of an underground economy. Bell's diary is filled with citations to Irish and black residents of Orange Street for selling goods without licenses or for fencing stolen property.[41] A number of smaller trades were interracial. For example, hairdressers, whom Mooney advised arriving Irishmen were "generally black, or copper coloured men," was an interracial occupation by 1860; of 29 listed barbers in the Sixth Ward, 12 were Irish, 9 were African American, and 8 were from France, Italy, or Germany. Irish and black men shared the labors of public waiters and scavengers.[42]

All of these trades were fairly low in status. In contrast, a more lucrative trade remained segregated. Butchers were another licensed occupation losing their exclusive monopolies. Once famous for their solidarity, the butchers found their earning power and potential now tied to ownership of a stall or, in the new setup, stores. Stall owners remained ensconced at older markets downtown. Stores became the venue for ethnic butchers, especially German ones, who operated beyond the scope of the butcher's downtown monopoly. Many of the younger butchers living in the downtown wards were journeymen without shops or stalls. These changes were not as apparent as in other trades. Possessed of political strength, stronger trade unity, a bank, and a boisterous culture, butchers resisted industrialism until after the Civil

Table 10.2

Sixth Ward Groceries and Porterhouses

	1846		1851		1860	
	Grocer-ies	Porter-houses	Grocer-ies	Porter-houses	Grocer-ies	Porter-houses
North (Anthony)	11	15	17	25	7	9
Centre	10	15	2	12	8	37
Cross	7	9	16	13		
Elm	7	4	24	13	10	11
Leonard	4	2	9	12	8	2
Mulberry	42	7	28	25	33	37
Mott	29	19	26	12	46	25
Orange (Baxter)	33	6	40	28	24	31
Bowery					18	50
Walker					24	
Other	43	6	46	19	19	44

Sources: Doggett's New-York Directory for 1846 & 1847 . . . (New York, 1846).

War. While class differences were a distant threat, meat cutting remained a preserve for New Yorkers of European descent. As the Irish shared opportunities with Anglo-Americans, Dutch, and Germans, the door was closed to women and to blacks. There were no women of any race or black men listed among 1,208 butchers in the 1860 directory. Although they seldom worked with blacks, butchers were steady customers at Five Points and Bowery dives.[43]

Perhaps the most public mixing occurred at porterhouses and groceries, which the Sixth Ward housed in abundance. Table 10.2 indicates the number of grocers and porterhouses by street. In 1850 the ward had a population of 24,000, 204 groceries, and 169 licensed porterhouses, which meant that 1 out of every 60 residents of the ward was selling liquor to the rest. Although every street in the ward had a few groceries and porterhouses, the majority were bunched along Mulberry, Mott, and Orange (Baxter). The nature of the two businesses meant that generally all races and genders were acceptable customers. In one example, Michael Crown, a grocer working at the corner of Anthony and Little Water Street in the heart of the Five Points, was about to close at two o'clock in the morning when someone asked for admission to his shop. In his subsequent testimony, Crown noted that he "knew the person calling to be one Alexander Davis, who was in the practice of coming about the store." After drinking some whiskey at the grocery, Davis and a second black man, Samuel Daily, attempted to rob Crown. Crown called for help and a mob of whites chased the pair down the street. Was this an example of racial violence? Perhaps, but the testimony also attested to easy familiarity between the grocer and his black customers.[44]

Grocers catered to the laboring class of the ward, selling items in infinitesimal quantities and remaining open 18 hours a day. Credit was necessary to secure return customers. Grocers gained their greatest profits not from food but from the sale of alcohol, legal after 1841. Despite attempts to curb liquor sales in 1836 and 1856, which temporarily reduced the numbers of groceries and alehouses, their numbers steadily increased. The huge increase in porterhouses and grocers did not mean a broader base of wealth because the hundreds of ale and food vendors in the Sixth Ward were usually employees of a distant landlord.[45]

The previous examples have emphasized public interaction among African Americans and Irish. Inside New York's homes, gender and racial equality were common. In the Sixth Ward, Irish women dominated the boardinghouse trade, with 10 entries in the 1860 directory to 7 for Irish males, and scattered German, Italian, and English keepers. Black boardinghouses were known by word of mouth rather than print. George Thompson maintained a house sheltering seven sailors and three dressmakers. Next door Andrew Coleman, a black carter, rented part of his house to an Irish cigar maker and his wife.[46]

Similar shared experiences took place among domestics working in the middle-class houses of the city. Although a few males worked in the field, domestic service seemed the most promising opportunity for Irish and black women. During the colonial and early national period, African Americans were the largest body of domestics. Attitudes toward servants became intertwined with racial hatred, which later influenced ethnophobic attitudes toward the Irish.[47] Domestic service expanded exponentially between 1830 and 1870. Two factors fueled this transformation. First, growing racism after the final extinction of slavery in New York State in 1827 and the ensuing social disintegration of the African American community pushed the black population out of the city. Second, as slavery ended, newly freed black women asserted their independence by constant shuttling between domestic employments. Third, as married women of New York's growing middle class discarded postrevolutionary antipathies against household work and sought relief from the unending chores, vast if ill-paid opportunities opened. As early as 1826 the Society for the Encouragement of Faithful Domestic Servants noted the growing significance of Irish women in the occupation. By 1855 Irish women accounted for 92 percent of the domestic work force.[48]

Domestic work had few rewards. The work was unceasing and drab. Domestics hauled water and firewood, disposed of human and other waste, washed, cleaned floors, and minded children in an atmosphere of hostility and exploitation, at the beck and call of their mistresses. Nonetheless, young Irish women arriving in New York preferred the $4 to $7 per month plus room and board they received for domestic work to the harsh, unhealthy, and insecure conditions of factory labor. Like laborers, domestics moved readily from job to job. The exploitative nature of the work negated any feelings of loyalty, and female domestics quickly learned to bargain for their value. Mooney asserted that domestics who quickly learned American modes of housewifery and who displayed loyalty and hard work could expect up to $7 a month plus board in a comfortable home, "where she will be treated nearly as an equal by the Lady of House." Despite his cheery words, Irish women were less sanguine and displayed what Mooney called their Irish spirit by frequently changing masters and mistresses.[49] At the bottom of domestic work, blacks and Irish women worked together as washerwomen. The 1860 directory lists eight Irish and eight black washerwomen living in the Sixth Ward.[50]

Boredom, poor conditions and wages, and shrill mistresses produced a rapid turnover. Yet the occupation remained attractive because black and Irish domestics shared equally poor chances for marriage and family life. The demand for domestics in the colonial period and after the American Revolution caused a gender imbalance in the city's black population. With many black men employed as sailors, the numbers of black families with female-headed households far exceeded those of whites. Among blacks between the ages of 15 and 40 in 1860, females outnumbered males in New York County by 4,267 to 2,672. Females accounted for 56 percent of the black population. Similarly, 58 percent of the city's Irish were female in 1855. Irish and black female domestics shared a second demographic trait. Few had children. In 1860, there were ten percentage points fewer black women

Table 10.3

Female Census of Tombs, 1860

Occupation	Irish	Black	Other*
Prostitute	183	14	60
Servant	93	2	52
Seamstress	38	0	29
Housekeeper	156	8	54
Day Worker	125	19	40
Washerwoman	47	14	16
Millner	5	0	1
Whitewasher	8	7	0
Pauper	8	11	3

Source: 1860 Manuscript Census, 6th Ward, 4th District, pp. 149–168.
*Includes Native-born Americans, Germans, French, and Italians.

with children than white females. Domestic work also lowered the Irish birth rate. As poverty, drinking, fighting, and desertion undermined marital relations, matrimony became devalued, and Irish female-headed families became common.[51]

The decline of family life produced an advantage for a few women. Delayed marital patterns, access to education, and cultural influences trickling down from the mistress enabled black and Irish domestics to move up in society. As modern forms of education and medicine blossomed, single or late-marrying women found opportunity and class mobility in school teaching and nursing.[52] Irish women and a few blacks gained employment as typists in emerging businesses. Sadly, such successes were rare. For those who did not marry, illness and old age presented problems of support. Lacking children to look after them, cut off from their communities and support networks, the single Irish and black women who inhabited the prisons, asylums, and the poorhouse were invariably spent domestics.[53]

A look at the census taken in the Tombs in 1860 dispels any illusions about the conditions for women in the Sixth Ward (Table 10.3). As might be expected, Irish prostitutes were the greatest perpetrators of minor crimes of intoxication, public lewdness, petty larceny, and, sadly, pauperism. Reflecting the troubles of their status, however, there are significant numbers of servants, housekeepers (domestics), day laborers, and washerwomen whose crimes commonly included petty larceny and intoxication.

Weary of their poverty and the exploitative routine of factory piece-work or the relentless harassment of domestic service, and with the gender imbalance for black and Irish women, many of these women either flirted with prostitution or embraced it. Love for sale could be an avenue of mobility for women. To the despair of moralists, prostitutes frequently earned more than their factory and domestic sisters. Despite their lives of desperation, prostitutes had career paths to follow and successes were folk heroes. Although prominent families actually owned many brothels, the most common individual female property owners in the ward were madams. The center of love markets was the Five Points. Here, historian Timothy Gilfoyle has charted at least 17 domiciles for sex at the crossroads of Anthony, Leonard, Orange, and Center in each of the four decades from 1820 to 1859.[54]

Five Pointers articulated their tough, raucous lives through a special night speech known as "flash talk," used to describe fast food places, drinking holes, dance halls, gambling halls, pawnshops, lodging houses, prostitutes, scams, and sports. "Going the rounds" or "on a bender" meant a drinking spree. Professional thieves were known as "crossmen," while burglars were called "crackmen," who worked together "on the dub . . . to crack a can" or break into a house. Streets had slang names. Anthony Street from Centre Street to the Five Points was Cat Hollow; Little Water, the southern edge of Paradise Square, occupied by two black and two Irish taverns, was called Dandy Lane.[55]

Language became song and dance at the markets, hotspots in the public economy, where black and Irish hucksters sold many varieties of food and filled the air with their poignant cries and songs while Irish butchers watched as blacks "danced for eels" at the nearby Catherine Market. Black and white female fruit and corn sellers shared territories on the streets, respecting each other's monopoly over favored corners. Originally a black tradition dating back into the eighteenth century, hot corn girls became universal during tough times in the 1840s. Legends grew about beautiful young women of indeterminate ethnicity selling corn and being the beloved of gang leaders.[56]

Tavern life, a staple since the earliest colonial days, shook races, classes, and genders in a rum punch. In Five Points bars, Irish and black revelers danced, sang, and courted to popular melodies composed from European and African rhythms. One visitor to a black tavern noted the mingling of black and white musical styles: "In the negro melodies you catch a strain of what has been metamorphosed from such Scotch or Irish tune, into somewhat of a chiming jiggish air." One Irishman is said to have "commenced humming, in a low tone, the popular negro melody of 'Mary Blane,' " but it seems "there was nothing in this to arrest particular attention." Walt Whitman argued in his Daybooks and Notebooks, that such mixing of cultures presaged a "native grand opera in America."[57]

Dance halls, attended by local blacks, Irish, and sailors, created a racial blend. George Foster described the hot music played at Peter Williams': "That red-faced trumpeter . . . looks precisely as if he were blowing glass, which needles [of sound] penetrating the tympanum, pierce through and through the brain without remorse . . . the bass drummer . . . sweats and deals his blows on every side, in all violation of the laws of rhythm." Another attraction was the fabled dancer, Juba, whom Dickens described dancing as Williams, performing the "single shuffle, double shuffle, cut and cross cut . . . spinning about on his toes and heels like nothing but the man's fingers on the tambourine." Juba and Peter Williams became so well known by 1850 that local sports regarded them as tame, preferring a dark cellar known as the Diving Bell. Located in a remote cellar on the Bowery, here "blacks mixed in freely with the gang" as interracial rowdies danced.[58]

Equally shocking to the middle classes was the neighborhood's predilection for what the nineteenth century termed amalgamation. Interracial love was sparked in such bordellos as the Diving Bell, Swimming Beach, and Arcade on Orange Street, and in the nearby Yankee Kitchen, Cow Bay, and Squeeze Gut Alley. Recording his visit of the early 1840s, Charles Dickens beckoned to his readers, "Let us go on again . . . and plunge into the Five Points." Accompanied by two policemen on a visit to Peter Williams' tavern, Dickens gaped as Irish and black men and women drank, danced, and made love. After Dickens, no popular construction of the Five Points was complete without a description of a love affair between a black man and an Irish woman.[59]

Brothels and dance halls were not the only venues for interracial love. Although Irish kinship ties in the Sixth Ward were very strong, occasionally Irish men and women took partners from other ethnic groups. A few brave Irish defied social sanctions and even married blacks. In the years after the 1834 riot, mixed couples appeared regularly in the Sixth Ward. One early indication of such unions was the children who fell into the clutches of the House of Refuge after 1840.[60] Peter Williams, a fifty-three year old Danish seaman, lived openly with his wife Deborah, a black woman from Maryland. Another union was blessed with young children. William Moore, a black male laborer, married an Irish woman, Winnifred. They lived with a 12–year-old son and a 2–year-old daughter at 228 Mulberry Street. Perhaps the bravest was John Baker, a black carter married to an Irish woman named Julia. Baker faced burly opposition on the street while living in a marriage which could provoke assault from thugs.[61] In 1860, 10 years after the Fugitive Slave Act, which sent hundreds of New Yorkers fleeing to Canada, Stephen Sanders, a black chimney sweep from Virginia, his wife Mary, from Ireland, hosted assorted boarders from Germany, Ireland, and New York City. One home sheltered two interracial couples. John DePoyster, a black laborer and his wife, Bridget, from Ireland, shared a house with John Francis of Virginia and his Irish wife Susan.[62]

Even in the late 1860s, several years after the fierce attacks on blacks during the Draft Riots, assaults that often took on a psychosexual tenor, interracial couples thrived in the Sixth Ward. When only 203 blacks lived in the entire ward, surrounded by almost 12,000 Irish, the presence of 11 interracial couples stands out. The men worked as laborer, seaman, boardinghouse keeper, carter, porter, servant, sweep, and liquor dealer. Six had Irish wives.[63] These marriages are not significant numerically but have great symbolic importance. Irish men and women, from a people not known for intermarriage, wedded African Americans and defied the racist conventions of their times to build genuine relationships and at times families. Although popular commentators generally sneered at such marriages, the men's occupations suggest serious commitment rather than casual romance.[64]

In sum, the relations of Irish and African Americans were polyvalent, but there is no easy explanation for them. Although they competed economically and lived closely together, Irish and black coexisted far more peacefully than historians have suggested. Day-to-day contact was as harmonious as could be in a tough, urban slum, while nighttime leisure produced a syncretic culture. A few brave souls intermarried. The example of the Sixth Ward contrasts with James O. Horton's interesting findings on relations between blacks and Germans in Buffalo, New York, in the nineteenth century.[65] Blacks and whites in Buffalo apparently got along when there was little competition for work or housing; blacks and Irish in the Sixth Ward cohabited in a slum where work was scarce and casual. Daily contact created a toleration not present in wards of greater segregation, which produced, for example, the draft rioters of 1863 and their racial terrorism.[66] Although disharmony and conflict abounded, there were also many points of cooperation and exchange. In their mutual experiences in the crowded Sixth Ward, black and Irish found common ground and affection.

Appendix to Chapter 3

Table A-1

Age and Sex of Blacks in Bergen County, New Jersey, 1830

	Hacken-sack	New Barbadoes	Harring-ton	Lodi	Bergen	Franklin	Pompton	Saddle River	Total
Slave									
Male									
0–10	0	0	0	0	0	0	0	0	0
10–24	0	0	0	0	0	0	0	3	3
24–36	26	13	11	9	7	4	9	20	99
36–55	20	17	7	12	8	14	9	30	117
55–100	6	9	11	12	4	3	11	81	137
Female									
0–10	0	0	0	0	0	0	0	3	3
10–24	0	1	0	0	0	0	0	1	2
24–36	25	9	10	5	4	7	5	16	81
36–55	18	11	5	19	9	11	8	26	107
55–100	20	7	16	7	12	8	1	14	85
Free									
Male									
0–10	57	30	75	32	56	63	28	76	417
10–24	59	27	64	35	66	67	22	65	405
24–36	17	13	26	7	31	19	5	19	137
36–55	10	8	9	5	13	13	1	7	66
55–100	4	3	11	6	4	4	0	5	37
Female									
0–10	54	33	63	24	28	47	19	69	337
10–24	44	36	54	27	36	33	16	48	294
24–36	10	14	23	4	14	15	4	9	93
36–55	7	2	14	4	20	7	0	4	58
55–100	6	1	9	3	7	4	0	5	35

Source: Manuscript Census of 1830, Bergen County, New Jersey.

Table A-2

Population of Bergen County, New Jersey, 1830

	Hacken-sack	New Barbadoes	Haring-ton	Lodi	Bergen	Franklin	Pompton	Saddle River	Total
Total Population	2,200	1,693	2,581	1,356	4,646	3,449	3,085	3,397	22,407
White	1,798	1,462	2,175	1,146	4,319	3,129	2,955	2,966	19,950
Black	402	231	406	210	327	320	130	431	2,457
Black									
Slaves									
Male	71	36	27	32	27	22	21	64	300
Female	63	28	31	31	25	26	14	60	278
Total	134	64	58	63	52	48	35	124	578
Free Dependent									
Male	100	50	98	75	99	108	36	131	697
Female	82	54	80	51	40	68	23	100	498
Free Independent									
Male	47	31	87	10	71	58	20	41	365
Female	39	32	83	11	65	38	16	35	319
Total Free Blacks	268	167	348	147	275	272	95	307	1,879
Total No. of Households Containing									
Free Blacks	127	81	134	60	113	117	36	120	788
Dependent Households	111	68	99	53	86	101	29	107	654
Independent Households	16	13	35	7	27	16	7	13	134
Heads of Independent Households	16	13	35	7	27	16	7	13	134
Male	13	11	32	7	26	14	6	12	121
Female	3	2	3	0	1	2	1	1	13

Source: Manuscript Census of 1830, Bergen County, New Jersey.

Table A-3

Age and Sex of Blacks in Bergen County, New Jersey, 1840

	Saddle River	Washington	New Bardadoes	Lodi	Hackensack	Harrington	Franklin	Total
Slave								
Male								
0–10	0	0	0	0	0	0	0	0
10–24	0	0	2	1	0	0	0	3
24–36	0	0	0	0	0	0	0	0
36–55	6	12	17	9	18	1	9	72
55–100	3	3	14	2	14	3	4	43
Female								
0–10	0	0	0	0	0	0	0	0
10–24	0	0	1	0	0	0	0	1
24–36	0	0	0	0	0	0	0	0
36–55	7	6	17	5	5	2	4	46
55–100	3	7	21	4	13	4	5	57
Free								
Male								
0–10	18	37	34	29	53	36	44	251
10–24	29	46	37	33	59	45	65	314
24–36	13	24	25	12	31	16	43	164
36–55	7	14	12	9	23	18	10	93
55–100	0	3	2	1	7	4	4	21
Female								
0–10	12	30	34	24	40	23	52	215
10–24	18	39	38	15	53	29	51	243
24–36	14	18	29	13	26	23	27	150
36–55	2	8	7	4	19	8	13	61
55–100	2	3	1	2	7	4	3	22

Source: Manuscript Census of 1840, Bergen County, New Jersey.

Table A-4a

Status and Living Patterns of Free Blacks and Slaves, Bergen County, New Jersey, 1860 Part A

	Saddle River	Frank- lin	New Barbadoes	Harring- ton	Hacken- sack
Total population	1,012	2,321	3,558	1,565	5,488
Whites	952	2,252	3,239	1,377	5,193
Blacks	60	69	319	188	295
Slaves	3	0	4	4	11
Free dependent blacks					
Male	24	30	28	27	52
Female	12	17	37	14	34
Total dependent	36	47	65	41	86
Free independent blacks					
Male	11	10	135	71	95
Female	10	12	115	72	103
Total Independent	21	22	250	143	198
Total free blacks	57	69	315	184	284

Source: Manuscript Census for Bergen County, New Jersey, 1860.

Table A-4b

Status and Living Patterns of Free Blacks and Slaves, Bergen County, New Jersey, 1860 Part B

	Washing- ton	Hohokus	Union	Lodi	Total
Total population	2,273	2,352	961	2,070	21,600
Whites	2,044	2,078	903	1,928	19,966
Blacks	229	274	58	142	1,634
Slaves	0	0	0	0	22
Free dependent blacks					
Male	34	42	11	21	269
Female	33	28	7	25	207
Total dependent	67	70	18	46	476
Free independent blacks					
Male	82	100	20	52	576
Female	80	104	20	44	560
Total Independent	162	204	40	96	1,136
Total free blacks	229	274	58	142	1,612

Source: Manuscript Census for Bergen County, New Jersey, 1860.

Table A-5a

Age/Sex Breakdown for African-American Population, Bergen County, New Jersey, 1860 Part A

	Saddle River	Frank-lin	New Barbadoes	Harring-ton	Hacken-sack
Dependent blacks—(Male/female (total))					
Age					
1–9	2/1	5/1	8/5	4/1	2/0
10–19	11/1	11/7	5/12	12/7	17/14
20–29	4/2	3/4	6/10	7/3	17/12
30–39	0/3	3/3	1/4	2/2	5/2
40–49	1/2	4/2	4/3	—	5/3
50–59	2/1	4/0	3/1	1/0	5/2
60–69	2/1	—	1/1	0/1	1/0
70–79	2/0	—	0/1	—	—
80–89	0/1	—	—	—	—
90–100	—	—	—	—	0/1
Totals	24/12 (36)	30/17 (47)	28/37 (65)	27/14 (41)	52/34 (86)
Independent blacks (male/female (total))					
Age					
1–9	3/1	2/1	44/24	23/27	25/35
10–19	1/3	1/3	25/26	14/11	14/20
20–29	1/2	3/3	15/15	7/8	19/15
30–39	3/1	3/1	17/21	10/10	17/10
40–49	2/1	0/1	19/17	11/11	3/9
50–59	1/0	0/1	10/4	5/1	14/10
60–69	0/1	0/1	2/3	1/2	2/3
70–79	—	1/1	3/4	0/2	1/1
80–89	0/1	—	0/1	—	—
90–100	—	—	—	—	—
Totals	11/10 (21)	10/12 (22)	135/115 (250)	71/72 (143)	95/103 (198)

Source: Manuscript Census for Bergen County, New Jersey, 1860.

Table A-5b

Age/Sex Breakdown for African-American Population, Bergen County, New Jersey, 1860 Part B

	Washing-ton	Hohokus	Union	Lodi	Total
Dependent blacks—(Male/female (total))					
Age					
1–9	3/5	15/3	1/0	5/6	45/22 (67)
10–19	17/17	16/3	1/3	5/7	95/81 176)
20–29	5/3	6/6	4/0	5/2	57/42 (99)
30–39	3/5	3/3	2/2	1/2	2-/26 (46)
40–49	2/3	1/1	1/1	3/2	21/17 (38)
50–59	3/0	1/0	2/0	1/2	22/6 (28)
60–69	1/0	0/2	—	0/1	5/6 (11)
70–79	—	—	0/1	1/1	3/3 (6)
80–89	—	—	—	—	0/1 (1)
90–100	—	—	—	0/2	0/3 (3)
Totals	34/33 (67)	60/28 (88)	11/7 (18)	21/25/46	269/207 (476)
Independent blacks (male/female (total))					
Age					
1–9	29/29	38/45	9/7	12/17	185/186 (371)
10–19	10/14	21/19	3/4	19/5	108/105 (213)
20–29	14/12	7/11	1/1	4/3	71/70 (141)
30–39	10/11	12/16	4/6	6/9	82/85 (167)
40–49	9/3	12/16	2/0	2/4	60/52 (112)
50–59	4/6	6/3	0/2	4/3	44/30 (74)
60–69	5/4	3/3	1/0	3/1	17/18 (35)
70–79	0/1	1/1	—	1/1	7/11 (18)
80–89	1/0	—	—	—	1/2 (3)
90–100	—	—	—	1/1	1/1 (2)
Totals	82/80 (162)	100/104 (204)	20/20 (40)	52/44 (96)	576/560 (1,136)

Source: Manuscript Census for Bergen County, New Jersey, 1860.

Notes

Introduction

1. David Roediger, *The Wages of Whiteness* (New York, 1993); Graham Russell Hodges, *New York City Cartmen, 1667–1850* (New York, 1986).

2. Graham Russell Hodges, *Slavery and Freedom in the Rural North: African Americans in Monmouth County, New Jersey, 1660–1870* (Madison, WI, 1997).

Chapter 1   Legal Bonds of Attachment: The Freemanship Law of New York City, 1648–1801

1. Allan Nevins, ed., *The Diary of Philip Hone, 1828–1851,* 2 vols. (New York, 1927), 2: 715.

2. The best overall review of the freemanship and its causes is Robert Seyboldt, *The Colonial Citizen of New York* (Madison, 1917). For good comment on the identification of freemanship with citizenship, see Chilton Williamson, *American Suffrage from Property to Democracy, 1760–1869* (Princeton, 1960), 115.

3. Beverly McAnear, "The Role of the Freeman in Colonial New York," *New York History* 21 (1940): 418–30, is the standard study. More contemporary works using his conclusions include Gary B. Nash, *The Urban Crucible: Social Changes, Political Consciousness, and the Origins of the American Revolution* (Cambridge, MA, 1979), and Jacob Price, "Economic Function and the Growth of American Port Towns in the Eighteenth Century," *Perspectives in American History* 8 (1974). For a slightly different perspective, see Hendrik Hartog, *Public Property and Private Power: The Corporation of the City of New York in American Law, 1730–1870* (Chapel Hill, NC, 1983). A recent study by Edward Countryman, *A People in Revolution* (Baltimore, 1981), does not mention the freemanship. A contemporary study that does give significance to the freemanship is Milton Klein, *Politics of Diversity: Essays in the History of Colonial New York* (Port Washington, NY, 1974), 21–23, 32.

4. Isaac S. Lyon, *Memoirs of an Ex-Cartman* (1872; rpt. New York, 1984), 6, 3. For the Angel Hendricksen incident, see *Second Annual Report of the Historian of the State of New York* (Albany, 1897), 243–52.

5. James Kent, *The Charter of the City of New York with Notes* (New York, 1836), 152.

6. For "Dun and Scot" provision, see Seyboldt, *Colonial Citizen,* 10. For

New York law restricting freemanship to naturalized Englishmen, see *Minutes of the Common Council,* 1: 371–72. See also T.J. Davis, "Slavery in Colonial New York City," (Ph.D. diss., Columbia University, 1974), 75.

7. Jon C. Teaford, *The Revolution in Municipal Government in America, 1650–1825* (Chicago, 1975), 9, 22–23, 38; Seyboldt, *Colonial Citizen,* 4–10; H.W. Merewether and A.J. Stevens, *The History of the Boroughs and Municipal Corporations* (1835; rpt. 1972), I: 9. The best account of corporate New York remains Arthur Everett Peterson, *New York as an Eighteenth-Century Municipality prior to 1731* (New York, 1917), and George William Edwards, *New York as an Eighteenth Century Municipality, 1731–1736* (New York, 1917). See also Hartog, *Public Property,* 21–23.

8. "Burgers and Freemen of New York," *NYHS* Coll. 18 (New York, 1885), 4.

9. *Ibid.,* 4–7, 19–26.

10. For a description of the takeover, see Thomas J. Archdeacon, *New York City, 1664–1710: Conquest and Change* (Ithaca, NY, 1976); Michael Kammen, *Colonial New York: A History* (New York, 1975), 73–100. For comment on the ease of transition, see William Smith, *History of the Province of New York from Its Discovery to the Appointment of Governor Colden in 1762,* 2 vols. (New York, 1829), 1: 20–30; and Robert C. Ritchie, *The Duke's Province: A Study of New York Politics and Society, 1664–1691* (Chapel Hill, NC, 1977), 18–26, 32–34.

11. Graham Hodges, *New York City Cartmen 1667–1850* (New York, 1986), 30–31, 174.

12. The material in this and the following two paragraphs was compiled from "Burgers and Freemen of New York" and from "Licenses for Cartmen, Tavernkeepers and Porters," in License Book of Mayor John Cruger, 1756–1765," New-York Historical Society.

13. Hodges, *New York City Cartmen,* 62.

14. Samuel B. McKee, *Labor in Colonial New York* (New York, 1935), 38–39.

15. Hodges, *New York City Cartmen,* 36–50; and *Minutes of the Common Council,* passim.

16. Petition of "Sundry Freemen of the City of New York to the Governor Against the Practices of Mechanics Coming from New Jersey and Other Provinces After the Laying of Our Taxes," Apr. 2, 1747, Daniel Horsmanden Papers, New-York Historical Society. The Common Council's reaction is in *Minutes of the Common Council,* 7: 177. See also Edwards, *New York as an Eighteenth-Century Municipality,* 89–90.

17. Hodges, *New York City Cartmen,* 45; Milton Klein, ed., *The Independent Reflector* (Cambridge, MA, 1964), 124.

18. Edwards, *New York as an Eighteenth-Century Municipality,* 22.

19. Nash, *Urban Crucible,* 57; Price, "Economic Function and Growth," 158–59, 173; Kammen, *Colonial New York,* 278–305.

20. "Licenses for Cartmen, Tavern-keepers and Porters."

21. For a sketch of Cruger, see John Stevens, *The Chamber of Commerce of Colonial New York: Biographical and Historical Sketches, 1768–1784* (New York, 1882); "Commissaries and Paymasters of the Province of New York, 1760–70," John Cruger Papers, New-York Historical Society.

22. See Hodges, *New York City Cartmen,* 62–64, for totals.

23. "Burgers and Freemen of New York," 170–210; "License Book of Cartmen, Tavern-keepers and Porters."

24. "Burgers and Freemen of New York," 201–7.

25. Nash, *Urban Crucible*, 364–68; Kammen, *Colonial New York*, 360–70, 407–8.

26. Hodges, *New York City Cartmen*, 62–64. See "Account Books of the British Quarter Master General in New York City, 1775–1783," New-York Historical Society. Costs for carters and wagoners often ran more than thirty thousand continental dollars per quarter.

27. Oscar T. Barck, *New York City during the War for Independence* (New York, 1931), 98–120; Stevens, *Chamber of Commerce*, 210, 234. On banning of wartime freemanships see *Minutes of the Common Council*, 1: 117.

28. Williamson, *American Suffrage*, 109.

29. This view is most recently expressed by Nash, *Urban Crucible*, and Eric Foner, *Tom Paine and Revolutionary America* (New York, 1976); for freemanship see McKee, *Colonial Labor in New York*, 179.

30. For discussion of the uneven development of society, see E.P. Thompson, "Eighteenth Century English Society: Class Struggle without Class?" *Social History 3* (1978): 149–80; and Barry Bluestone, "Economic Crisis and the Law of Uneven Development," *Politics and Society* 3 (1972): 65–82. The clearest demonstration of uneven development is Thompson, "Patrician Society, Plebeian Culture," *Journal of Social History* 7 (1974): 382–406.

31. Hodges, *New York City Cartmen*, 74–76; Mary O'Connor English, "New York City, 1783–1786" (Ph.D. diss., Fordham University, 1971); and Sidney Pomerantz, *New York: An American City, 1783–1901* (New York, 1939), 3–40.

32. Hodges, *New York City Cartmen*, 66–67; *Independent New York Gazette,* Nov. 28; Dec. 6, 1783; Pomerantz, *New York,* 20–30; and Oscar Handlin and Mary Handlin, *Commonwealth: A Study of the Role of Government in the American Economy, Massachusetts, 1774–1861*, rev. ed. (Cambridge, MA, 1969), 68.

33. For announcement by Duane, see *Independent Gazette,* June 18, 1784. For admission of cartmen as freemen, see *Minutes of Common Council,* 1: 24–48.

34. "Burgers and Freemen of New York," 275–86.

35. Hodges, *New York City Cartmen*, 82–83.

36. *New York Packet,* Apr. 7, 1785.

37. Hodges, *New York City Cartmen*, 83–84.

38. Ibid., 141–43, 139; and *Varick's License Book.*

39. *Daily Advertiser,* Jan. 13, 1791.

40. Alfred F. Young, *The Democratic-Republicans of New York: The Origins* (Chapel Hill, NC, 1967), 283–84, and Williamson, *American Suffrage,* 162.

41. *Daily Advertiser,* Sept. 24, 25, 1791.

42. *New York Journal,* Apr. 7, 10, 1792.

43. For Lamb, see Hodges, *New York City Cartmen*, 91–93.

44. *New York Journal,* Apr. 29, 1795; *Daily Advertiser,* Apr. 30, 1795.

45. Hodges, *New York City Cartmen*, 93–97.

46. For these controversies see Young, *Democratic-Republicans,* 429–55, and Hodges, *New York City Cartmen*, 95–98. For accusations against Lamb for intimidating cartmen and supporting Federalist war policies, see *New York Argus,* Apr. 26, 1796.

47. *Daily Advertiser,* Nov. 20, 1797; "Broadside of the Mayor's Proclamation Concerning the Laws Governing Carts and Cartmen," Nov. 1, 1797, New York Public Library.

48. *"Laws of the City of New York Governing Carts and Cartmen"* (New York, 1799).

49. *American Citizen,* Aug. 28–Sept. 8, 1801, includes a series of articles denouncing Varick and recalling past misdeeds. For official passage of office to Livingston see *Minutes of the Common Council,* 3: 57.

50. *Republican Watchtower,* Oct. 29, Dec. 8, 1801.

51. *Restoration of Liberty in the City of New York* (n.d. [1804]).

52. See "Report of the Common Council on the Request of the Committee of Cartmen," Offices and Officers File, 1816, New York Municipal Archives.

53. *Minutes of the Common Council,* 15: 429–30.

54. For black victories see petitions on hack-driving and chimneysweeps in Laws File for 1811, 1814, 1816, and 1817, New York Municipal Archives. For later discrimination see Rhoda Golden Freemen, *The Free Negro in New York City in the Era before the Civil War* (New York, 1994); *New York Emancipator,* May 5, 1836. For the twentieth century, see George Edmund Haynes, "The Negro at Work in New York City" (Ph.D. diss., Columbia University, 1912), 73–77, and Herbert R. Northup et al., *Negro Employment in Land and Air Transport* (Philadelphia, 1971). For racism in Republican theory, see Ronald Takaki, *Iron Cages: Race and Culture in Nineteenth-Century America* (New York, 1979), 3–16.

Chapter 2   In Retrospect: Richard B. Morris and *Government and Labor in Early America* (1946)

1. On the demand for cuts, see Dorothy M. Swart to Richard B. Morris (RBM), Dec. 20, 1944; for quote, see RBM to Charles G. Proffitt, Apr. 25, 1945, both in Papers of RBM, Box 21, Rare Book Room, Butler Library, Columbia University.

2. Joseph Rosenfarb, *Harvard Law Review* 59 (July 1946): 1019. For other reviews, see compilation in Mertice M. James and Dorothy Brown, eds., *The Book Review Digest,* vol. 42 (1947): 593.

3. For survey, see *Mississippi Valley Historical Review* 39 (Sept. 1952): 300. Editions of *Government and Labor* appeared in 1946, 1965, 1966, and 1981.

4. Stephen Botein, "Scientific Mind and Legal Matter: The Long Shadow of Richard B. Morris's Studies in the History of American Law," *Reviews in American History* 13 (June 1985): 303–15. For Morris's career, see Peter Coclanis, "Richard B. Morris," in *Twentieth-Century American Historians,* Clyde N. Wilson, ed., vol. 17, *Dictionary of Literary Biography* (1983), 307–14. For labor law, see Christopher Tomlins, *Law, Labor, and Ideology in the Early American Republic* (1993); Robert J. Steinfeld, *The Invention of Free Labor: The Employment Relation in English and American Law and Culture, 1350–1870* (1991); Karen Orren, *Belated Feudalism: Labor, the Law, and Liberal Development in the United States* (1991).

5. For comments, see Gary B. Nash to author, Apr. 23, 1996, in author's possession.

6. Louis Hartz, *The Liberal Tradition in America: An Interpretation of American Political Thought since the Revolution* (1955), 89.

7. Daniel Vickers, *Farmers and Fishermen: Two Centuries of Work in Essex County, Massachusetts, 1630–1850* (1994), 26–27. For comment on cities, see his essay in *The Cambridge Economic History of the United States,* vol. 1: *The Colonial Era,* Stanley L. Engerman and Robert E. Gallman, eds. (1996), 241. For debate on transition and on moral economy, see Winnifred Barr Rothenberg, *From Market-Places to a Market Economy: The Transformation of Rural Massachusetts, 1750–1850* (1992).

8. See, for example, Sean Wilentz, "The Rise of the American Working Class, 1776–1877: A Survey," in *Perspectives on American Labor History: The Problems of Synthesis,* J. Carroll Moody and Alice Kessler-Harris, eds. (1989), 86–88. On Morris's ideas, see Alfred F. Young, "American Historians Confront 'The Transforming Hand of Revolution,' " in *The Transforming Hand of Revolution: Reconsidering the American Revolution as a Social Movement,* ed. Ronald Hoffman and Peter J. Albert (1996), 408.

9. Edmund S. Morgan, *American Slavery, American Freedom: The Ordeal of Colonial Virginia* (1975).

10. For exceptions, see Graham Russell Hodges, *New York City Cartmen, 1667–1850* (1986); Howard B. Rock, *Artisans of the New Republic: The Tradesmen of New York City in the Age of Jefferson* (1979), 151–83. For influences on western cities, see Richard C. Wade, *The Urban Frontier: Pioneer Life in Early Pittsburgh, Cincinnati, Lexington, Louisville, and St. Louis* (1959), 79–83; and Jon C. Teaford, *The Municipal Revolution in America: Origins of Modern Urban Government, 1650–1825* (1975).

11. David Roediger, *The Wages of Whiteness: Race and the Making of the American Working Class* (1991).

12. Jesse Lemisch, *Jack Tar vs. John Bull: The Role of New York's Seamen in Precipitating the American Revolution.* See also, Jesse Lemisch, "Jack Tar in the Streets: Merchant Seamen in the Politics of Revolutionary America," *William and Mary Quarterly* 25 (1968), and "The American Revolution Seen from the Bottom Up," *Towards a New Past: Dissenting Essays in American History,* Barton Bernstein, ed. (1968), 3–45. Marcus Rediker, *Between the Devil and the Deep Blue Sea: Merchant Seamen, Pirates, and the Anglo-American Maritime World, 1700–1750* (1987).

13. Richard Dunn, "Servants and Slaves: The Recruitment and Employment of Labor," in *Colonial British America: Essays in the New History of the Early Modern Era* (1984), 158; Abbott E. Smith, *Colonists in Bondage: White Servitude and Convict Labor in America, 1607–1776* (1947); Sharon V. Salinger, *"To Serve Well and Faithfully": Labor and Indentured Servants in Pennsylvania, 1682–1800* (1987); Bernard Bailyn, *Voyagers to the West: A Passage in the Peopling of America on the Eve of the Revolution* (1986); David Galenson, *White Servitude in Colonial America* (1981); A. Roger Ekirch, *Bound for America: The Transportion of British Convicts to the Colonies, 1718–1775* (1987).

14. *Government and Labor,* 444–48, 458. For unpublished tables, see Morris Papers, Box 11, 24. Butler Library, Columbia University.

15. Samuel B. McKee, Jr., *Labor in Colonial New York, 1664–1776* (1935); Lawrence William Towner, *A Good Master Well Served: A Social History of Servitude in Massachusetts* (New York, 1998).

16. *American Historical Review* 52 (Oct. 1946).

Chapter 3   Slavery and Freedom Without Compensation: African Americans in Bergen County, New Jersey, 1660–1860

1. See Bergen County Petitions to the Legislature Requesting the Appeal of the New Jersey Abolition Act of 1804, Jan. 4–Feb. 6, 1806, nos. 421–28, State Library and Archives (New Jersey Archives), Trenton, NJ.

2. Arthur Zilversmit, *The First Emancipation: The Abolition of Slavery in the North* (Chicago, IL, 1967), 192–99.

3. For a recent review of New Jersey's halting approach to abolition of slavery, see my *Slavery and Freedom in the Rural North: African Americans in Monmouth County, New Jersey, 1660–1870* (Madison, WI, 1997). For Delaware, see Patience Essah, *A House Divided: Slavery and Emancipation in Delaware, 1638–1865* (Charlottesville, VA, 1996); and William H. Williams, *Slavery and Freedom in Delaware, 1639–1865* (Wilmington, DE, 1996).

4. John C. Pomfret, *Colonial New Jersey: A History* (New York, 1973), 13–15.

5. Carl Nordstrom, "Slavery in a New York County: Rockland County, 1686–1827," *Afro-Americans in New York Life and History* 1 (1977), 145–47. Old Tappan is on the northern edge of New Jersey; Tappan is now in Rockland County New York.

6. For Roberts, see Peter Wacker, *Land and People, A Cultural Geography of Preindustrial New Jersey: Origins and Settlement Patterns* (New Brunswick, NJ, 1975), 203. For Jochem Antony, see *Holland Society Yearbook for 1915* (New York, 1915), 62, 83. For the Van Donks, see Howard I. Durie, *The Kakiat Patent in Bergen County New Jersey* (Pearl River, NY, 1970), 50–52. The Van Donk holdings lasted until well after the American Revolution.

7. Oliver A. Rink, *Holland on the Hudson: An Economic and Social History of Dutch New York* (Ithaca, NY, 1986), 169.

8. Peter O. Wacker and Paul G.E. Clemens, *Land Use in Early New Jersey: A Historical Geography* (Newark, NJ, 1995), 95, 109, 179–182.

9. Pomfret, *Colonial New Jersey,* 97.

10. Pomfret, *Colonial New Jersey,* 22–31; Peter O. Wacker and Paul G.E. Wacker, *Land Use in Early New Jersey* (Newark, NJ, 1995), 89–92; and Wacker, *Land and People,* 190–91.

11. For court case, see New York Colonial Manuscripts XXIX, 218, New York State Library, Albany.

12. Randall Balmer, *A Perfect Babel of Confusion: Dutch Religion and English Culture in the Middle Colonies* (New York, 1989), 157.

13. *The Judgement of the Synode Holden at Dort, Concerning the Five Articles . . .* (London, 1619). For apposite discussions of the Synod of Dort, see Oliver Rink, *Holland on the Hudson, An Economic and Social History of Dutch New York* (Ithaca, NY, 1986), 17–18; George L. Smith, *Religion and Trade in New Netherland: Dutch Origins and American Development* (Ithaca, NY, 1973), 60–64; Keith L. Sprunger, *Dutch Puritanism: A History of English and Scottish Churches of the Netherlands in the Sixteenth and Seventeenth Centuries* (Leiden, 1982), 355–57; Jonathan Israel, *The Dutch Republic: Its Rise, Greatness, and Fall, 1477–1806* (Oxford, UK, 1995), 293 and Orlando Patterson, *Slavery and Social Death A Comparative Study* (Cambridge, MA, 1982), 276.

14. Rink, *Holland on the Hudson,* 62.

15. For retention of Roman Catholic influence in Holland, see J.L. Price, *Culture and Society in the Dutch Republic During the Seventeenth Century* (London, 1974), 27–34; Pieter Geyl, *The Revolt of the Netherlands, 1555–1609* (London, 1932), 1–26. Many slaves from the Spanish Caribbean were baptized. See the discussion in Herbert S. Klein, "Anglicanism, Catholicism and the Negro Slave," in Ann J. Lane, ed., *The Debate Over Slavery: Stanley Elkins and his Critics* (Urbana, IL, 1971), 137–90.

16. For baptism traditions, see Klein, "Anglican, Catholicism and the Negro Slave," 141–57; Thornton, *Africa and Africans,* 269 and Robert C.-H. Shell, *Children of Bondage: A Social History of the Slave Society at the Cape of Good Hope, 1652–1838* (Middletown, CT, 1994), 333. Religious requirements for manumission have been studied more thoroughly elsewhere. For example, in Cape Town, South Africa, slaves followed a specific track of acculturation toward freedom. Requirements included fluency in Dutch and membership in the Dutch Reformed Church. Each freeman paid annual dues of 100 florins. See A.J. Boescher, *Slaves and Free Blacks at the Cape, 1658–1700* (Cape Town, SA, 1977), 81–82; Robert Ross, *Cape of Torments: Slavery and Resistance in South Africa* (London, 1983); and Nigel Worden, *Slavery in Dutch South Africa* (New York, 1985), 97, 143–44.

17. *The Judgement of the Synode Holden at Dort, Concerning the Five Articles,* 38–41.

18. David Martin, *Tongues of Fire: The Explosion of Protestantism in Latin America* (Oxford, UK, 1990), 20–21.

19. Shell, *Children of Bondage, 333.* For the creation of patriarchal power in the New World, see Mary Beth Norton, *Founding Mothers & Fathers: Gendered Power in the Forming of American Society* (New York, 1996). See in particular Norton's comments on maternal attitudes toward servants at 170–71 and on familial authorities, 289–95. For masters' power over servants, see Robert J. Steinfeld, *The Invention of Free Labor: The Employment Relation in English and American Law and Culture, 1350–1870* (Chapel Hill, NC, 1991), 56.

20. Shell, *Children of Bondage,* 332–335. For automatic emancipation in the Netherlands, see Seymour Drescher, "The Long Goodbye: Dutch Capitalism and Antislavery," *American Historical Review,* 99:1 (Feb., 1994), 49.

21. Ibid., 60, 107. See also Pomfret, *Colonial New Jersey,* 107.

22. Elias Neau to Secretary of S.P.G., Apr. 30, 1706, S.P.G. Papers, Rhodes Library, Oxford University.

23. Balmer, *A Perfect Babel,* 101; and Joyce D. Goodfriend, *Before the Melt-*

ing Pot: Society and Culture in Colonial New York City, 1664–1730 (Princeton, NJ, 1993), 36–37, 90, 97–98. See also G.T. Van Duersen, *Plain Lives in a Golden Age: Popular Culture, Religion, and Society in Seventeenth-Century Holland* (Cambridge, UK, 1991), 83.

24. Bernard Bush, compiler, *Laws of the Royal Colony of New Jersey, 1704–1775*, 5 vols. (Trenton, NJ, 1975–1986), II, 28–30. In 1709 the Privy Council disallowed a second New Jersey law of 1708 requiring castration for black rapists, noting that such punishment "was never allowed by or known in the Laws of this Kingdom." For Privy Council action, see "Lords of Trade to Governor Hunter, Dec. 23, 1709, *Doc. Rel.,* V, 57. For discussion of Privy Council actions toward excessively severe punishments, see Elmer B. Russell, *The Review of American Colonial Legislation by the King in Council* (New York, 1915), 144–47.

25. Peter Kolchin, *American Slavery* (New York, 1993), 38–41.

26. For slave prices, see Zilversmit, *First Emancipation,* 231; for tax evidence see Wacker and Clemens, *Land Use,* 101.

27. For examples in Dutch architecture see Rosalie Fellows Bailey, *Pre-Revolutionary Dutch Homes and Families in Northern New Jersey and Southern New York* (New York, 1936), 269–381 and especially 272–75, 306, 314, 326–27, 370, 377. For other modes of housing see Adaline C. Sterling, *The Book of Englewood* (Englewood, NJ, 1922), 16. For slaves living in caves and tents, see Osborn, *Life in the Old Dutch Homesteads of Saddle River* (Paramus, 1967 reprint of 1919 edition), 25–29.

28. *Journal of Lieutenant Isaac Bangs, Apr. 1–July 29, 1776* (Boston, MA, 1890), 51.

29. For information and numbers of fugitive slaves, see Graham Russell Hodges and Alan Edward Brown, eds., *"Pretends to Be Free": Runaway Slave Advertisements from Colonial and Revolutionary New York and New Jersey* (New York, 1994). All ensuing fugitive notices from the colonial and revolutionary period are taken from this volume. For nearly one hundred revolutionary fugitives, see Graham Russell Hodges, ed., *The Black Loyalist Directory: African Americans in Exile after the American Revolution* (New York, 1996).

30. For Powellse, see *Zenger's Weekly Journal,* June 10, 1734; for Robin, see *The New York Gazette Revived in the Weekly Post-Boy,* July 3, 1749. For general comments on Dutch penuriousness in Bergen County, see Richard B. Lenk, "Hackensack New Jersey, From Settlement to Suburb, 1686–1804," unpublished doctoral dissertation, New York University, 1968, 161–64.

31. *New York Weekly Post-Boy,* Oct. 30, 1752, May 28, 1759. See also Aesop, runaway from Lawrence Janse Van Buskirk, of Hackensack in *New York Mercury,* Dec. 1, 1755; and Hack of Ramapough, *New York Journal* or *General Advertiser,* June 18, 1767.

32. See Cuff, in *Weekly Post-Boy,* June 6, 1757; Peter and York, in *Weekly Post-Boy,* May 28, 1759; and Harry, in *New York Gazette,* June 20, 1768. For the importance of fiddlers, see Sterling A. Stuckey, *Slave Culture, Nationalist Theory and the Foundations of Black America* (New York, 1987), 18, 21, 107, 370.

33. *Weekly Post-Boy,* Apr. 23, 1753.

34. *Weekly Post-Boy,* Sept. 9, 1762.

35. For trials and testimonies, see *Minutes of the Justices and Freeholders of Bergen County, New Jersey, 1716–1795* (River Edge, NJ, 1924), 21–23, 30–33,

36–40, 44–49. See also *Pennsylvania Gazette* (Philadelphia), June 8, 1738; *Boston Weekly Post-Boy,* June 4, 1744; *Pennsylvania Journal* (Philadelphia), Mar. 10, 1757; *New York Gazette and Weekly Post-Boy,* Dec. 25, 1752; and *Pennsylvania Gazette* (Philadelphia), Jan. 9, 1753.

36. For Dinar and Pero, see "Court of Oyer and Terminer for Bergen County, 18th Century," manuscript, Johnson Free Public Library, Hackensack and J.M. Van Valen, *History of Bergen County, New Jersey* (New York, 1900), 52–53. For punishment by mosquito torture, see W. Woodford Clayton, *History of Bergen and Passaic Counties, New Jersey* (Philadelphia, 1882), 345.

37. *The New York Journal or General Advertiser,* Oct. 29, 1767; and *New York Mercury,* Nov. 9, 1767.

38. For employment of blacks, see Force, *American Archives,* 5th Series, 1:486, 2:252, 3:109, 266 and "Proceedings of a Board of General Officers of the British Army at New-York, 1781," in *Collections of the New-York Historical Society for 1916* (New York, 1917), 112, 118, 125–26, 130–31, 134, 136–39, 141–42, 174, 210. For Jack, see Leiby, *Revolutionary War in the Hackensack Valley,* 200–202; and Clayton, *History of Bergen County,* 344.

39. Leiby, *Revolutionary War in the Hackensack Valley,* 75–87.

40. Ibid., 93–99.

41. For a discussion of the massive amounts of goods taken by the armies, see *New Jersey Journal,* Aug. 4, 1829, reprinted in *Bergen County History Annual,* 1976, 7–24.

42. Richard Varick to Philip Van Renssalaer, Oct. 30, 1778, Varic Papers, New-York Historical Society.

43. Leiby, *Revolution in the Hackensack Valley,* 190–99. Leiby omits mention of black participation. See Clayton, *History of Bergen and Passaic Counties,* 56–65; Mary A. Demarest and William H.S. Demarest, *The Demarest Family,* 67–68; Mildred Taylor, *The History of Teaneck* (Teaneck, 1977), 34. For the attack on Closter, see *Royal Gazette,* May 12, 1779.

44. Gaine's *Mercury,* June 20, 1779.

45. See George Fenwick Jones, "The Black Hessians: Negroes Recruited by the Hessians in South Carolina and Other Colonies," *South Carolina Historical Magazine,* 83:4 (1982), 287–302; William A. Calnek, *History of the County of Anapolis* (Toronto, 1897), 214; "Journal of Lt. John Charles Philip Van Kraft, 1776–1784," *Collections of the New-York Historical Society for 1883* (New York, 1884), 83 and Henry B. Livingston to Governor Trumbull, in Force, *American Archives,* 5th series, 2:252.

46. See Jeffrey J. Crow, *The Black Experience in Revolutionary North Carolina* (Raleigh, 1977); Wood, "The Dream Deferred"; Nash, *Forging Freedom,* 49. For organization in New York City, see Allen, *Loyal Americans,* 71; Walker, *Black Loyalists,* 22; and, using his evidence with different emphasis, Philip Ranlet, *The New York Loyalists* (Nashville, TN: 1986), 116–17.

47. See Theodore G. Tappert and John W. Doberstein, *The Journals of Henry Melchior Muhlenburg,* 3 vols. (Philadelphia, PA, 1942–1958), 3:105. For Black Brigade members see Hodges, ed., *The Black Loyalist Directory.*

48. For discussion of the severity of the winter, see David Ramsay, *History of the American Revolution,* 2 vols. (London, 1789), 191.

49. "Proclamation of Sir Henry Clinton, K.B.," *Royal Gazette,* July 3, 1779,

running through Jan. 7, 1780. For runaways, see "Embarkation Lists," M247 Reel 66, and M332 Reel 7.

50. Adrian C. Leiby, *The Revolutionary War in the Hackensack Valley, the Jersey Dutch, and the Neutral Ground* (New Brunswick, NJ, 1962), 190–209.

51. See "A Book for Registering the Inventories of Damages Done by the British in Bergen County," New Jersey State Archives, Trenton, Petition No. 11.

52. See the various arrests for consorting with the enemy in "Ancient Indictments," 1779–1782, Bergen County Historical Society.

53. For the Cuyler letter, see "Letter Book of James Patterson," in *Collections of the New-York Historical Society for 1875* (New York, 1876), 397; for American warning, see *New Jersey Gazette*, June 5, 1780; for martial law, see Carl Prince et al., *Papers of William Livingston*, 5 vols. (Trenton and New Brunswick, 1978–1988), 3:421; for slaves running away, see *Burlington New Jersey Journal*, June 13, 1780; and *Pennsylvania Evening Post*, June 23, 1780; Charles H. Winfield, *History of the County of Hudson, New Jersey* (New York, 1874), 140, 152; and *idem., The Block House by Bull's Ferry* (New York, 1904), 5. For method of escape see Dan Van Winkles, *Old Bergen, History and Reminicenses* (Jersey City, 1902), 122.

54. Leiby, *Revolutionary War in Hackensack*, 256–58; for Tye, see Quarles, *Negro in the American Revolution*, 147–48. For Bleuke, see Robert S. Allen, ed., *The Loyal Americans: The Military Role of the Loyalist Provincial Corps and Their Settlement in British North America, 1775–1784* (Ottawa, 1983), 71. For biography of Tom Ward, see E. Alfred Jones, *The Loyalists of New Jersey, Their Memorials, Petitions, Claims, Etc. from English Records* (Newark, 1927), 240.

55. See Clayton, *History of Bergen*, 59.

56. Ibid., 262–66.

57. For Prince William's visit, see Clayton, *History of Bergen*, 66–67.

58. King is quoted in Allen, *The Loyal American*, 14. See Boston King, "Memorial of the Life of Boston King, A Black Preacher," *The Methodist Magazine*, 21 (1798).

59. This neglected subject is best discussed in Arnett G. Lindsay, "Diplomatic Relations Between the United States and Great Britain Bearing on the Return of Negro Slaves, 1783–1828," *Journal of Negro History* 5 (Oct. 1920): 391–419.

60. For the murder of Hessius, see Reverend Dirck Romeyn to Richard Varick, July 20, 1782, Varick Papers, New-York Historical Society. For the slaves going to Novy Koshee, see Valentine, ed., *Manual for 1870*, 808–9. In a similar incident the slave of Jacob Duryea of Dutchess County refused to return with his master from New York City after making a delivery. After Duryea tied the slave to his boat, the slave was rescued on the Hudson River by Colonel Cuff and helpful Hessian soldiers. The slave was freed, and Duryea was taken back to New York City and court-martialed. See "An Excerpt from a Letter on the Banks of the Hudson," July 9, 1783 in Valentine, ed., *Manual for 1870*, 794. For black mobs, see Paul Gilje, *The Road to Mobocracy, Popular Disorder in New York City, 1763–1834* (Chapel Hill, NC, 1987), 147–53.

61. For a good account of this, see Quarles, *Negro in the American Revolution*, 160–81.

62. For names, see Hodges, *Black Loyalist Directory;* and for overall percentages, see Kruger, "Born to Run," 668–70. Kruger's account of the evacuation

(654–723) is especially instructive. See also Mary Beth Norton, Herbert Gutman and Ira Berlin, "The Afro-American Family in the Age of Revolution," in Berlin and Hoffman, *Slavery and Freedom*, 175–93.

63. For the best coverage of the passages to Nova Scotia and Sierra Leone, see Ellen Wilson, *The Loyal Blacks* (New York, 1976); James W. St. G. Walker, *The Black Loyalists: The Search for a Promised Land in Nova Scotia and Sierra Leone, 1783–1870* (New York, 1976) and Robin W. Winks, *The Blacks in Canada, A History* (New Haven, CT, 1971), 24–96.

64. Walker, *Black Loyalists*, 66–76.

65. For John, Isaac Taylor, and the Freelands, see Hodges, *Black Loyalist Directory*.

66. *Pennsylvania Packett*, Oct. 28, 1783 (italics added). For British reaction to this attack, see David T. Valentine, ed., *Manual of the Corporation of the City of New York for 1870* (New York, 1870), 817.

67. This statement presumes a black population of around 1,000 in Bergen County during the Revolutionary War and the loss of 120 blacks to Nova Scotia.

68. See Quarles, "American Revolution as a Black Declaration of Independence," in Berlin and Hoffman, *Slavery and Freedom*.

69. See the fine material on the post-revolutionary era in Lenk, "Hackensack," 165–73.

70. Professor John Gwaltney of Syracuse University forcefully informed me of the family memories passed along from generation to generation in Surrey County, Virgina, of black family members gone on to Nova Scotia and Sierra Leone. "Interview with Professor John Gwaltney," Dec. 7, 1987, author's file.

71. Leon Litwack, *North of Slavery: The Free Negro in the North* (Chicago, 1961); Arthur Zilversmit, *The First Emancipation* (Chicago, 1967); Ira Berlin, *Slaves Without Masters: The Free Negro in the Antebellum South* (New York, 1974); and David Brion Davis, *The Problem of Slavery in the Age of Revolution* (Ithaca, NY, 1967).

72. Gary B. Nash and Jean R. Soderlund, *Freedom by Degrees: Emancipation in Pennsylvania and Its Aftermath* (New York, 1991), 74; Jean Soderlund, *Quakers and Slavery: A Divided Spirit* (Princeton, NJ, 1985), 13; Hodges, *Slavery and Freedom in the Rural North*.

73. Shane White, *Somewhat More Independent: The End of Slavery in New York City, 1770–1810* (Athens, GA, 1991), 50–54.

74. Hodges, *Slavery and Freedom in the Rural North;* Essah, *A House Divided;* T. Stephen Whitman, *The Price of Freedom: Slavery and Manumission in Baltimore and Early National Maryland* (Lexington, KY, 1997).

75. For tax data, see "Tax Ratables for Bergen County, 1784–1814," State Archives, Trenton. For John Rutherford, see Wacker and Clemens, *Land Use,* 97. For land cultivation, see Wacker and Clemens, *Land Use,* 72–77.

76. Manuscript Wills for Bergen County, 1783–1800, State Archives, Trenton.

77. For the constitution of the Reformed Church, see *Tricentenary Studies of the Reformed Church in America* (New York, 1918), 401; John Pershing Luidens, "The Americanization of the Dutch Reformed Church" (Ph.D. dissertation, University of Oklahoma, 1969), 331.

78. Reginald McMahon, *Jack Was Earnest* (Hackensack, NJ, 1984), 3, 5, 9–11.

79. McMahon, *Jack Was Earnest,* 11, 15, 19, 21; Joan H. Geismar, *The Archaeology of Social Distingration in Skunk Hollow A Nineteenth-Century Rural Black Community* (New York, 1982), 18–21; and David Steven Cohen, *The Ramapo Mountain People* (New Brunswick, NJ, 1974), 42–49.

80. John Van Buskirk, Inventory 3950B; Adrian Rost, Inventory 3967B; Jerry Van Riper, Inventory 4009B; James Outwater, Inventory 4166B. Wills and Inventories of Bergen County, 1814–1832, State Archives, Trenton.

81. Bergen County Court Indictments, June term, 1793, Oct. term 1795, Bergen County Historical Society. See also *People v. Pero, A Negro Man Slave,* Mar. 4, 1785, sentenced to 200 lashes for beating the wife of Daniel McCormick.

82. For eighteenth-century references to *Pinkster,* see "Baptisms in the Lutheran Church, New York City, from 1725," *New York Genealogical and Biographical Record,* 98 (1967), 109, 99 (1968), 105. These church records included activities in Hackensack. For argument about folklore, see Sterling Stuckey, *Going Through the Storm: The Influence of African American Art in History* (New York, 1994), 3–19.

83. For discussion on the importance of the markets, see Graham Russell Hodges, *Root and Branch: African Americans in New York and East Jersey, 1613–1863* (Chapel Hill, NC, forthcoming 1999).

84. The material on market dancing comes from Thomas F. DeVoe, *The Market Book* (New York, 1862), 344–45. See also Cohen, "In Search of Carolus Africanus Rex," 156–57; and Shane White, "A Question of Style: Blacks in and Around New York City in the late Eighteenth Century," *Journal of American Folklore* 102 (Spring 1989): 23–44.

85. See Appendixes 1 and 2.

86. Geismar, *The Archaeology of Social Distingration,* 202–10.

87. See Appendix 3.

88. A convenient source for these numbers is Gilles Wright, *Afro-Americans in New Jersey, A Short History,* (Trenton, 1988), 82–87.

89. See Appendixes 4 and 5.

90. See, for example, John Mack Faragher, *Sugar Creek* (New Haven, CT, 1988); Eric Foner, *Free Soil, Free Labor, Free Men: The Ideology of the Republican Party Before the Civil War* (New York, 1970).

91. Robert Farris Thompson, *Flash of the Spirit: African and Afro-American Art and Philosophy* (New York, 1983), chapter 2; and Margaret Washington Creel, *A Peculiar People: Community-Culture Among the Gullah* (New York, 1988), 45–58, 311–18. For local evidence, see "The Old Slave Cemetery, Cedar Street, Bergenfield," Notebook, 1987, Bergen County Historical Society, and grave site at Gethsemane, Little Ferry, New Jersey. For percentages, see Wright, *Afro-Americans in New Jersey,* 88–92.

Chapter 4   Violence and Religion in the Black American Revolution

1. See for example the essays collected in Ira Berlin and Ronald Hoffman, ed., *Slavery and Freedom in the Age of the American Revolution* (1983) and Ronald Hoffman and Peter J. Albert, *Women in the Age of the American Revolution*

(1989), 293–447, which discuss the effect of the revolution on blacks but rarely touch upon the war itself.

2. Among the best works on the subject are Peter H. Wood, " 'The Dream Deferred': Black Freedom Struggles on the Eve of White Independence," in Gary Y. Okihiro, ed., *In Resistance: Studies in African, Caribbean and Afro-American History* (1966), 166–68; Gary B. Nash, *Forging Freedom The Formation of Philadelphia's Black Community 1720–1840* (1988), 38–66; Margaret Washington Creel, *"A Peculiar People": Slave Religion and Community-Culture Among the Gullahs* (1988), 113–67 and two articles by Sylvia Frey, "Between Slavery and Freedom: Virginia Blacks in the American Revolution," *Journal of Southern History* 49 (1983): 375–98 and "The British and the Black: A New Perspective," *Historian* 38 (1976): 225–38. Two books which focus on Black Loyalists are James W. St. G. Walker, *The Black Loyalists: The Search for a Promised Land in Sierra Leone and Nova Scotia 1783–1870* (1976) and Ellen Gibson Wilson, *The Loyal Blacks* (1976).

3. Wood, "Dream Deferred," 168–69.

4. Herbert Aptheker, *American Negro Slave Revolts* (1944).

Chapter 5   Black Revolt in New York City and the Neutral Zone: 1775–83

1. From a hymn sung by black loyalists as quoted in Wallace Brown and Hereward Senior, *Victorious in Defeat: The American Loyalist in Exile* (New York, 1984), 170.

2. For the roster of black loyalists on *L'Abondance* see "Book of Negroes Inspected on the 30th of Nov. . . . on Board the fleet laying near Statten Island"; *Papers of the Continental Congress, 1774–1789,* National Archives microcopy 247, reel 66, item 53 (published as Graham Russell Hodges, *The Black Loyalist Directory* [New York, 1996], 195–214). See also Esther Clark Wright, "The Evacuation of the Loyalists from New York in 1783," *Nova Scotia Historical Quarterly* 4 (1984): 5–27; and *Loyalists of New Brunswick* (Frederickton, New Brunswick, Canada, 1955), 249.

3. Wright, *Loyalists of New Brunswick,* 290–93.

4. See Eugene Genovese, *From Rebellion to Revolution: Afro-American Slave Revolts in the Making of the Modern World* (Baton Rouge, 1979), 11–12; David Barry Gaspar, *Bondsmen and Rebels: A Study of Master-Slave Relations in Antigua with Implications for Colonial British America* (Baltimore, 1985) and Philip Morgan, "Black Society in the Lowcountry, 1760–1810," in Ira Berlin and Ronald Hoffman, ed., *Slavery and Freedom in the Age of the American Revolution* (Charlottesville, VA, 1983), 83–143. See also Michael Craton, *Testing the Chains: Resistance to Slavery in the British West Indies* (Ithaca, NY, 1982) and the classic and most sympathetic studies of C.L.R. James, *The Black Jacobins: Toussaint L'Overture and the San Domingo Revolution,* 2d ed. (New York, 1963) and Herbert Aptheker, *American Negro Slave Revolts* (New York, 1944).

5. Quoted in Phyllis Blakely, "Boston King: A Black Loyalist," in *Eleven Exiles: Accounts of Loyalists in the American Revolution* (Toronto, 1982), 266.

6. See William H. Nelson, *The American Tory* (Oxford, 1961), 111–12 and

Theodore G. Tappaert and John W. Doberstein, eds., *The Journals of Henry Melchior Muhlenberg*, 3 vols. (Philadelphia, 1942–58), 3: 53, 105.

7. "Lee Papers," 4 vols., *Collections of the New-York Historical Society* (New York, 1871–74), 1: 379, 410.

8. James W. St G. Walker, "Blacks as American Loyalists: The Slaves' War for Independence," in *Historical Reflections/Reflections Historiques* 2 (1975): 53–54; Peter Wood, "The Dream Deferred: Black Freedom Struggles on the Eve of White Independence," in Gary Okihiro, ed., *In Resistance: Studies in African, Caribbean and Afro-American History* (Amherst, MA, 1986), 167–87.

9. For laws regulating behavior of blacks in New York see *Colonial Laws of New York from 1664 to the Revolution*, 5 vols. (Albany, NY, 1894), 1: 158, 519, 588, 1073; and for New Jersey see Bernard Bush, ed., "Laws of Royal Colony of New Jersey, 1703–1769," *Documents Relating to the Colonial History of the State of New Jersey* (hereafter *New Jersey Archives*), 3d ser., vols. 2–4 (Trenton, NJ, 1900–82), 2: 27–30, 138–40, 163–64, 496; and John C. Pomfret, *The Province of East New-Jersey, 1609–1702, The Rebellious Proprietary* (Princeton, NJ, 1962), 292, 297. For a discussion of rigor and cruelty of laws see T.J. Davis, "Slavery in Colonial New York City" (Ph.D. diss., Columbia University, 1974), 20; Edgar J. McManus, *Black Bondage in the North* (Syracuse, NY, 1976), 73–88.

10. See Tappert and Doberstein, *Journals of Henry Melchior Muhlenberg*, 3: 105.

11. See Robert D. Bass, *The Green Dragon: The Lives of Banastre Tarleton and Mary Robinson* (New York, 1957), 40–58; J.W. Fortescue, *History of the British Army*, 13 vols. (London, 1910–30), 3: 259.

12. For coverage of the 1712 revolt see Davis, "Slavery" (Ph.D., diss., Columbia University, 1974), 99–113; Kenneth Scott, "The Slave Insurrection in New York of 1712," *New-York Historical Society Quarterly* 45 (1961): 43–74; Aptheker, *American Negro Slave Revolts*, 172; McManus, *Black Bondage*, 127–32.

13. The 1741 conspiracy is receiving new attention from scholars who emphasize its potential rather than its failure. For coverage of the 1741 conspiracy see T.J. Davis, ed., *The New York Conspiracy* by Thomas J. Horsmanden (Boston, 1971); Davis, *A Rumor of Revolt* (New York, 1985); Davis, "These Enemies of Their Own Household: A Note on the Troublesome Slave Population in Eighteenth Century New York City," *Journal of the Afro-American Historical and Genealogical Society* 5 (1984): 133–47; and Marcus Rediker and Peter Linebaugh, "The Many-Headed Hydra: Sailors, Slaves and the Atlantic Working Class in the Eighteenth Century," *Journal of Historical Sociology* 3 (1990): 225–52. For a discussion of the 1734 plot see *The New-York Gazette*, 25 Mar. 1734; *The American Weekly Mercury* (Philadelphia), 5 Mar. 1734; *The Weekly Rehearsal* (Boston), 8 Apr. 1734. For murders see *American Weekly Mercury*, 14–20 Jan. 1729; *New York Gazette*, 1–8 June 1730; *Pennsylvania Gazette* (Philadelphia), 28 Feb.-7 Mar. 1737; *Boston Weekly News-Letter*, 18–25 Jan. 1739.

14. Anthony Benezet to David Barclay, 29 Apr. 1767, as quoted in Betty Fladeland, *Men and Brothers: Anglo-American Antislavery Cooperation* (Urbana, IL, 1972), 15–16.

15. For black conspiracies with the Indians see Alexander M. Flick, *The Papers of Sir William Johnson*, 13 vols. (Albany, NY, 1931), 2: 165–66, 174–75,

201; 4: 424, 431, 439–40, 495–97, 500; *New-York Weekly Post-Boy,* 18 July 1765. For gangs in Westchester County see *New-York Weekly Post-Boy,* 29 Dec. 1746. For Bergen County see *Boston Weekly Post-Boy,* 4 June 1744 and *Pennsylvania Gazette* (Philadelphia), 10 Mar. 1754.

16. The work of the Anglican church and its missionary arm, the Society for the Propagation of the Gospel, has recently renewed attention after decades of neglect. See Patricia Bonomi, *Under the Cope of Heaven: Religion, Society and Politics in Colonial America* (New York, 1986), 119–22; John C. Van Horne, *Religious Philanthropy and Colonial Slavery; The American Correspondence of the Associates of Dr. Bray, 1717–1777* (Urbana, IL, 1985), 22, 34–36, passim. For older and still very useful studies see Nelson R. Burr, *The Anglican Church in New Jersey* (Philadelphia, 1954), 24–28; Frank Klingberg, *Anglican Humanitarianism in Colonial New York* (Philadelphia, 1940), 124–39; William W. Kemp, *The Support of Schools in Colonial New York by the Society of the Propagation of the Gospel* (New York, 1913), 234–61; Charles Briggs, "Elias Neau, the Confessor and Catechist of Negro and Indian Slaves," *Proceedings of the Huguenot Society of America* 3 (1903): 103–16.

17. See *New York Journal or General Advertiser,* 13 Oct. 1774. For the importance of black preachers see Albert J. Raboteau, "The Slave Church in the Era of the American Revolution," in Berlin and Hoffman, *Slavery and Freedom,* 193–217.

18. For this point see Gary B. Nash, "Forging Freedom: The Emancipation Experience in the Northern Seaports, 1750–1820," in his *Race, Class and Politics: Essays in American Colonial and Revolutionary Society* (Urbana, IL, 1986), 284–88.

19. Here I am employing the models for slave revolts developed by Marion D. deB. Kilson, "Towards Freedom: An Analysis of Slave Revolts in the United States," *Phylon 25* (1964): 175–87 and extended by Genovese, *From Rebellion to Revolution,* 1–51.

20. See Clement A. Price, *Freedom Not Far Distant: A Documentary History of Afro-Americans in New Jersey* (Trenton, NJ, 1980), 56–60. For Somerset County troubles see the many citations in "Docket of Jacob Van Noorstrat, J.P., Somerset County," *Genealogical Magazine of New Jersey 43* (1968); 65–67. For early colonization plans see Eli Seifman, "A History of the New-York State Colonization Society" (Ph.D. diss., New York University, 1965), 17.

21. See "New Jersey Provincial Congress to John Hancock, NAM 247 reel 82, item 68, 169, 173. For the hanging of blacks see *New England Chronicle* (Cambridge, MA), 1 June 1775. For incidents in northern New York see Jeptha R. Simms, *The Frontiersmen of New York,* 2 vols. (Albany, NY, 1882–83), 2: 176; James Sullivan, ed., *Minutes of the Albany Committee of Correspondence, 1775–1778,* 3 vols. (Albany, NY, 1970), 1: 24, 649–50. For rebellious conditions on Long Island see Richard Shannon Moss, *Slavery on Long Island: Its Rise and Decline during the Seventeenth through Nineteenth Centuries* (New York, 1994), 232–52.

22. See Samuel S. Forman, "Memoirs," 3 vols. 1765–1867, 1: 16, New-York Historical Society Manuscript Collection.

23. See Larry R. Gerlach, *New Jersey in the American Revolution, 1763–1783: A Documentary History* (Trenton, NJ, 1975), 147–50. Colonel Breeze

could not have done that good a job because a year later his slave, Samuel Smith, left him to join the British army. See Hodges, ed., *Black Loyalist Directory,* 189.

24. For a computation of New Jersey colonial runaways see Harry B. Weiss, *The Personal Estates of Early Farmers and Tradesmen of Colonial New Jersey, 1670–1750* (Trenton, NJ, 1970), 17.

25. This is based upon comparison of the slave notices in *New Jersey Archives,* 1st ser., vol. 31, 2d. ser., 1–5 and the New Jersey slaves leaving with the British in 1783 listed in the embarcation lists in Hodges, ed., *Black Loyalist Directory.* Thus it is a conservative estimate.

26. Historians of the southern provinces have noted that only about one of every four runaways was advertised and argue that costs, distances to newspapers, and the belief that slaves could be captured quickly and locally cut down on the number of notices. See Margaret Washington Creel, *A Peculiar People: Slave Religion Among the Gullah* (New York, 1988); Philip Morgan, "Black Life in Eighteenth Century Charleston," *Perspectives in American History,* n.s. 1 (1984): 187–232 and Betty Wood, *Slavery in Colonial Georgia, 1730–1775* (Athens, GA, 1984), 147–50, 168–87.

27. See, for example, *Pennsylvania Gazette* (Philadelphia), 14 Sept. 1774; *Pennsylvania Packett* (Philadelphia), 25 Aug. 1778 for extended discussion of macaroni hairstyle. For a discussion of the used-clothing markets of New York City see Shane White, "A Question of Style: Blacks in and Around New York City in the late Eighteenth Century," *Journal of American Folklore* 102 (Jan. 1990): 23–44.

28. See *New Jersey Archives,* 2d ser., 1: 17 and 4: 419.

29. For buckskin breeches see New Jersey Archives, 2d ser., 1: 209, 335–36, 2: 78–79; 3: 14, 73–74, 225, 235, 273; 4: 169, 267; 5: 116, 183, 196. For beaver hats see 1: 134, 498–99; 2: 78–79, 364–66 (This description of Harry includes a two-page discussion of the "maccaroni" style), 4: 197, 419; 5: 326. For women see 2: 511, 612; 3: 14, 400; 4: 176, 180, 193, 255, 272.

30. For the Van Sayls see Hodges, ed., *Black Loyalist Directory,* 81; for the Couwenhoven brothers book, 5, 103, 132, 151–152; for John Sipe's losses book, 102. That the five were traveling together suggests a relationship. For the Collins see 9, 202. For a discussion of the extended nature of the black family during revolutionary era see Mary Beth Norton, Herbert G. Gutman and Ira Berlin, "The Afro-American Family in the Age of Revolution," in Berlin and Hoffman, *Slavery and Freedom,* 175–93; for an important study of the black family in New York City see Vivien Kruger, "Born to Run: The Slave Family in Early New York, 1626–1827" (Ph.D. diss., Columbia University, 1985).

31. See Kenneth Scott, ed., *Rivington's New York Newspaper* (New York, 1973); Hodges, ed., *Black Loyalist Directory,* 81.

32. For Stephen and Margaret Bleuke see Ibid., 88; for Joseph Paul and family, 108.

33. Ibid., 36.

34. Ibid., 73.

35. Ibid., 43.

36. Donald L. Robinson, *Slavery in the Structure of American Politics, 1765–1820* (New York, 1971), 54–98; F. Nwabueze Okoye, "Chattel Slavery as the Nightmare of the American Revolutionaries," *William and Mary Quarterly,* 3d ser., 37 (1980): 3–28.

37. The best review of American use of blacks remains Benjamin Quarles, *Negro in American Revolution* (Chapel Hill, NC, 1960), 68–111 and Sylvia Frey, *Water From the Rock: Black Resistance in a Revolutionary Age* (Princeton, NJ, 1991).

38. See William Kelby, ed., "Orderly Book of Three Battalions of Loyalists," in *Collections of New-York Historical Society* (New York, 1916), 6; "Lee Papers," 1: 369, 372, 379, 410, 425; 2: 104–05. See also Quarles, *Negro in American Revolution,* 94–110, 156 and black reminiscences in Jon C. Dann, *The Revolution Remembered: Eyewitness Accounts of the War for Independence* (Chicago, 1980), 46–48, 390–99.

39. The phrase is Quarles's in his *Negro in American Revolution,* 94–111.

40. See Jeffrey J. Crow, *The Black Experience in Revolutionary North Carolina* (Raleigh, NC, 1977); Gary B. Nash, *Forging Freedom: The Formation of Philadelphia's Black Community* (Cambridge, MA, 1987); Wood, "Dream Deferred," in Okihiro, ed., *In Resistance,* 167–87. For Black Pioneers arriving in Canada see Robert S. Allen, ed., *The Loyal American: The Military Role of the Loyalist Provincial Corps and their Settlement in British North America, 1775– 1784* (Ottawa, 1983), 12, 14, 71, 83. For a good portrait of the slave-soldier see Gary B. Nash, "Thomas Peters: Millwright, Soldier and Deliverer," in his *Race, Class and Politics,* 269–83. See also James W. St. G. Walker, *The Black Loyalists: The Search for a Promised Land in Nova Scotia and Sierra Leone, 1783– 1870* (New York, 1976), 1–17 and Ellen Wilson, *The Loyal Blacks* (New York, 1976), 1–41.

41. For company organization see the many pay vouchers for the Black Pioneers in the British Headquarters Papers, Public Record Office (hereafter PRO)/55/57 fol. 6492; PRO 30/55/57 fol. 6480; PRO 30/55/79, fol. 891; "Return of Strength and Distribution of His Majesty's Provincial Troops, 1779," Cortlandt Skinner Papers, Library of Congress. Further evidence of Black Pioneer presence in New York from Aug. 1779 until June 1780 comes from the account book of William D. Faulkner, brewer. Faulkner supplied beer to the British troops and sold more than 260 gallons to the Black Pioneers in that time. See William D. Faulkner Account Book, 1773–1790, Faulkner Manuscripts, New-York Historical Society, 76, 110, 112–19, 130, 139–46. For organization in New York City see Allen, *Loyal Americans,* 71; Walker, *Black Loyalists,* 22; and using his evidence with different emphasis, Philip Ranlet, *The New York Loyalists* (Nashville, TN, 1986), 116–17.

42. "Return of Troops in the North Fit For Duty, Apr. 2, 1776," Clinton Papers, 19: 40; "The State of the Black Company of Pioneers as Given up by Captain Martin to Capt. Stewart, July 13, 1777," Clinton Papers, 41: 29, Clements Library; Mackensie Papers, 10 May 1776, 19 Aug. 1776, Clements Library; "Muster Roll of Butler's Rangers," *New York Genealogical and Biographical Record* 31 (1900): 13, 16; Wilson, *Loyal Blacks,* 34.

43. Quarles, *Negro in the American Revolution,* 92–97, 134–54; Peter Michael Voeltz, "Slave and Soldier: The Military Impact of Blacks in the Colonial Americas" (New York, 1993), 57–67, 92, 126–31, 178–81. For black executions of Hessian soldiers see "Intelligence," Green Manuscripts, 5 Nov. 1782, Clements Library, Ann Arbor, Mich., and Rodney Atwood, *The Hessians: Mercenaries from Hessen-Kassel in the American Revolution* (New York, 1980), 193. For

discovery of conspiracy see Thomas H. Edsall, ed., *Journal of John Charles Phillip Von Kraft, 1776–1784* (New York, 1888), 104.

44. "List of the Names of Negroes belonging to Capt. Martin's Company, whom they Belonged to, and the Respective Places They Lived At," Gold Star Manuscripts, no. 30, Clements Library; PRO Audit Office Records, "Transcript for Benjamin Whitecuff," 41: 223; Hugh Edward Egerton, *The Royal Commission on the Losses and Service of American Loyalists, 1783–1785* (New York, 1971 reprint), 132; Robert Ernst, "A Long Island Black Tory," *Long Island Forum* 41 (1978): 18–19. For other spies see John Bakeless, *Turncoats, Traitors and Heroes* (Philadelphia, 1959), 100, 148, 260.

45. "Extract of General Orders Given by His Excellency General Sir Henry Clinton, Commander in Chief of the Army in America," Mackensie Letter Book E., Clements Library.

46. Voeltz, *Slave and Soldier,* 8, 19, 35–41, 640–48.

47. For Howe's proclamation see Wilson, *Loyal Blacks,* 29. Clinton's proclamation ran for several months in the *Royal Gazette* (New York), 3 July 1779–25 Sept. 1779.

48. See *New Jersey Journal* (Chatham), 20 July 1779. As with Patriot commanders, British officers were sometimes inconsistent about offering places in their armies to blacks. Oliver DeLancey, for example, a Loyalist given a key position in the British army, declared in 1777 that "all Negroes Mullattoes and other Improper Persons who have been admitted to the Corps be immediately discharged." See Kelby, ed., "Orderly Book of Three Battalions of Loyalists," *Collections of the New-York Historical Society* (1916), 6. Also E. Alfred Jones, "A Letter Regarding the Queens' Rangers," *Virginia Magazine of History and Biography* 30 (1922): 369–70.

49. For black housing see Thomas A. Jones, *History of New York during the Revolutionary War,* 2 vols. (New York, 1879–80), 2: 76; William A. Stone, *History of New York City from Discovery to the Present Day* (New York, 1872), 232; Kruger, "Born to Run," 674.

50. For descriptions of Corlies's land see George H. Moss, *Nauvoo to the Hook* (Trenton, NJ, 1964), i and "Conveyance Records," vol. G-2; 331–34, New Jersey State Archives, Trenton.

51. For a good coverage of Monmouth's problems and the doubtful loyalty of its citizens see Dennis Ryan, "Six Towns: Continuity and Change in Revolutionary New Jersey, 1770–1792" (Ph.D. diss., New York University, 1974), 127–28, 178, 181–83; Francis Lundlin, *New Jersey: Cockpit of the Revolution* (New Brunswick, NJ, 1960), 291. For George Washington's doubts about Monmouth see John C. Fitzpatrick, ed., *Writings of Washington,* 30 vols. (Washington, DC, 1932), 5: 226–27.

52. For this incident see John Stillwell, *Historical Genealogical Miscellany of New York and New Jersey,* 5 vols. (New York, 1903), 5: 290. For the British custom of informally awarding titles see Craton, *Testing the Chains,* 52–99.

53. See *New Jersey Archives,* 2d ser., 4: 504. For Moody's participation see *Lieutenant James Moody's Narrative of His Exertions and Suffering in the Cause of Government since the Year 1776,* 2d ed., (London, 1783), 11–12; for the fear of uprising in Elizabethtown see *Gaine's Weekly Mercury* (New York), 23 June 1780 and Edward F. Hatfield, *History of Elizabeth Town, N.J.* (New York, 1868), 476 and Aptheker, *Negro Slave Revolts,* 89.

54. For Loyalist plots and anger see Edward H. Tebbehoff, "The Associated Loyalists: An Aspect of Militant Loyalism," *New-York Historical Society Quarterly 63* (1979): 115–44. See also *Royal Gazette* (New York), 5, 23 June 1779.

55. For weather and crops in New York City see David Ramsay, *The History of the American Revolution,* 2 vols. (London, 1789), 2: 181–84, 191.

56. *Pennsylvania Evening Post* (Philadelphia), 12 Apr. 1780.

57. For removal of blacks to interior regions see *New Jersey Gazette* (Burlington), 5 June 1780. For mass exodus of blacks see *New Jersey Journal* (Chatham), 13 June 1780, *Pennsylvania Post* (Philadelphia), 23 June 1780. For Loyalist confidence see William Smith, *Historical Memoirs* (New York, 1971), 261, 286, 289, 314–17. For Livingston see Carl Prince et al., eds., *Papers of William Livingston,* 5 vols. (New Brunswick, NJ, 1979–89), 1: 427.

58. For an account of Murray's death see Franklin Ellis, *The History of Monmouth County, New Jersey* (Philadelphia, 1885), 209.

59. For the attack on Smock see Ellis, *Monmouth County,* 209. For the British attack see *Pennsylvania Packett* (Philadelphia), 13 June 1780. For cannon see *New Jersey Archives,* 2d ser., 4: 434–35. For the importance of spiking cannon see Ernest Mandeville, *The Story of Middletown, New Jersey* (Freehold, NJ, 1927), 63. For Smock's damage claims see "An Account of Captain Barnes Smock for Loss of Arms," Miscellaneous Manuscripts, nos. 1059, 1077, 1092, New Jersey State Archives, Trenton. See also "David Forman to William Livingston," 9 June 1780, in *Livingston,* 3: 423, and "Asher Holmes to William Livingston," 12 June 1780, Monmouth County Historical Association. For martial law see "Acts of Assembly of the State of New Jersey," 29 Oct. 1779–19 July 1780, (Trenton, NJ, 1780), 243 and "William Livingston to the Assembly," 7 June 1780 in *Livingston* 3: 421; for a nice description of Tye's attack see Sidney Kaplan, *The Black Presence in the Era of the American Revolution* (New York, 1973), 66–67.

60. *Pennsylvania Evening Post* (Philadelphia), 30 June 1780.

61. *New Jersey Archives,* 2d ser., 4: 603.

62. For accounts of this famous battle see "Nathaniel Scudder to Joseph Scudder," 11 Sept. 1780, New-Jersey Historical Society Manuscript Collection, Newark, NJ; *Gaines Weekly Mercury* (New York City), 25 Sept. 1780; *Pennsylvania Packett* (Philadelphia), 3 Oct. 1780.

63. For first reports on Huddy's capture see *New Jersey Gazette* (Burlington), 24 Apr. 1782 in which Tye's death in 1780 is prominently mentioned. The article describes Tye as "justly to be more feared and respected than any of his breathern of a fairer complexion." For part of the voluminous literature on the Huddy-Asquill case see Charles Forman, *Three Revolutionary Soldiers* (Cincinnati, OH, 1902), 12–15 and Allan J. Donor, "The Melancholy Case of Captain Asquill," *American Heritage* 31 (1970): 81–92.

64. See, for example, John H. Barber, *Historical Collections of New Jersey; Past and Present* (New Haven, CT, 1865), 365; Ellis, *Monmouth County,* 88.

65. See *New Jersey Archives,* 2d ser., 5: 446.

66. For damage to slavery in New York see Kruger, "Born to Run," 640–41, 650–53, 690–91; for New Jersey see Arthur Zilversmit, "Liberty and Prosperity: New Jersey and the Abolition of Slavery," *New Jersey History* 88 (1970): 215–27; for the region see McManus, *Black Bondage,* 159; for racial attitudes see Shane White, "Impious Prayers: Elite and Popular Attitudes towards Black and

Slavery in the Middle Atlantic States, 1783–1810," *New York History* 67 (1986): 261–85. For the tenor of abolition in these areas see Robert Fogel and Stanley Engerman, "Philanthropy at Bargain Prices: Notes on the Economics of Gradual Emancipation," *Journal of Legal Studies* 3 (1974): 377–401 and Claudia Goldin, "The Economics of Emancipation," *Journal of Economic History* 33 (1973): 66–86, esp. 68–71.

67. See "Register of Marriages in Trinity Church," 1: 149–53, passim; "New York City Manumission Society Standing Committee Reports," 1785–95, New-York Historical Society; Carleton Mabee, *Black Education in New York State* (Syracuse, NY, 1979), 20–21.

68. See especially, James W. St. G. Walker, "The Establishment of a Free Black Community in Nova Scotia," in Martin Kilson and Robert J. Rotberg, ed., *The African Disapora* (Cambridge, MA, 1976) and for Bleuke see Wilson, *The Loyal Blacks* 70, 85, 202–19 and Wilson, *John Clarkson and the African Adventure* (New York, 1980).

69. Herbert Aptheker, ed., *One Continual Cry: David Walker's Appeal to the Colored Citizens of the World* (New York, 1965), 114.

Chapter 6   Gabriel's Republican Rebellion

1. Peter S. Onuf, ed., *Jeffersonian Legacies* (1993), esp. 183–86.

2. See Herbert Aptheker, *American Negro Slave Revolts* (1943), 218–35; Gerald W. Mullin, *Flight and Rebellion: Slave Resistance in Eighteenth-Century Virginia* (1972), ch. 5; Philip J. Schwarz, *Twice Condemned: Slave and the Criminal Laws of Virginia, 1705–1865* (1988).

3. Sylvia Frey, *Water from the Rock: Black Resistance in a Revolutionary Age* (1991).

4. Eugene Genovese, *From Rebellion to Revolution: Afro-American Slave Revolts in the Making of the Modern World* (1979); David Barry Gaspar, *Bondmen & Rebels: A Study of Master-Slave Relations in Antigua With Implications for Colonial British America* (1985).

5. Thomas J. Davis, *A Rumour of Revolt: The "Great Negro Plot" in Colonial New York* (1985). For recent use of this testimony, see Marcus Rediker and Peter Linebaugh, "The Many-Headed Hydra: Sailors, Slaves, and the Atlantic Working Class in the Eighteenth Century," *Journal of Historical Sociology* (1990).

6. Robin Winks, *The Blacks in Canada: A History* (1971), 114–16.

Chapter 7   Reconstructing Black Women's History in the Caribbean

1. See for example Jacqueline Jones, "Race, Sex and Self-Evident Truths: The Status of Slave Women in the Era of the American Revolution," in *Women in the Age of the American Revolution,* ed. Ronald Hoffman and Peter J. Albert, eds. (Charlottesville, Va., 1989), 293–338, and Lois Green Carr and Lorena S. Walsh, "Economic Diversification and Labor Organization in the Chesapeake, 1650–

1820," in *Work and Labor in Early America,* Stephen Innes, ed. (Chapel Hill, NC, 1988), 144–189.

2. Carr and Walsh, "Economic Diversification," 182–183.

3. See Susan Lebsock, *The Free Women of Petersburg: Status and Culture in a Southern Town, 1784–1860* (New York, 1984), 136–138.

4. Thomas J. Davis, ed., *The New York Conspiracy by Daniel Horsmanden* (Boston, 1971).

5. See David Warren Sabean, "The History of the Family in Africa and Europe: Some Comparative Perspectives," *Journal of African History,* 24 (1983): 163–171, for need for flexibility.

6. See Richard Dunn, "The Recruitment and Employment of Labor," in *Colonial British America: Essays in the New History of the Early Modern Era,* Jack P. Greene and J.R. Pole, eds. (Baltimore, 1983), 174–175.

7. Albert Hurtado, *Indian Survival on the California Frontier* (New Haven, Ct., 1988), 182–186. See also Hazel V. Carby, *Reconstructing Womanhood: The Emergence of the Afro-American Novelist* (New York, 1987), 20–40.

Chapter 8   Flaneurs, Prostitutes, and Historians: Sexual Commerce and Representation in the Nineteenth-Century Metropolis

1. "The Man of the Crowd," in Edgar Allan Poe, *Poetry and Tales* (New York, 1984 ed.), 388–97.

2. For apposite efforts, see Judith Walkowitz's pioneering work, *Prostitution and Victorian Society: Women, Class, and the State* (New York, 1980); Alain Corbin, *Women for Hire: Prostitution and Sexuality in France after 1850* (Cambridge, 1990; first published in Paris, 1978); Jill Harsin, *Policing Prostitution* (Princeton, 1984).

3. For an apt discussion of such problems see "Introduction," in *History from Crime,* ed. Edward Muir and Guido Ruggiero (Baltimore, 1994).

4. Jonathan Mayne, trans. and ed., *The Painter of Modern Life and other Essays by Charles Baudelaire* (London, 1964), 1–40, esp. 26–38.

5. See for example, Hilary M. Beckles, *Natural Rebels: A Social History of Enslaved Black Women in Barbados* (New Brunswick, NJ, 1989).

6. Elizabeth Blackmar, *Manhattan for Rent, 1785–1850* (Ithaca, NY, 1989).

7. Paul A. Gilje, *The Road to Mobocracy: Popular Disorder in New York City, 1763–1834* (Chapel Hill, NC, 1987), 85–91, 237–9, 272–6.

8. Lillian Faderman, *Odd Girls and Twilight Lovers: A History of Lesbian Life in Twentieth-Century America* (New York, 1991), 30–3; and John D'Emilio and Estelle B. Freedman, *Intimate Matters: A History of Sexuality in America* (New York, 1988), 120–3.

9. Gilje, *Road to Mobocracy,* 253–64; Richard B. Stott, *Workers in the Metropolis: Class, Ethnicity, and Youth in Antebellum New York City* (Ithaca, NY, 1990), 247–76.

10. See George Chauncey, *Gay New York: Gender, Urban Culture, and the Making of the Gay Male World, 1890–1940* (New York, 1994), 292.

11. L. Perry Curtis, Jr., "Review of City of Dreadful Delight: Narratives of

Sexual Danger in Late-Victorian London," *American Historical Review* (1993): 1199–1201.

12. Enid Starkie, *Baudelaire* (New York, 1933), 69–81.

Chapter 9   The Decline and Fall of Artisan Republicanism in Antebellum New York City: Views from the Street and Workshop

1. George Rude, *The Crowd in History: A Study of Popular Disturbances in France and England, 1730–1848* (New York, 1964); E.P. Thompson, "The Moral Economy of the English Crowd in the Eighteenth Century," *Past and Present* 50 (1971), 76–136; Gordon S. Wood, "A Note on Mobs in the American Revolution," *William and Mary Quarterly,* 3rd ser., 23 (1966), 635–642.

2. Edward S. Countryman, *A People in Revolution: The American Revolution and Political Society in New York, 1760–1790* (Baltimore, 1981), 392.

3. Sean Wilentz, *Chants Democratic: New York City and the Rise of the American Working Class, 1788–1850* (New York, 1984).

4. Leonard L. Richards, *"Gentlemen of Property and Standing": Anti-Abolition Mobs in Jacksonian America* (New York, 1970), 150–155.

5. For critique of Gilje see Roger Lane, "A Trip Through Riot, Rout, and Tumult in New York," *Reviews in American History* 16 (1988), 380–385; Robert Fogleson, *America's Armories: Architecture, Society, and Public Order* (Cambridge, 1989).

6. Bruce Laurie, *Working People of Philadelphia, 1800–1850* (Philadelphia, 1980); Wilentz, *Chants Democratic,* 61–107; Amy Bridges, "Becoming American: The Working Classes in the United States Before the Civil War," in Ira Katznelson and Aristide R. Zolberg, eds., *Working-Class Formation: Nineteenth Century Patterns in Western Europe and the United States* (Princeton, NJ, 1986), 194–195.

7. Wilentz, *Chants Democratic,* 386–87. More recently, another scholar has uncovered artisanal republicanism roots among German immigrants to New York City. See Stanley Nadel, *Little Germany: Ethnicity, Religion, and Class in New York City, 1845–80* (Urbana, 1990), 15.

8. Robert Ernst, *Immigrant Life in New York City, 1825–1863* (New York, 1949), 215.

9. For his discussion of labor strife in 1850, see Wilentz, *Chants Democratic,* 363–389.

Chapter 10   "Desirable Companions and Lovers": Irish and African Americans in the Sixth Ward, 1830–1870

1. George Foster, *New York by Gaslight* (New York, 1850), 56–57.

2. For classic examples see Robert Ernst, *Immigrant Life in New York City: 1825–63* (New York, 1949), 105, 173; Carl Wittke, *The Irish in America* (Baton Rouge, LA, 1956), 125–35; Florence E. Gibson, *The Attitudes of the New York Irish Toward State and National Affairs, 1848–1892* (New York, 1951); Carl N.

Degler, "Labor in the Economy and Politics of New York City, 1850–1860" (Ph.D. diss., Columbia University, 1952); Phyllis F. Field, *The Politics of Race in New York: The Struggle for Black Suffrage in the Civil War Era* (Ithaca, NY, 1982). For popular histories that accept the presence of racial lore see Herbert Asbury, *Gangs of New York* (New York, 1927), 3–15; and Alvin F. Harlow, *Old Bowery Days* (New York, 1931), 180–82.

3. David Roediger, *The Wages of Whiteness: Race and the Making of the American Working Class* (London, 1991), 133–67, esp. 140–43, and "Labor in White Skin," in Roediger, *Towards the Abolition of Whiteness* (London, 1994), 21–39; Barbara Jeanne Fields, "Slavery, Race, and Ideology in the United States of America," *New Left Review* 181 (1990): 95–118.

4. Amy Bridges, "Becoming American," in Ira Katznelson and Aristide R. Zolberg, eds., *Working-Class Formation: Nineteenth-Century Patterns in Western Europe and the United States* (Princeton, NJ, 1986), 195.

5. For this view see Carol Groneman, "Working-Class Immigrant Women in Mid-Nineteenth Century New York: The Irish Women's Experience," *Journal of Urban History* 4 (1978): 255–71; Sean Wilentz, *Chants Democratic: New York City and the Rise of the American Working Class, 1788–1850* (New York, 1984); Christine Stansell, *City of Women: Sex and Class in New York: 1789–1860* (New York, 1986); Peter George Buckley, "To the Opera House: Culture and Society in New York City, 1820–1860" (Ph.D. diss., State University of New York at Stony Brook, 1984), 5–6, and Iver Bernstein, *The New York City Draft Riots: Their Significance for American Society and Politics in the Age of The Civil War* (New York, 1990), 23–24, 31–40. On pursuers of the American dream see Stuart Blumin, *The Emergence of the Middle Class Social Experience in the American City, 1760–1800* (New York, 1989), 230–257; Richard B. Stott, *Workers in the Metropolis: Class, Ethnicity, and Youth in Antebellum New York City* (Ithaca, NY, 1990), 237–42, 252.

6. George Walker, *The Afro-American in New York City, 1827–1860* (New York, 1993), 50.

7. Degler, "Labor in the Economy," 140–41 and Lawrence Costello, "The New York City Labor Movement, 1861–1873" (Ph.D. diss., Columbia University, 1967), 130–33. For black advising whites see Walker, *The Afro-American in New York City,* 51.

8. Carol Groneman, "The 'Bloudy Ould Sixth,' A Social Analysis of a Mid-Nineteenth-Century Working-Class Community" (Ph.D. diss., University of Rochester, 1978), 61.

9. Foster, *New York by Gaslight,* 56. On Cartmen's Ward see Graham Russell Hodges, *New York City Cartmen, 1667–1850* (New York, 1986); for percentages see Groneman, "Bloody Ould Sixth," 23–24; and Elizabeth Blackmar, *Manhattan for Rent, 1785–1850* (Ithaca, NY, 1989), 68–71, 93.

10. Ernst, *Immigrant Life,* 214–17. For an updating see Stott, *Workers in the Metropolis,* 92. For transformation of crafts see Wilentz, *Chants Democratic.* For black artisans see Shane White, *Somewhat More Independent: The End of Slavery in New York City, 1790–1810* (Athens, GA, 1991), 158; and Walker, *The Afro-American in New York City,* 40–65. On paucity of blacks in manufacturing see Stott, *Workers in the Metropolis,* 92. On "communitas" see Victor Turner, *Structure and Anti-Structure* (Chicago, 1969), 131–32.

11. Ernst, *Immigrant Life in New York,* 38–42; Groneman, " 'Bloudy Ould Sixth,' " 35.

12. For the importance of laborers in crafts in transition see David Montgomery, *The Fall of the House of Labor* (New York, 1987), 58–62. For union movement see Wilentz, *Chants Democratic,* 250–51; and Stott, *Workers in the Metropolis,* 58–61.

13. Degler, "Labor in the Economy," 19–23, 40–53; Amy Bridges, *A City in the Republic: Antebellum New York and the Origins of Machine Politics* (New York, 1984), 99–100.

14. Groneman, " 'Bloody Ould Sixth,' " 100, 155, 164; Stott, *Workers in the Metropolis,* 196–97, 204.

15. For businesses see *Doggett's New York City Street Directory for 1851 . . .* (New York, 1851). For tabulation see Edward K. Spann, *The New Metropolis: New York City, 1840–1857* (New York, 1981), 343.

16. On boardinghouses see Blackmar, *Manhattan for Rent,* 122–26; for a classic description of boardinghouses see Thomas B. Gunn, *The Physiology of New York Boarding-Houses* (New York, 1857).

17. *Rode's New York City Directory for 1850–1851* (New York, 1850), appendixes; James D. McCabe, *Lights and Shadows of the Great City* (New York, 1872), 401, 412–21. For career of the Five Points Mission see Carol Smith-Rosenberg, *Religion and the Rise of the American City: The New York Mission Society, 1812–1870* (Ithaca, NY, 1971), 225–44.

18. Blackmar, *Manhattan for Rent,* 93; Groneman, " 'Bloody Ould Sixth,' " 23–8.

19. Foster, *New York By Gaslight,* 52–63. For comment on pornography see Stansell, *City of Women,* 174–75. On historical descendants of Five Points see Eileen Southern, *The Music of Black Americans: A History* (New York, 1971), 120–22.

20. For the texture of community life in lower wards see Kenneth A. Scherzer, *The Unbounded Community: Neighborhood Life and Social Structure in New York City, 1830–1875* (Durham, NC, 1992), 211–13; and Paul A. Gilje, *The Road to Mobocracy: Popular Disorder in New York City, 1763–1834* (Chapel Hill, NC, 1987), 160–61.

21. For Orange Street see *Doggett's New York City Street Directory for 1851* (New York, 1851), 260. For other examples see Anthony Street, 15–17; Centre Street, 94; Cross Street, 121–22; and Mott Street, 264–66.

22. For Washington see 1850 Manuscript Census, Sixth Ward, National Archives Microfilm, 101; for Downey 1860 Manuscript Census, Sixth Ward, Second District, 167. For street conversation see John D. Vose, Esq., *Seven Nights in Gotham* (New York, 1852), 78. For comment on blacks in white homes, see White, *Somewhat More Independent,* 172–76.

23. Robert S. Pickett, *House of Refuge, Origins of Juvenile Reform in New York State, 1815–1857* (Syracuse, NY, 1969). For apprentices see "Apprentices File," Common Council Papers, Reel 81, New York Municipal Archives.

24. John Griscom, *The Sanitary Condition of the Laboring Population of New York with Suggestions for Its Improvement* (New York, 1845), 18. For an accounting of the dismal statistics of Irish and black lives see Leonard Curry, *The Free Black in Urban America, 1800–1850* (Chicago, 1981), 40–41, 53–54, 7: 3, 79.

25. Kenneth Scott, compiler, "Coroner's Reports for New York City, 1823–1842," Collections of the New York Genealogical and Biographical Society, 12 (New York, 1989). For death rates see John Duffy, *A History of Public Health in New York City, 1625–1866* (New York, 1966), 536–37. For children see "Book of Indentures of the Association for the Benefit of the Colored Orphan Asylum, vol. 1 (1835–66), Mss., New-York Historical Society (N-YHS); J.D.B. De Bow, compiler, *Mortality Statistics of the Seventh Census of the United States, 1850 . . .* (Washington, 1855), 161–63, 171–87. For missionary efforts see Smith-Rosenberg, *Religion and the Rise of the American City,* 240.

26. For number of murders see David T. Valentine, ed., *Manual of the Common Council of New-York 1854* (New York, 1854), 332. For image of Five Points in Literature see Adrienne Siegel, *The Image of the American City in Popular Literature 1820–1870* (Port Washington, NY, 1981). For a good study of gang culture see Eliott J. Gorn, "Good-Bye Boys, I Die A True American: Homicide, Nativism, and Working Class Culture in Antebellum New York City," *Journal of American History* 74 (1987): 388–411.

27. Gilje, *The Road to Mobocracy,* 138–39, 152.

28. Ibid., 166–68. For reports see *New York Commercial Advertiser,* July 10–12, 1834. For composition of mobs see Leonard L. Richards, *"Gentlemen of Property and Standing": Anti-Abolition Mobs in Jacksonian America* (New York, 1970), 141–45. For Irish as targets see Harlow, *Old Bowery Days,* 294–300.

29. *Commercial Advertiser,* June 22–25, 1835; *New York American,* June 22–25, 1835; *New York Sun,* June 22–25, 1835. For arrests see "Watch Returns, June 22–25, 1834," New York Municipal Archives, Reel 22.

30. *Diamond* 2 (July 1840): 19.

31. *Irish-American,* Nov. 11, 1849; Buckley, "To the Opera House," 5–7; Bernstein *New York City Draft Riots,* 334–38. On the Dead Rabbit Riots see Asbury, *Gangs of New York,* 1112–18.

32. "William H. Bell Diary," Jan. 8, 1851, N-YHS; cf. n. 25.

33. *Political Bulletin and Miscellaneous Repository,* May 10, 1810, and Jan. 2, Feb. 16, 1811; *Diamond,* 2 (July 1840). See the *Irish-American,* Aug. 10, 1849, for opposition to slavery; Aug. 21, 1850, for a description of Douglass and approval of colonization. On the comparison of slavery and the Irish condition see Philip S. Foner and Herbert Shapiro, eds., *Northern Labor and Antislavery: A Documentary History* (Westport, CT, 1994).

34. For the fullest coverage of black struggles over the vote see Walker, *Afro-Americans in New York City,* 188–211; and Field, *Politics of Race.* For number of voters see *Census of the State of New York for 1845 . . .* (Albany, 1846). See also Jerome Mushkat, *The Reconstruction of the New York Democracy, 1861–1874* (Rutherford, NJ, 1981), 70, 120–37.

35. Minutes of the Common Council of the City of New York, 1784–1831, 22 vols. (New York, 1930), 15: 406, 429–30, 467, 492.

36. For general comments see Stott, *Workers in the Metropolis,* 235–38; Bridges, *A City in the Republic,* 132. For transformation of government see Jon C. Teaford, *The Municipal Revolution* (Baltimore, 1975). For specific occupations see Hodges, *New York City Cartmen,* chap. 7; James F. Richardson, *The New York Police: Colonial Times to 1901* (New York, 1970). For firemen see Stott, *Workers in the Metropolis,* 242–43. For appointive office, see *The City Election*

Handbook Votes for Mayor from 1834 to 1863 (New York, 1864).

37. For Loco-Foco effect of Democrats and party attitudes on blacks see Jerome Mushkat, *Tammany: The Evolution of a Political Machine, 1789–1865* (Syracuse, NY, 1971), 158–67, 231–33; Wilentz, *Chants Democratic,* 193–96.

38. [Thomas Mooney], *Mooney's Nine Years in America in a Series of Letters* (Dublin, 1850), 152–54. Similar sentiments can be found in Isaac Lyon, *Memoirs of an Old Cartman* (Newark, 1872).

39. Compare *Superintendant of Carts License Book,* New York Municipal Archives and Records Center (MARC), J-40–A with Ernst, *Immigrant Life,* 217; and Groneman, " 'Bloudy Ould Sixth,' " 100, 115, 118.

40. For discussions on integrating carting see Hodges, *New York City Cartmen.* For Fernando Wood see Stott, *Workers in the Metropolis,* 226. For 1900 figures see George E. Haynes, *The Negro at Work in New York City: A Study in Economic Progress* (New York, 1912), 69–72. For porters see Mooney, *Nine Years,* 85–87.

41. For policeman see "William H. Bell Diary," 1850–51, N-YHS. For licenses see "List of Licensed Pawnbrokers in City of New York, 1823–41"; "Licensed Dealers in Second-Hand Articles"; "List of Carts Licensed to Keepers of Junk"; "Licensed Dealers in Second-Hand Articles, 1842–1860," all in MARC, J-40–A. For numbers on Orange Street see David T. Valentine, ed., *Manual of the Common Council for the City of New York, 1854* (New York, 1854), 330–32. For anti-Semitic descriptions of junk dealers and intelligence offices see [George Foster], *New York in Slices by an Experienced Carver* (New York, 1849), 30–32, 37.

42. For comments see Mooney, *Nine Years,* 81. For counts of various occupations see *Wilson's Business Directory of New York City* (New York, 1860), 229–34.

43. The classic work on butchers is Thomas F. Devoe, *The Market Book* (New York, 1861). For good articulation of their culture, see also Gorn, "Good-Bye Boys, I Die A True American"; and Wilentz, *Chants Democratic,* 137–39.

44. See *People v. Alexander Davis,* Sept. 14, 1842, Box MDA 411, and *People v. Samuel Daily,* Sept. 11, 1842, Box MDA 427, both in District Attorney Indictment Papers, MARC. I am grateful to Michael Kaplan for these references.

45. For comments on grocers see Luc Sante, *Low Life: Lures and Snares of Old New York* (New York, 1991), 105–6. For reform efforts see Blackmar, *Manhattan for Rent,* 136, for 1836; and Spann, *The New Metropolis,* 373, for 1856.

46. For Irish keepers see *Wilson's Business Directory,* 26–32. For blacks see 1860 Manuscript Census, Sixth Ward, Fourth District, 114.

47. For attitudes about manual laborers and domestics see Jonathan Glickstein, *Concepts of Free Labor in Antebellum America* (New Haven, CT, 1991), 175–77, 237. For ethnophobia and racial attitudes see Dale T. Knobel, *Paddy and the New Republic: Ethnicity and Nationality in Antebellum America* (Middletown, CT, 1986).

48. Blackmar, *Manhattan for Rent,* 57–62, 116–20, 311–13; Stansell, *City of Women,* 156–68; Glickstein, *Concepts of Free Labor,* 175–77, 424.

49. Blackmar, *Manhattan for Rent,* 119–20; Stansell, *City of Women,* 161–63; Hasia R. Diner, *Erin's Daughters in America: Irish Immigrant Women in the Nineteenth Century* (Baltimore, 1983), 93; Mooney, *Nine Years,* 87.

50. *Wilson's Business Directory of New York City* (New York, 1860), 478–81.

51. For antebellum patterns of black family see Scherzer, *Unbounded Community,* 117–19; Walker, *Afro-Americans in New York City,* 10. For Irish women and marriage see Diner, *Erin's Daughters,* 7–13, 52–58, 77, 92.

52. Diner, *Erin's Daughters,* 94–96. For black and Irish nurses see *Wilson's Business Directory for 1860.*

53. For Irish see Diner, *Erin's Daughters,* 110. For blacks see Mary Thompson, *Sketches of the Colored Old Folks Home* (New York, 1851).

54. Timothy Gilfoyle, *City of Eros: New York City, Prostitution, and the Commercialization of Sex, 1790–1920* (New York, 1992), 36–42; Marilyn Wood Hill, *Their Sisters' Keepers: Prostitution in New York City, 1830–1870* (Berkeley, CA, 1993), 55–58, 352n., 70, 71,190–91.

55. See "Bell Diary." For a good assortment of terms see Vose, *Seven Nights,* 32–3. For comments see Irvin Lewis Allen, *The City in Slang* (New York, 1993), 21–23, 57–71, 149–77. For cant names see Harlow, *Old Bowery Days,* 180.

56. For hot corn see *Life in New York In Doors and Out of Doors, Illustrated with Forty Engravings by the late William Burns* (New York, 1851); Solon Robinson, *Hot Corn* (New York, 1855); Foster, *New York by Gaslight,* 122. For "dancing for eels" see Vose, *Seven Nights,* 88; and Devoe, *The Market Book,* 344–45. For legends see Asbury, *Gangs of New York,* 7–8.

57. The quotation is from Charles Dickens, *American Notes for General Circulation* (London, 1842). For humming see Ned Buntline (pseud. of E.Z.C. Judson), *The G'Hals of New York: A Novel* (New York, 1850), 7. Whitman quoted in Graham Hodges, "Muscle and Pluck, Walt Whitman's Working Class Ties," *Seaport Magazine,* 26, no. 1 (1992).

58. Gilfoyle, *City of Eros,* 38–46; Foster, *New York by Gaslight,* 74–76; McCabe, *Lights and Shadows,* 596–600. For the Diving Bell see Vose, *Seven Nights,* 85–88. For tameness of Juba and Peter Williams see Robert C. Toll, *Blacking Up: The Minstrel Show in Nineteenth-Century America* (New York, 1974), 43.

59. For the descriptions in this paragraph see *The Old Brewery and the New Mission House at the Five Points by Ladies of the Mission* (New York, 1854), 33, 45. For comments on interracial love see Asbury, *The Gangs of New York,* 21–25; updated in Sante, *Low Life,* and in Eric Lott, *Love and Theft: Blackface Minstrelsy and the American Working Class* (New York, 1993), 47.

60. For marriage between ethnic groups see Groneman, " 'Bloody Ould Sixth,' " 70–73. For interracial children see cases 1973, 2097, 2496, 2701, and 2996 in House of Refuge Papers, New York State Library, Albany.

61. For 1850 interracial couples see Manuscript Census for 1850, National Archives Microfilm, Sixth Ward, 36, 37, 76 (John and Francis Hall), 101, 153, 162, 163.

62. For Sanders, DePoyster, and Francis see Manuscript Census for 1860, Sixth Ward, Second District, 213. For others see First District, 16; Second District, 80, 158, 160; Fourth District, 116.

63. See entries for Moses Roper, Frederick Hill, Manuel Gilbert, Sylvester White, Perry Cooper, Henry Willis, Frederick Mingo, Joseph Armstrong, Daniel Young, and Benjamin Hosley, Manuscript Census of 1870, Sixth Ward of New York City, National Archives Microfilm, 54, 56, 80. A few couples appear in

popular novels of the 1850s. See, for example, Robinson, *Hot Corn,* 71, 94–97; and Harriet E. Wilson, *Our Nig; or Sketches from the Life of a Free Black* (1859; New York, 1983).

64. Commentary on interracial marriages in the urban north is scanty, but see the useful comments, in a different context, in James O. Horton, *Free People of Color: Inside the African American Community* (Washington, DC, 1993), 175.

65. Ibid., chap. 8.

66. It is striking how few residents of the Sixth Ward were involved in the Draft Riots of 1863. For the residences of those killed, injured, and arrested see Adrian Cook, *The Armies of the Streets: The New York City Draft Riots of 1863* (Lexington, KY, 1974), 213–16; and Bernstein, *New York City Draft Riots,* 28, 31–36.

Index

Vickers, Daniel, 21-22
Virginia, 33, 62, 78
Vose, John D., 129

Waddell, William, 77
Wade, Richard, 24
Wage regulation, 21-22
Waiters, 123
Waldron, Adolph, 46
Walker, David, 86
Walkowitz, Judith, 101-10
Walsh, Mike, 120
Ward, Tom, 44, 47
War of 1812, 91
Washerwomen, 140
Washington, Adelaide, 130
Washington, George, 13-14, 43, 48,
   62, 82, 90
Washington, George (resident of Five
   Points), 130
Weldon, Georgianna, 109
Westchester County, 67, 85

Westervelt, Jacobus, 43
Whigs, 10, 12, 135
White, Shane, 51
Whitecuff, Benjamin, 78
Whitman, T. Stephen, 51
Whitman, Walt, 142
Wilentz, Sean, 21, 115, 117-9
Willett, Marinus, 10
Williams, Deborah, 143
Williams, Peter (tavern owner), 129, 143
Williams, Peter, Jr.(minister), 91
Winslow, Cato, 6
Women's history, 93-97
Wood, Fernando, 135
Wood, Gordon, 112
Wood, Peter, 60
Workingmen's Movement, 134

York Rebellion, 23

Zabriskie, Hendrick Christians, 42
Zabriskie, John, 41